LITERATURE AND HISTORY

Edited by

Leonard Schulze
Walter Wetzels

UNIVERSITY
PRESS OF
AMERICA

LANHAM • NEW YORK • LONDON

Copyright © 1983 by

University Press of America,™ Inc.

4720 Boston Way
Lanham, MD 20706

3 Henrietta Street
London WC2E 8LU England

Library of Congress Cataloging in Publication Data
Main entry under title:

Literature and history.

Bibliography: p.
Includes index.
1. Literature and history. I. Schulze, Leonard. II.
Wetzels, Walter D., 1930–
PN50.L57   1983   801'.9   83–6746
ISBN 0–8191–3280–2
ISBN 0–8191–3281–0 (pbk.)

TABLE OF CONTENTS

INTRODUCTION

When we proposed this project to ourselves, it seemed to us that it was time for a more differentiated look at the relations between literary and historical discourse. There has, of course, been no dearth of theoretical speculation and occasionally some methodological hand-wringing among literary scholars concerning the historical status (or lack of it) of the "art," or, more recently, the "texts" allotted to their disciplinary purview. And historians, in turn, teach their students to be cautious when they use literary texts as evidence.

But midst the jostling among the humanities and social sciences to assure themselves respectability and legitimacy, one often has the feeling that scholars are trying not so much to generate discourse as to establish a hierarchy of privilege among scholarly languages. Every generation or so (more quickly, lately), we struggle particularly through a rethinking of the relations between literature and history. And such rethinking always has to do with the value, not only of specific questions, but of the terms in which questions might be posed.

It was surely a relief for literary scholars to be told, by John Crowe Ransom and others, that they did not have to feel guilty about the sketchiness of their historical knowledge, or about their methodological indifference to history. They were free to enjoy the exhilaration of establishing a "new" criticism, and the satisfaction of working out the systematic, immanent structures of meaning in literary texts: such are the ahistorical joys of formalism. That poetic space might be subject to some temporal dimension was trivial--what made it poetic was precisely its escape from history, its ability to translate experience into form. When Northrop Frye tried to historicize the literary corpus, he produced an almost Jungian structure of archetypes and displacement, a structure which revealed only too clearly the essential formalism of his enterprise. Once again, the literary imagination was "demonstrated" to have priority over the historical. The defense of literature's privilege over history could be told in any number of chapters, among them some entitled, for example, "Structuralism" and "Deconstruction," with an array of supporting characters such as "anthropology" and "linguistics."

Of course, the story of privilege can also be told from the perspective of modern history, where, in the tradition of Ranke, the degree of discourse's proximity to the facts, "wie es eigentlich gewesen," constitutes its legitimacy, whereby "facts" are understood as something firmly unique in the temporal flux, bearing, presumably, no relation to archetypes or other literary-philosophical or linguistic notions. When Hayden White attempted to show historians that their nineteenth-century forebears could emplot the same sets of facts so as to make them tell radically different stories, however, he raised once again the claim that the literary has a certain hegemony over the historical. Predictably, though White is a practicing historian and not "merely" a historiographer, he was ostracized by the professional journals and societies of historians.

It is around such figures as White, and around increasing discomfort with the methodology of formalism and structuralism, that any contemporary attempt to address the relation between literature and history will inevitably coalesce. But we did not want simply to retrace old battle lines; we wanted to try, at least, to generate new discourse. While we did not shy away from methodological confrontations, we wanted also to provide new constellations and alternative perspectives: to review, for example, traditional literary notions such as Aristotle's concept of plot, to hear from a social historian about literature and science, to invite a philosopher to speak about redemption, a classicist about Tacitus, a social scientist about the historical relation between literature and the social sciences. The breadth of issues addressed by the essays in this book is therefore no accident, and we believe that thoughtful readers will find, as we have, resources for rethinking their own assumptions about literary and historical studies, as well as the relationship between them.

A word about our own biases: aside from theoretical issues, the texts dealt with stem almost exclusively from German literature and philosophy. There are historical reasons why a project such as this should be undertaken in a German context. From about 1770 on, history--its definition, its meaning, its pursuit--has been a central concern to German literature. From the locus classicus in Herder through Schiller's praxis as poet, playwright, and historian, through Hegel's grand view of the progress of spirit, to Nietzsche's views on history a century later, one might write a history of German literature from the point of view of what history meant to it. In short, there is, in German literature and philosophy, a peculiarly strong preoccupation with history and historiography.

The volume is divided into a theoretical section containing four contributions, and a section presenting five specific case studies. Ilse Bulhof first retraces the contours of the antagonistic relationship between those historians who hold that history describes the past and those who claim that history constructs a past. For the former, faithful documentation tells <u>the</u> story; for the latter, it is only with guided and guarded imagination that <u>a</u> story can be told. The author then proposes to transform the controversy into an investigation of interpretation in history. It is the concept of interpretation which should be of common concern for both the factual and the fictional.

Margaret Rose is concerned with history both as judgment about the past and as a (fictional) text. She approaches the issue by delineating the concept of history as farce, that is, as the parody of itself "the second time around," beginning with the idealist philosopher of history, Hegel, moving to the materialist interpreter of history, Marx, and going on to the structuralist analyst of history, Foucault.

Wolf Lepenies investigates the role of literature in the history of two scientific disciplines: that of sociology and psychiatry. Not only did Balzac's novels as sociograms precede the academic discipline of sociology, but they were the storehouse for social data from which sociological research could feed for a long time. Similarly, it was largely from the character descriptions in literature (where earlier scientific attempts at psychology had survived), that Freud gained his insights into the relationship of the conscious and the unconscious.

Finally, Louis Mackey rethinks the Aristotelian distinction between history as the account of that which did happen, and poetry of that which might happen, and the dictum that poetry is, therefore, more philosophical than, that is, superior to history. If philosophy is able to offer essential truth, then the imaginative hypotheses of poetry are supposed to be closer to the essence of reality than the factualness of history. The ancient question of truth in history and poetry is then recast and reopened in the contexts of Hayden White's and Northrop Frye's writings, among others. The ultimate issue is that of the notion of truth itself, its origin and its purpose in human life.

The specific case histories presented in the volume begin with an interpretation of Tacitus' description of the Germanic tribes, his <u>Germania</u>, by Gwyn Morgan. It appears that the question whether Tacitus' account of Germany is a reliable historical document or a piece of fiction is not so much unanswerable as, given the political context in which it was written, irrelevant. The dominance of rhetoric in Roman political life redirects the issue. In the <u>Germania</u>, seen as a rhetorical treatise in a concrete political situation, the (modern) antagonism between literature and history appears suspended. Even more revealing than Gwyn Morgan's description of the role of rhetoric in the <u>Germania</u> is his account of the history of the reception of the work in Germany's development to a nation state, including the national-socialist state.

Peter Uwe Hohendahl investigates the way in which literary history can be and was molded by political and social conditions: his example is Wilhelm Dilthey, and he locates the roots of and conditions for the seemingly most apolitical, most intimately artistic approach to literary history, in the post-revolutionary period of Germany after 1848. A comparison of representative literary histories before and after 1848 shows the differences in accepted literary canons, aesthetic theories and norms. Political history clearly informs literary history.

The remaining three essays focus on central themes and figures in Germany after the catastrophe of World War I, when historical events had shattered not only the political system of the past but also the established culture of that past. At the same time new voices appeared in the political and intellectual vacuum the Great War had left. John Zammito presents the most significant intellectual and particularly literary currents which rose in Berlin as a response to the political disaster of 1918, specifically the apparently contradictory orientation toward the Russian Revolution on the one hand and Americanism on the other. He further shows the underlying affinity of these two intellectual and political focal points as far as the German intelligentsia of the time was concerned.

In his analysis of Thomas Mann's diaries, using mainly the 1918-1921 diary which Mann had meant to burn, Hans Mayer shows Mann's bewildered, slow, and only partial awakening to the Republic. A keen observer of the revolutionary events in Bavaria, Thomas Mann is at once repelled and exhilarated by the new political and intellectual forces in society. The turmoil of these years, however, does not yet break down the ideological defenses of this "unpolitical man," and it will only later find its finely filtered expression in the Magic Mountain. It is during this most stormy period of Germany after World War I that Thomas Mann writes the two most idyllic pieces of his oeuvre, a story of his dog and a poem about his baby daughter.

The final essay, David Bathrick's contribution on Brecht, first presents Brecht's basic aesthetic tenet, namely that poetic representation is in itself historical representation. Aristotelian drama theories of the nineteenth century present a bourgeois reading of history; Brecht's own epic drama attempts a Marxist reading of history. Thus dramatic and political theory appear to necessitate each other. Yet while the stated correlation is successfully at work in many of Brecht's didactic plays, it reveals its limits in the dramatic treatment of the Nazi-phenomenon by Brecht. Bathrick's analysis of the play "Resistible Rise of Arturo Ui" shows how Brecht succeeds in the portrayal of Hitlerism only by reverting to classical dramatic techniques and only by subverting his stated dramatic paradigm from within. His "rationalist historiography" cannot come to terms with the non-economic, the anti-semitic, the emotional, the cultic components of the Nazi-movement.

The spectrum of the essays in this volume is broad and the approach is interdisciplinary. We have attempted to present the old Aristotelian question concerning the relationship between literature and history as refracted in the thoughts of our authors from the disciplines of philosophy, intellectual history, and literary history. Without the rigor and patience of our contributors, this volume would have remained a mere projection. Our special gratitude goes to Jennifer Oppenheim, for the expertise, precision, and cheerfulness with which she assisted us in the preparation of the manuscript.

LGS, WDW
Austin, Texas
November, 1981

x

I.

LITERATURE, HISTORY, AND THE QUESTION OF TRUTH:

THEORETICAL PERSPECTIVES

IMAGINATION AND INTERPRETATION IN HISTORY

Ilse N. Bulhof

...and thus I hope that history might recognize its significance not in generalizations,
seen as a kind of flowering and fruition, but
rather that its value is precisely that of ingen-
iously re-presenting a well-known, perhaps
banal subject, of raising it, or elevating it into
an encompassing symbol, and thus allowing a
whole world of profundity, power and beauty
to be perceived in the original subject.*
                    Friedrich Nietzsche,
                    The Use and Abuse
                    of History

Ever since the founder of modern historical scholarship, Leopold von Ranke, stated that he wanted to avoid imagination in his
historical writing, to stick to the facts, and to describe faithfully
what had happened, professional historians have scorned the usage
of the imagination in their renderings of the past. These days historians may realize that Ranke's version of historical realism was
somewhat naive, that, for instance, describing the past always
involves selection of the facts that go into the story, and that for
that reason exact descriptions are impossible. But nevertheless
they still purport to reconstruct rather than construct the past.
Thus it comes as no surprise that Hayden White's advocacy in
Metahistory of the literary imagination for the writing of history has
met with marked disapproval from the profession. After a lengthy
analysis of the literary devices used not only by eminent
nineteenth-century philosophers of history such as Hegel,
Nietzsche and Marx, but also by respectable historians such as
Ranke himself, Michelet and Burckhardt, White adds a
little-appreciated prescription for today's historians, admonishing
his colleagues to free themselves from the spell of the cautious
"ironic mode" of writing history caused by their misplaced desire to

*Editors' translation. See Friedrich Nietzsche, Werke in Drei
Bänden, ed. Karl Schlechta (Munich: Hanser, 1960), I, 249.

be objective and scientific.[1] Historians, White believes, should raise their linguistic consciousness, explore other literary modes for their narratives--modes which are consistent with their existential choices--and reanchor history in the literary imagination. This would remedy the dullness and sterility of ivory-tower historical research, and again give history a place in contemporary life.

Most historians, however, shudder upon hearing such pleas for the fictionalization of history. The approach of White and his like would, in the words of Adrian Kusminski, who in a recent issue of History and Theory claims to speak for the "silent majority" of historians, make history "indistinguishable from literature,"[2] "muffle" the cry of past actors, and reduce what has been said in the past from an end in itself to a mere means.[3] Another historian, John S. Nelson, writes disapprovingly that White unbridles a "Nietzschean imagination."[4]

What are the issues at stake in this debate? In exploring this question I will first try to show why historians tend to reject the use of imagination--by which I mean the introduction of elements not supported by the evidence--namely because they consider it to be their first and foremost obligation to do justice to the actors of the past. Next, I will suggest that by reorienting the debate from the topic of imagination to that of interpretation--by which I mean the elucidation of the meaning of the evidence--the discussion between the two parties might become much more rewarding. From the perspective of interpretation, another type of imagination might be given a place in historical practice: not the imagination of the writer who creates a fictional world, but that of the reader who imaginatively responds to a text. Let us begin by investigating Ranke's attitude toward literature.

Ranke's rejection of the use of literary language for the writing of history had three components. It was, first, a rejection of Hegelian philosophy of history; second, a rejection of history's literary past; and, third, an expression of the period's new sense of responsibility toward the past's actors. As Ranke's aversion to phi-

---

[1]   Hayden White, Metahistory: The Historical Imagination in Nineteenth Century Europe (Baltimore: Johns Hopkins, 1973), p. 434.

[2]   Adrian Kusminski, "Defending Historical Realism," History and Theory: Studies in the Philosophy of History 18 (1979), p. 322. Kusminski has made the same point, but in a less forceful manner, in his review article of Metahistory, "A New Science?," Comparative Studies in Society and History 18 (1976), pp. 129-143.

[3]   Kusminski, "Defending Historical Realism," p. 323.

[4]   John S. Nelson, rev. of Metahistory, by Hayden White, History and Theory: Studies in the Philosophy of History 14 (1975), p. 89.

losophy of history is well known, I will concentrate on his rejection of literary language for historical writing, and on his new attitude toward the past. We may recall that while teaching classics at a Gymnasium, he began to realize that history had not stopped with Classical Antiquity, that, although they were not described by prestigious authors, important events nevertheless had taken place since the fall of Rome.[5] Determined to chart this unknown sea stretching between Classical Antiquity and the present world, he was struck by the discrepancy between the portraits two different historians made of the same historical figures, Louis XI and Charles the Bold. This prompted him to consult sources of the time itself, such as documents and eyewitness reports. To his amazement, he found "...by comparison that the truth was more interesting and beautiful than the romance"; he now "resolved to avoid all intention and imagination" in his works and "to stick to the facts."[6] From that moment on, he wanted the past to speak for itself, by recording exactly what had happened, "wie es eigentlich gewesen."[7] Ranke wanted to picture the past in words as it offered itself to the observer's view, in exactly the same manner as the natural historians of his time began to prefer exact illustrations of the phenomena of nature over the traditional literary descriptions.

In Buffon's Natural History, published during the years 1750-1774, the left page of the book is occupied by a learned and elegant literary description of a natural phenomenon, while the right page is occupied by its illustration--a woodcut, drawing, or painting. In the transition from Buffon's traditional natural history to modern biology around 1800, the illustration gradually came to be considered as more instructive than the literary text. With an allusion to Buffon, Johann Andreas Naumann in his Naturgeschichte der Vögel Deutschlands (1822) stated that his book contained no illustrations of birds he had himself not observed, and he warned

---

[5] On Ranke, see Leonard Krieger, Ranke: The Meaning of History (Chicago: University of Chicago Press, 1977); Georg G. Iggers, The German Conception of History: The National Tradition of Historical Thought from Herder to the Present (New York: Columbia University Press, 1968), pp. 63-124. Iggers has also collected Ranke's scattered references to his theory of history in The Theory and Practice of History, ed. with an introduction by Georg G. Iggers and Konrad von Moltke. New translations by Wilma S. Iggers and Konrad von Moltke (Indianapolis: Bobbs-Merrill, 1973).
[6] Quoted by G.P. Gooch, History and Historians in the Nineteenth Century (London, New York: Longmans, Green, 1952), p. 74.
[7] Leopold von Ranke, "Preface to The Histories of the Latin and Germanic Peoples," in The Varieties of History: From Voltaire to the Present, ed. Fritz Stern (New York: Random House, 1973), p. 57.

his readers not to expect stylistic elegance in his work, as he "was more at home in rendering birds (Vogelstellen) than in literary writing (Schriftstellen)," and preferred the exploration of nature over that of books."[8] Similarly, the Rankean historian did not have to be versed in literature in order to write history. As Ranke put it, "where the events themselves speak, where the pure coherence shows how everything is connected, one does not have to use many words."[9] The only attribute a historian needed to have was a gift for empathy, an open mind to perceive the often amazing events and figures of the past. Ranke thus became the father of antiliterary realism, the school that maintains that the good historian faithfully describes the historical past, rather than imaginatively constructs or "creates" it, as the later revisionists maintain.

The first fruit of Ranke's labors was his Histories of the Latin and Teutonic Peoples, published in 1824. This landmark in historical scholarship is not an exciting literary achievement. But Ranke in his introduction proudly maintained that history should indeed not be written in a more graceful manner; a description of the particulars of history could not be other than "harsh, disconnected, colorless, and tiring," because that is what they themselves were. "The strict representation of facts, contingent and unattractive though they may be, is undoubtedly the supreme law."[10]

We may make three remarks at this point. To begin, the historian as the teller of the story, meting out praise and blame to the past actors, and offering his comments on events, had disappeared from Ranke's texts. Secondly, art had disappeared, too. In a straightforward descriptive language, the text simply depicted the truth, which in itself supposedly was already so beautiful that it required no embellishments to charm the reader. Thirdly, Ranke, in describing the past, did not feel he was interpreting it. The unadorned truth, after all, is the uninterpreted truth. The past in itself not only seemed beautiful to Ranke, but was so "eloquent," so to speak, that it sufficed for the historian simply to reconstruct it in words. Although Ranke, like his contemporaries, was well aware of the difference between the worlds of past and present, he did not feel alienated from the past. On the contrary, he felt part of the continuous stream of unfolding historical life. For Ranke the past world was a "text," different from the text of the present, but written by the same beneficent God and in the same language as the

---

[8] Wolf Lepenies, Das Ende der Naturgeschichte. Wandel kultureller Selbstverständlichkeiten in den Wissenschaften des 18. und 19. Jahrhunderts (Munich: Hanser, 1976), pp. 73-74.
[9] Quoted in Eberhard Kessel, "Rankes Idee der Universalhistorie," Historische Zeitschrift 178 (1954), p. 298.
[10] Ranke, "Preface to The Histories of the Latin and Germanic Peoples," p. 57.

present. Empathy and openmindedness were sufficient requirements to understand it. What was so fascinating about the past's
naked truth that he felt compelled to devote his life to the
description of a past that for centuries nobody had cared about?
Ranke and his contemporaries felt a new responsibility toward the
past.

Ranke was by nature a religious man. In his first publication,
he often perceived the hand of God hovering above the life of the
Latin and Teutonic peoples.[11] He discerned in every existent and in
every situation something "eternal" that "comes from God."[12] God's
presence in the past inspired the historian with "a certain respect
for what has passed, disappeared."[13] God's presence in nature
inspired the natural historian with a similar respect for the infinitely complex design of nature's creatures. But Ranke's religiosity
does not yet explain his devotion to the past; he could, after all,
also have found God in the present. His urge to recall the forgotten history back to memory was due to a new feeling that the
historian must redeem the past by remembering it.

As was the case with many intellectuals of his age, Ranke's
faith was no longer that of a traditional Lutheran. It was, in fact,
more of a pious mood affirming life's goodness than a creed affirming Christ as the Savior. It had become the task of man and the
historian in particular, to "save" man by remembering him. "Much
of what has been described has been lost," Ranke wrote. "Everything is threatened by death; only those who are remembered by
history have not completely died, their essence and existence are
still effective to the extent that they are perceived (aufgefasst).
Only with the disappearance (Erlöschen) of memory, death proper
begins."[14]

Nineteenth-century historians were concerned with the frightening possibility of total oblivion which, it was felt, would reduce
man's labor on earth to vanity. Jacob Burckhardt, for instance,
experienced despair over the fate of those peoples who perished
through the armies of Alexander the Great, who had not even left
their name. The aim of history, Michelet declared, is
"resurrection";[15] to Carlyle, history's aim was to revoke "the Edict
of Destiny, so that Time shall not utterly, not so soon by several
centuries have dominion over us."[16] The priestly task of guarding
the memory of the dead was behind the efforts of the Rankean his-

[11] Ibid., p. 57.
[12] Kessel, p. 295.
[13] Ibid., p. 296.
[14] Ibid., p. 302.
[15] White, Metahistory, p. 152
[16] Ibid., p. 146.

torian to restore to memory the forgotten past as it has been. It also inspired the requirement that the historian be just in his approach to the past.

Ranke urged historians to allow each of the past's struggling parties to speak for itself, and to give them an impartial hearing.[17] To be impartial was to be just. Rankean scientific history, indeed, had two components, a technical one of empirical research and factual description, and a moral one of justice.

Thus we may conclude that Ranke's anti-philosophical and anti-literary historical realism was rooted not only in the effort to make the discipline of history empirical and scientific but also in the effort to redeem the past by correctly remembering it. This moral dimension distinguishes history then and now from the natural sciences, and, according to J.H. Hexter, from the social sciences as well.[18] It also distinguishes history from literature; for how could a work of fiction save the past?

Since Ranke first outlined the new discipline of history, his conception of history, in particular its scientific nature, has been challenged seriously from various quarters. Doubts began to be raised from the end of the nineteenth century concerning whether the history of mankind really culminated in the civilization of the West, whether the storyline of history really evidenced such a progressive pattern. Thus, thinkers like Dilthey began to wonder how historians could discover the real story of history. In particular, five methodological questions were raised. Can the past, in view of the limitations of the human mind, be described objectively? Which is history's appropriate method of knowing the past: causal thinking, empathy, or hermeneutic understanding? Can the past be

[17] Kessel, p. 301. See also Leopold von Ranke, Author's preface to Memoirs of the House of Brandenburg and History of Prussia, trans. by A. and D. Gordon (New York: Greenwood Press, 1968), p. ix. In his essay, "On the Use and Abuse of History," Nietzsche castigated the historians of his time for their facile sympathizing. But he rightly saw that it was justice that was at stake. "The search for truth is often thoughtlessly praised, but it has something great in it only if the seeker has the sincere unconditional will for justice. Its roots are in justice alone" (F.W. Nietzsche, The Use and Abuse of History, trans. by Adrian Collins (Indianapolis: Bobbs-Merrill, 1957), p. 35). It may be said that the last judgment at the second coming of the Christian era was replaced by the judgment of history in which people have such a "happy faith," as Ranke wrote (Kessel, p. 299).

[18] J.H. Hexter, "History and the Social Sciences," Doing History (Bloomington: Indiana University Press, 1971), p. 133.

described without being interpreted? Can a past which does not exist be described at all? What is the appropriate language for history: scientific, ordinary, or literary language? Philosophizing by such writers about history as Nietzsche, Dilthey, Oakeshott, Collingwood, Sartre, Becker and Beard--and, lately, Murrey Murphy, Harold Toliver, Hayden White and Roland Barthes--seemed in the eyes of most historians to undermine needlessly the serious professional historian's claim that history provides true knowledge. Worse, their constructionism seemed to lower history to the status of art--of literature which produces only subjective fantasies powerless to redeem a past crying out for justice.

It was existential despair, not hostility toward science or enthusiasm for literature, that prompted the revisionists of Rankean history to give up the ideal of historical realism. Carl Becker is an example. His challenge to Rankean objective history clearly originated in his own despair over life's unintelligibility and over his helplessness in face of the sufferings of the past. He suffered from the same existential nausea so poignantly described by Sartre in his novel Nausea, in which--not accidentally--a historian who lost faith in the possibility of objective historical knowledge figures as the hero. In his memorable essays "Everyman His Own Historian," and "What Are Historical Facts," Becker explained the subjectivity of historiography by comparing history to memory. As memory is an essentially subjective type of knowing, in which one remembers only what one needs, or is compelled to remember, while the rest sinks back into oblivion, so is history.

Becker did not in the least glorify the limitations of collective historical memory. Ruefully he stated that the most striking historical events "must inevitably, for posterity, fade away into pale replicas of the original picture, for each succeeding generation losing, as they recede into a more distant past, some significance that once was noted in them, some quality of enchantment that once was theirs."[19] Concerning the facts which, according to Ranke, had to speak for themselves, Becker said that they were mute--"the miserable things couldn't say anything, would say just nothing at all."[20] Justice to past generations therefore was an illusion: every new generation of historians "must inevitably play on the dead whatever tricks it finds necessary for its own peace of mind."[21]

[19] Carl L. Becker, "Everyman His Own Historian," in Everyman His Own Historian: Essays in History and Politics (New York: F.S. Crofts, 1935), p. 255.
[20] Carl L. Becker, "What Are Historical Facts?," in Detachment and the Writing of History: Essays and Letters of Carl L. Becker, ed. Phil L. Snyder (Ithaca: Cornell University Press, 1958), p. 54.
[21] Becker, Everyman His Own Historian, p. 253.

The more a historian became aware of what he was doing, so it seemed, the more impossible his discipline became. It was clearly better not to think about history, and to consider history a craft, a skill to be learned by patiently practicing it, than to speculate about it.[22] The wicked attention to self-conscious theories of interpretation (as opposed to the praiseworthy work of plain description) serves, so writes Kusminski, the latest defender of historical realism, "to blunt the forces of the historical narrative, to deaden historians to the significance of the events, to skew their moral judgment and scramble their sensibilities, to drain the writing of history of its truth and vividness."[23] The "emotive power and ineffable significance"[24] of historical events such as the Holocaust simply is there for us to see, Kusminski claims, and it should be given to the reader uninterpreted, in the raw. Kusminski's reference to the victims of the Holocaust proves that today's defenders of historical realism still resist considering the role of the imagination in writing history, because of a deeply felt sense of responsibility towards the past's actors.

It may be countered that generally speaking today we no longer live in an age used to the comforting belief that God would remember everything, and that the majority of today's historians no longer feel the obligation to be just toward the past. And furthermore, it might be countered that today's social history discourages a concern for doing justice to the past's individual actors. Reacting to the impossibility of finding history's storyline, social historians are getting rid of the story element in history altogether, becoming more "scientific," more social-science oriented, and preferring to describe long-range historical processes, or topics such as population growth, the history of the family, of sexuality, of childhood. As a result of the anonymous nature of these topics, historians these days seldom comment on the question of justice. There is one notable exception: J.H. Hexter. In a seminal article entitled "The Rhetoric of History," Hexter claims that the peculiar-

---

[22] See, for instance, Marc Bloch, The Historian's Craft, trans. by Peter Putnam (New York: Knopf, 1962). Bloch refuses to give a definition of history: "What serious workman has ever burdened himself with such articles of faith?" (p. 21). He presents his essay as a "memorandum of a craftsman," "the notebook of a journeyman who has long handled the ruler and the level, without imagining himself to be a mathematician" (p. 19). In his short autobiography, J.H. Huizinga mentioned that he used to tell his students that they should not occupy themselves too much with the theory of history, because that would distract them "from the historian's real business" (J.H. Huizinga, "My Road to History," in Verzamelde Werken (Haarlem: H.D. Tjeenk Willink, 1948), I, 36).
[23] Kusminski, "Defending Historical Realism," p. 349.
[24] Ibid., p. 348.

ities of the study of history and of the way in which historical
knowledge is communicated to the reader will remain "wrapped in
mystery" if one does not realize that the historian's ultimate goal is
to pronounce a just judgment on the actors of the past.[25] But
although few historians comment on the problem, it would seem that
in our culture at large the memory of history's victims still
haunts--and perhaps also inspires--the survivors. The playwright
and poet Bertolt Brecht writes that the tombstone of the unknown
soldier serves as a daily reminder of the soldier's fate, that thus,
in spite of his death, the victim lives on.[26] The philosopher Marcuse, in Eros and Civilization, regrets that not even "the ultimate
advent of freedom can...redeem those who died in pain."[27] The literary scholar Hans Robert Jauß defends the traditional "history of
events" (histoire événementielle) with an appeal to justice--one
should write about events if indeed "one finally wants to do justice
to the great majority of suffering subjects. For these millions of
nameless actors undoubtedly would go down...if their historical
revival solely depended on their numerical or symbolical function in
economic processes, growth statistics, catastrophic wars and
natural disasters."[28] The novelist Alexander Solzhenitsyn dedicated

---

[25]   Hexter, Doing History, p. 133. But interestingly, he then
qualifies this statement by saying that perhaps to the dead "it may
not matter whether they receive justice at the hands of succeeding
generations" or not, but that it does matter to the living, to the
historian himself. "Not to be concerned with justice (in writing history) is to diminish not their human stature, but ours." According
to Karl Otto Apel, the language of science is not suited to communicate meaning, that is, the inter-subjective dimension of language.
[Karl Otto Apel, "The Apriori of Communication and the Foundation
of the Humanities," Man and World 5 (1972), p. 11].
    [26]   ...
    Entfernt wenigstens
    Diesen
        Stein über ihm
        ...
    Die wir den Erschlagenen
    Schon vergessen hatten, erinnert er
    Täglich aufs neue an euch, die ihr noch
    Lebt und die ihr
    Immer noch nicht erschlagen seid--
    Warum denn nicht?
        [Bertolt Brecht, Gesammelte Werke
        (Frankfurt am Main: Suhrkamp,
        1976), Vol. IX, p. 428.]
    [27]   Herbert Marcuse, Eros and Civilization: A Philosophical
Inquiry into Freud (Boston: Beacon Press, 1956), p. 237.
    [28]   Hans Robert Jauß, in Geschichte: Ereignis und Erzählung,
ed. Reinhart Koselleck and Wolf Dieter Stempel, pp. 559-560. This

his The Gulag Archipelago to "all who were tortured and murdered," to all those "who did not live to tell it," and he asks forgiveness "for not having seen it all nor remembered it all, for not having divined all of it."[29] To know that "everything will be told"[30] is to him the supreme consolation, salvation in short, for those who suffered. That Solzhenitsyn's conception of his task as a historian of the Russian labor camp system strikes a sensitive chord in today's realist historians is indicated by the lavish praise bestowed on the Gulag by Kusminski as a model to be emulated by historians.

It should be noted that in praising Solzhenitsyn, Kusminski is making an important concession to the self-conscious historical writers with theoretical and literary inclinations he disapproves of. He apparently deems it permissible again to use literary language in writing history. As long as a writer fulfills his function of being just toward the past, his literary language can be taken in stride. Hexter in his article "The Rhetoric of History" went even farther towards literature: he argued that the evocative but vague "rhetoric of history" is better equipped to do justice to the past's actors than the precise, controlled "rhetoric of science."[31] But before White, no historian had taken Hexter's advice to make a serious study of the rhetoric of history. Several circumstances still make it extremely difficult for historians to do so, the most important being that because historians honestly think that they are describing, not constructing the past, they cannot really see the "literary" nature of their writings. In our scientific culture literary language, with its figurative style and levels of meaning, is not considered an appropriate vehicle for telling "scientific" truth.

The second circumstance is that truth generally is considered in terms of logic. Something is true or it is not. Such simple truths can be expressed in simple and direct language, the unam-

passage occurs in discussion following a panel on the concept of the event in history. At this occasion Jauß had read a paper entitled "Geschichte der Kunst und Historie," in Geschichte: Ereignis und Erzählung (Konstanz: Universitätsverlag, 1976), pp. 174-211.
[29] Alexander I. Solzhenitsyn, The Gulag Archipelago 1918-1956. An Experiment in Literary Investigation (New York: Harper and Row, 1974), unnumbered page.
[30] Ibid., Preface, p. xi.
[31] Hexter suggests that the non-scientific way history is written not only has esthetic bearing, but "noetic bearing" as well (Doing History, p. 45); his aim in writing the essay was to alert historians to the fact that "the rhetoric of history...constitutes an appropriate response on the part of historians to their commitment to advance the knowledge and understanding of the past as it actually was" (Doing History, p. 75).

biguous language of science and logic. Literary language is either looked up to as a language for poets, a language too elevated to convey the elementary truths of ordinary life, or it is looked down upon as rhetoric.[32]

The third circumstance is that outside the literary profession, literary works are generally considered products of a gratuitous fancy which have little or nothing to do with ordinary reality. As Hexter puts it, as a self-contained work, a work of fiction can only be true or false to itself. A work of history, by contrast, is judged with regard to its congruence with the record of man's past.[33] The consequence for history of this supposed isolation of literary works from the "real world" is that historians do not expect that an understanding of literature can be of much value to them.

The historian's implicit concern for justice makes the profession's indignation over Hayden White's approach to history, which I mentioned in the beginning of this essay, seem less strange. For in his defense of literary language in historical writing, White goes much farther than Hexter: whereas Hexter takes pains to make clear that he wants the historian with his literary rhetoric to describe the past as it really has been,[34] White maintains that such a description is impossible. As far as the impossibility of exactly, or literally, describing the past is concerned, many historians might agree. But in stating that the historian's representation has nothing whatsoever to do with the past he purports to describe, White takes a position that is unacceptable to almost all historians.

According to White, every supposed historical description, falling short of a complete re-creation of the original, involves a selection of what is important and what is not, involves, in other words, interpretation. For that reason alone, the Rankean notion of a description of the past as it had really existed is impossible. Second, even if the past simply could be described as it had been, it would be useless to do so, for as a result of intervening historical changes, we are alienated from the past. The past is no longer

---

[32] In his essay, "History and Literature: Reproduction or Signification," in The Writing of History: Literary Form and Historical Understanding, ed. Robert H. Canary and Henry Kozicki (Madison: University of Wisconsin Press, 1978), pp. 4-7, Lionel Gossman describes how from the late eighteenth century on, literature has become increasingly esoteric.

[33] Hexter, Doing History, p. 48.

[34] In Style in History (New York: Basic Books, 1974), Peter Gay takes the same position.

directly intelligible to us without interpretation.[35] Thus, even if it could be done, reproduction would not work, for it is "the very strangeness of the original as it appeared in the documents," says White, "that inspired the historian's efforts to make a model of it in the first place."[36] Thirdly, the historian does not deal with the past strictly speaking, for that is gone forever. Thus a literal description of the past is impossible.

He observes that historical descriptions, the verbal images of the past as a whole, or of a specific set of events such as the French Revolution, can diverge widely; he then concludes that such supposedly descriptive narratives are constructs of the historian's creative literary imagination. History, he writes, is a poetic rather than an empirical enterprise. Historical narratives are "verbal fictions,"[37] poetic creations which have more in common with literary narratives than with scientific reports. Thus, White directly links history's unscientific or literary language to historical constructionalism.

His approval of Lévi-Strauss's statement that today's histories are the modern version of yesterday's myths[38] confirms the historian's worst suspicions that White wants to turn history into mere fiction. Historians might be less indignant if White, like Becker, had at least the excuse of suffering from existential despair over the meaninglessness of life and history. But he clearly rejoices over the freedom the historian has in shaping his story, and he happily encourages his colleagues to do the same.

White further alienates historians by charging that, to the extent that they do not realize the subtle means by which they smuggle personal interpretations into supposedly objective pictures, they evidence a deplorable "lack of linguistic self-consciousness."[39] So far, historians have shown little inclination to have their consciousness raised by White.

White has made great contributions to the study of history; but in one respect he perhaps overreacts to the Rankean ideal of anti-literary historical realism, namely in denying that no relationship whatsoever exists between the story and past events. In tak-

---

[35] Hayden White, "The Historical Text as Literary Artifact," in The Writing of History: Literary Form and Historical Understanding, ed. Robert H. Canary and Henry Kozicki (Madison: University of Wisconsin Press, 1978), p. 49.
[36] Ibid., p. 51.
[37] Ibid., p. 42.
[38] Ibid., p. 44.
[39] Ibid., p. 61.

ing this position, he ignores the role played by the evidence, the sources, in historical research.

According to White, historical facts have no intrinsic meaning. Historical factors may be defined in this context as the events that according to the general consensus of the historical community have occurred in the past, and function as the unquestioned supports of the stories historians tell. Because, according to White, history has always happened haphazardly and discontinuously, historical events "do not have built into them intrinsic meanings in the way that literary texts do."[40] The meaning of an event such as the assassination of President Kennedy derives exclusively from the place it occupies in a story as told by a historian.[41] In themselves events are "value-neutral."[42] Perhaps the assassination of President Kennedy cannot be plotted as a comedy, but it could be plotted equally well as a romance, a satire or a tragedy.[43]

[40] Ibid., p. 48.
[41] Ibid., p. 47.
[42] Ibid., p. 47.
[43] Ibid., p. 48. White's conception of historical narratives brings to mind Thomas Kuhn's conception of scientific theories during a scientific revolution. About events, the events of the French Revolution for instance, White writes, very different stories can be told, such as the accounts by de Toqueville or Michelet. Yet, as far as the underlying historical facts are concerned, these divergent versions are equally good history. One therefore cannot choose between them on purely historical grounds; external factors, including ideological preferences, also play a role in evaluating them (Metahistory, passim; see also "The Historical Text as a Literary Artifact," p. 48).
Kuhn likewise maintains that in times of scientific revolutions several theories are brought forward, each of which explain the facts equally satisfactorily, and that at those periods external factors co-determine which theory finally will be adopted by the scientific community (Thomas S. Kuhn, The Structure of Scientific Revolutions (Chicago: University of Chicago Press, 1962), pp. 144-159). In contrast to the scientist, however, the historian will always be confronted with different versions of the past to choose from; history therefore will never be comparable to a "normal" science.
A second similarity between White and Kuhn is that neither of them wants to jeopardize the foundations of the enterprises they analyze. White explicitly takes the standards of historical research for granted by stating that there is good and bad history. In evaluating history the historian has reliable criteria at his disposal, such as responsibility to the rules of evidence, the relative fullness of narrative detail, logical consistency ("The Historical Narrative as

It is unwarranted, however, to maintain that such a total separation exists between past human experience that at the time was
lived through as meaningful, and that is mediated to later periods
by still extant evidence, and the histories later told about it. In
White's approach to history, the formalist literary and linguistic
analysis of the end product of the historian's labor, the narrative,
obscures the interpretation of the meaning of the signifying evidence that lies at its basis.[44]

The succession of events in history may be haphazard, as
White claims, and hence they may not express an objective immanent
meaning of the type traditional philosophers of history were looking
for. But the events certainly have been meaningful for their participants; they therefore did have subjective meaning, and that
meaning the historian still attempts to understand.[45]

As the "meaningless" succession of events, the course of history thus may not be like a consciously written literary text; but as
a succession of meaningful experiences, it is not like a succession
of mere scribblings, a non-text. The experienced event, or cluster
of such events, can be likened more appropriately to a word or sentence uttered in a language with which the later reader is
insufficiently familiar. It is the business of the historian to learn
to understand the language of the evidence mediating these experienced events to the present and to listen to what the voices of the
past are saying by means of it. The evidence, as an objectified
expression of human experience, does not cease to signify, or to
communicate meaning, when the receiver to whom it may originally
have been addressed is no longer there to "read" it. Its function
of signifying remains intact. In order to be actualized as text, it
only needs someone to approach it with the intention to understand
it. The widening temporal gap between the lived experience on the
one hand, and the later historian on the other, does not undo the
evidence's power to communicate meaning. It will only make it more
difficult to interpret.[46] Moreover, language is by nature symbolic,

a Literary Artifact," p. 59). Kuhn likewise accepts the natural sciences as they are actually practiced these days.
  [44] As Leon J. Goldstein in Historical Knowing (Austin: University of Texas Press, 1976), pp. 141-143, points out, this strategy
characterizes the writings on the philosophy of history published in
the English speaking world in general. (See also Historical Knowing, p. 148.)
  [45] In hindsight, history's events appear to be linked causally.
To establish causal chains is usually an exciting but risky affair, as
the results can be neither confirmed nor disconfirmed.
  [46] The same mistaken conception of the evidence as saying nothing because of the ambiguity of its language is expressed by Roland
Barthes. In "The Discourse of History," Barthes distinguishes

and can therefore be interpreted in different ways. The circumstance that it is not always clear what the evidence is saying, or what kind of experience it is communicating, does in no way justify the conclusion that it communicates no meaning at all.

It is interesting to note, however, that with his constructionalism and his advocacy of a freer use of the literary imagination, White does not intend to open the door to wilful distortion of the past, or to turn history into an exercise in propaganda. On the contrary, White claims truth-value for the products of the historian's literary imagination: these histories make us understand the past better, not in the way science does (or at least, not in the way laymen think science does) but in the way works of literature do: "We experience the 'fictionalization' of history as an 'explanation' for the same reason that we experience great fiction as an illumination of a world that we inhabit along with the author."[47]

Unfortunately, White does not give the reader any explanation of how a work of imaginative history, or fiction for that matter, helps us to understand our world better. Here lies a serious deficiency in his defense of the literary imagination. For in order to convince the silent majority of realist historians that his view represents a way to further history's aim of doing justice to the past instead of subverting it, White should have explained just how the literary form of a historical narrative can do justice to the past, or, put in more general terms, how art is related to our human reality. As it stands now, White's offhand remark leads nowhere. As a

three kinds of "relics"--things which testify to the presence, or "reality," of the past: first, there are the "true relics" which are believed really to contain the sacred; second, there are the "secularized relics," which no longer contain the sacred in the original sense of the word, only the quasi-sacred which is "attached to the riddle of what has been"; these secularized relics no longer have a real presence, for as relics they are "no more"; they merely present themselves "as present signs of something dead" (Roland Barthes, "Le discours de l'histoire," Information sur les sciences sociales, 6 (1967), p. 74). Third, there are "profanized relics," things which once were containers of the sacred, which once had presence, but which presently no longer refer to anything. They are, we might say, too weak to say or signify anything, and therefore can be made to say everything a present historian wants them to say.

One can only wonder why a literary critic such as Barthes, and a historian with such a keen sensitivity for language as White, feel compelled to interpret the ambiguity of evidence as an indication of muteness, instead of its textual nature.

[47] White, "The Historical Text as Literary Artifact," p. 61.

result, the relationship between realist and literary history has become more strained than ever.

We have now identified the two root causes of the hostility many historians experience toward literarily inclined colleagues: the responsibility felt by the historian to do justice to past actors, and the feeling that works of literature with their fictitious stories have little or nothing to do with reality, past or present. At this impasse, I will suggest another approach to the debate between history and literature.

The fact that history is written on the basis of evidence does not mean that the imagination plays no part in the study of history. The historian indeed has a great deal of freedom in constructing his narrative. But, I will argue now, it is not the freedom of the novelist creating a world in words. It is the freedom of the interpreter reading a literary text, listening to what is actually said and trying to figure out what it means.

When in this debate attention is reoriented from the problem of historical imagination to that of historical interpretation, when history is seen as a hermeneutic discipline rather than either a scientific or a literary one, then the discussion between realist and literary historians begins to look rewarding in other ways besides that of the analysis of history's rhetoric. I would like to submit that historians might explore the experience of philosophers of literature in the field of literary interpretation in order to find out in which ways they could profit from this experience for their own study of history. In the following, I will illustrate how historians, especially realist historians, might benefit from a greater familiarity with literary theory in the areas of (1) the interpretation of the evidence and (2) historical praxis. I will do so by using the work of Thomas E. Hill and Hans-Georg Gadamer. I do this very eclectically and tentatively. For, being a historian, my experience in the field of literary interpretation is limited. First, we will consider interpretation in the area of historical evidence. For the understanding of what is going on in interpreting historical evidence--documents, letters, artifacts, mementoes, monuments, field patterns--I have found most useful the reflections of Thomas E. Hill on how signs, or "bearers of meaning," as he calls them, express meaning. In his book The Concept of Meaning,[48] Hill points out that signs bear meaning--often simultaneously--in two major ways: causal and intentional. Evidence bearing meaning in the causal way figures in logical discourse; evidence bearing meaning in the intentional way in hermeneutical discourse.

[48] Thomas E. Hill, The Concept of Meaning (New York: Humanities Press, 1971). See in particular pp. 1-60 and pp. 122-129.

Historians use evidence in logical discourse when they treat them as clues for the reconstruction of the causally connected and tightly knitted structure of past events. This usage can be likened to a detective's usage of bloodstains and fingerprints as clues in reconstructing a crime.

But the historian's task is not finished when he has logically established the sequence of events--that is to say, in having figured out who has done what, when and where. He also wants to understand the meaning of these happenings: what they have meant to the historical actors themselves, and what they now mean to his own generation. Historians, in other words, use the evidence also as what Hill calls "bearers of meaning in the intentional way," in hermeneutical discourse.

Historical evidence in the widest possible sense can therefore be likened to texts, or speech acts, whose meaning needs to be interpreted.[49] They are the outward manifestations of voices reaching us from the past--voices that continue to speak to later generations as long as the objects embodying them exist. Hill's distinction between the evidence's causal and intentional ways of bearing meaning further clarifies the seemingly unlogical approach of the last of the historical realists. Historical realists such as Kusminski, but also Peter Gay in Style in History, and Hexter in Doing History, feel that they not only causally reconstruct the structure of a past that they know very well is gone forever, cannot be described exactly as it has been, and has to be interpreted. Historians, I believe, feel that they listen to past voices that, fixated in the evidence, continue to speak to the present, and that by means of the evidence, they somehow really are in touch with the past.

The second area in which the historian may profit from an increased familiarity with literary interpretative theory is in the interpretation of what it is that historians are doing, the interpretation of historical practice. In exploring literary-interpretation

[49] Historians do not work with high quality texts only, such as the classical texts of historiography, religion, philosophy, jurisprudence or literature. They work with evidence, texts of a humbler nature, often not even linguistic. Consequently, the literary scholar focuses his attention on the text as such, and when studying its social context, is always drawn to return to his text; the historian, by contrast, is drawn irresistibly toward the past beyond the humble evidence, the past that once produced the evidence, and that the historian attempts to rescue from oblivion. More than anything else, this movement away from the humble evidence to the past he wants to understand creates the illusion that the historian describes the past.

theories, I have been struck by the similarities between Hans-Georg Gadamer's analysis of the function of the literary scholar's reading and interpreting historical evidence.[50] In the following exposition of these similarities, I will in each case first outline an aspect of Gadamer's theory of literature, and then tentatively explain how it compares with the historian's study of history.

A first similarity concerns Gadamer's view of the function of literary representation as a "re-presenting" of what is imaged. In Truth and Method, Gadamer stresses the representational nature of art. In making an image, verbal or other, the artist, according to Gadamer, makes the imaged subject become present; he literally "re-presents" what is represented. Gadamer states that a work of art participates in the being of what is represented.[51] He furthermore maintains that the imaged world, the subject matter of representation, presents itself, as it were, to the artist, inviting to be imaged. An image, a representation, he writes, can be made of a subject because it presents or discloses itself, or exists in a way worthy of being imaged.[52] According to Gadamer, Velasquez' painting of the surrender of Breda illustrates how an historical act was being performed with such solemnity, "almost like a sacrament," that the scene invited imaging. The ceremony was "bildhaftig," as he puts it.[53]

---

[50] In literature, currently two schools of hermeneutical interpretation theory exist: the school of E.D. Hirsch, according to whom the meaning of a text is identified as the author's conscious intention, and the school of Hans-Georg Gadamer, according to which meaning can be identified as the outcome of a dialogue between text and reader. I tend to agree with Gadamer's analysis because the meaning of a work of art always transcends an author's conscious intention, expressing the author's unconscious desires and testifying to social and cultural situations the author may not in the least be aware of, but at which a reader may grasp.

[51] Hans-Georg Gadamer, Wahrheit und Methode. Grundzüge einer philosophischen Hermeneutik (Tübingen: J.C.B. Mohr, 1960). "Was ein Bild ist, bleibt...eine Manifestation dessen, was es darstellt, auch wenn es dasselbe durch seine autonome Sagkraft zur Erscheinung kommen läßt" (p. 142). "Die im Spiel der Darstellung erscheinende Welt steht nicht wie ein Abbild neben der wirklichen Welt, sondern ist diese selbst in der gesteigerten Wahrheit ihres Seins" (p. 130).

[52] Ibid., p. 135. Gadamer writes about a public figure: "Nur weil er derart ein Sein im Sichzeigen hat, wird er ja eigens im Bilde dargestellt. Das Erste ist also gewiß Sich-Darstellen, das Zweite die Darstellung im Bilde, die dieses Sichdarstellen findet."

[53] Ibid., p. 142. "Es gibt eben Seiendes, das bildbedürftig und bildwürdig ist und das sich in seinem Wesen gleichsam erst vollendet, wenn es im Bilde dargestellt wird."

Seen from Gadamer's perspective of art as "re-representation," realist historians in describing the past seem to behave as if all past human experience was "bildhaftig." Ranke was the first historian to become alerted to the lasting invitation of the past to be "re-presented," and the modern historian's act of justice was then and still is to make the forgotten past present again by "re-presenting" what had happened.

Examples of events inviting representation are the atrocities perpetrated by Stalin and Hitler. As far as the Holocaust is concerned, this event is for many of us still too painful to be looked at and to be "read" again. But all of us are convinced, I think, that if any historical event should remain alive--present--in the memory of later generations, be it as warning or as an act of remembrance, it is the death of those millions. Such "imaging," such "re-presentation," one might think, is what Kusminski had in mind in calling for the plain description of historical events in all their "emotive power and ineffable significance."[54] Thus, from Gadamer's perspective of art as "re-presentation," even Kusminski's naive advocacy of pure description begins to make sense.

It may be remarked in this context that, unlike an official occasion such as the surrender of Breda, episodes in the life of the anonymous masses had invited no artists or historians to image the scenes. Sometimes such "unrepresented" episodes, however, have had witnesses who have written about what went on, and sometimes such episodes more or less accidentally have left behind linguistic or non-linguistic evidence. Later historians piece these together in order to reconstruct and understand what has happened. There are, of course, countless episodes that have left no evidence whatsoever. Because they were forever forgotten, these episodes haunted Burckhardt. Gadamer's theory of re-representing helps us to better understand his despair. For we might say that in cases in which life simply was lived--not self-consciously represented--the participants produced the events, the sequences of events that for us are histories, without knowing they were "writing a story." They behaved like private persons, without attempting to get any lasting meaning across. In cases in which the evidence has been destroyed by history's victors, we might say that the victims are deprived of the consolation that they will live on in the stories later generations will tell. Such people lived or "wrote" the story of their lives, of their generation and age, for nobody; and in many cases nobody ever will read their story; their lives, like screams in outer darkness, will never be heard and will receive no response. Ranke and historians ever since, it would seem, have responded to those who despaired of ever being heard--that is to say, to the despair of those for whom God, who used to remember them all, tru-

---

[54] Kusminski, "Defending Historical Realism," p. 348.

ly had died. In the same way, recently, several groups of anonymous people have been rescued from oblivion--women, blacks, the working class--causing whole new branches of history to emerge. We experience this as an act of justice.

A second similarity lies in the area of interpretation. Gadamer's conception of a work of art as a re-presentation of an original presence brings with it a conception of interpretation as the actualization, or, to use Gadamer's expression, "completion" of the work's intention, which, after all, has been written to be read. In reading, viewing, hearing--whatever the case may be--a work of art is completed by the observer. Brought to fruition, its potential is realized, made to work, given an opportunity to be effective. Gadamer states that many existents present themselves in order to be re-presented, to be imaged. Just like works of art, such existents are "in a fundamental sense completed when re-presented in an image."[55] Seen from that perspective, historical evidence, too, might be considered to come to fruition, to be completed, by the historian's reading of it and his act of communicating its meaning to the general public. This is particularly true with regard to the great historical monuments--Gettysburg, the Alamo, Stonehenge, the pyramids--which are like texts in requiring interpretation by the historian, and which only by means of such an act of interpretation become effective as monuments.

A third similarity lies in the area of the historical effect of a work of art, occasioning various interpretations. In order to fulfill its function of bringing the imaged subject into the present, the work (to limit ourselves to literary works) needs to be read and interpreted. As we have seen, the original text, itself a re-presentation of an original presence, is, according to Gadamer, re-presented in interpretation. But such re-presentation is not a simple repetition of the original texts. In each new situation the original text presents itself differently to later readers.

The readings and interpretations it receives in the course of time, Gadamer maintains, originate in the work and therefore belong to the work itself. The interpreter actualizes the work's potentialities. These successive interpretations are the work's "effective history" (Wirkungsgeschichte), its "way of being effective" (Weise von Wirkung).[56] In Gadamer's words: "Understanding (Verstehen) must be conceptualized as a part of the process in which meaning happens, [a process] in which the meaning of all utterances (Aus-

---

[55] Gadamer, Wahrheit und Methode, p. 136. "Wort und Bild sind nicht bloße nachfolgende Illustrationen, sondern lassen das, was sie darstellen, damit erst ganz sein, was es ist."
[56] Ibid., p. 323.

22

sagen)...is formed and completed."[57] But such completion is never finished, because, as a result of new life-experiences, the work will continue to inspire new interpretations. Interpretation is thus an ongoing process.[58] The greater the work, the more responses it will draw, the richer its effective history will be.

Seen from Gadamer's perspective on an effective history of works of art, the continuing stream of "readings," or interpretations by historians, too, can be considered the "effective" history of what are known as history's great events--the defeat of Athens in the Peloponnesian War, the fall of Rome, the modern revolutions, the Holocaust. As Jauß puts it, like works of art, events have a "horizon of possible meaning,"[59] an "open structure of meaning,"[60] and their understanding implies the same hermeneutic as the understanding of a work of art.[61] Like works of art, such events continue to influence the future, and are never "worked out," are never interpreted exhaustively.

A fourth similarity might be in the area of Gadamer's conception of interpretation as a kind of translation of a text--which in consequence of the lapse of time has become unintelligible--into an idiom the reader can understand.

In history, we may distinguish between two kinds of translation: linguistic and experiential. Linguistic translation is obviously indicated when the past experiences have been expressed in the evidence in a different language from that spoken by the historian and his readers. This may be a foreign language, or a language that from our point of view has become antiquated and so is unintelligible without the services of a translator. Experiential translation is indicated next, as many of the past experiences are alien to our contemporary way of life. Occultist beliefs and practices (as described by Francis Yates) have often been described by historians in terms of superstition, while at the time they represented profound philosophical insights. To describe them in terms of superstition, therefore, is clearly a mistranslation. Rendering them more adequately may involve much paraphrasing and commentaries, and even the creation of new linguistic forms. Robert F. Berkhofer, Jr. hopes that a "Picasso of history" will find such new forms.[62]

---

[57] Ibid., p. 157.
[58] Ibid., p. 282.
[59] Jauß, in Geschichte: Ereignis und Erzählung, p. 535.
[60] Ibid., p. 536.
[61] Ibid., p. 536.
[62] Robert F. Berkhofer, Jr., Behavioral Approach to Historical Analysis (New York: Free Press, 1969), p. 320.

23

Gadamer's perspective on the understanding of the past's literary texts as being a kind of translation process may induce realist historians to be somewhat more sympathetic to Hayden White. And so we return to the problem of the literary imagination in history. Like the interpreter of a work of art, the Whitean historian will experiment with language in order to find out which linguistic structure can best render the meaning of the past as he understands it. Such understanding is difficult, White stresses, because the data the historian works with are always "strange, not to say exotic, simply by virtue of their distance from us in time and their origin in a way of life different from ours."[63] A simple description, even if possible, would not help us to understand the past. The alien experiences of distant periods first have to be translated in terms that make sense to the historian and his contemporaries in their own present. Such translation has nothing to do with a free-floating imagination. Perhaps White in the final analysis might be considered a respectable hermeneutic historian after all. For let us remember also at this point, that White wanted to tell "true" stories, stories that further our understanding of our shared human reality.

The parallels existing between Gadamer's philosophy on the one hand, in which the speaking power of the work is so important, and on the other hand, the implied philosophy of realist historians in which the speaking voices of the past occupy such a crucial place, result from the fact that in both cases we are dealing with a philosophy of presence. Gadamer's theory of literature is, of course, but one of many such philosophies. It would be most interesting to undertake similar investigation of other literary theories, such as Jacques Derrida's, whose "grammatology," being a philosophy of absence, of the "trace," seems the exact counterpart of Gadamer's.[64] Perhaps such an investigation would illuminate other aspects of what it is today to write history, or what it might become tomorrow.

．　．　．　．　．

It is time to bring our exploration to an end. In the first part of this presentation we have identified the two root-causes of the prevailing animosity between the majority of realist historians claiming that history describes the past and the minority of historians

---

[63]   White, "The Historical Narrative as a Literary Artifact," p. 49.

[64]   In his Of Grammatology, trans. Gayatri Chakravorty Spivak (Baltimore: Johns Hopkins, 1977), Derrida rejects the "ontology of theology and the metaphysics of presence" (p. 50). He chastises the "exigent, powerful systematic, and irrepressible desire for the transcendental signified" (p. 49).

claiming that history imaginatively constructs it: the responsibility felt by many historians to do justice to the past, and their conception of literature as mere fancy. In the second part I have suggested that when attention is reoriented from imagination to interpretation, the discussion might become more rewarding. Such a discussion is being made easier these days through the development by literary scholars--such as Yuri Lotman and Hans Robert Jauß--of theories of literature stressing the relationship between literature and the worlds in which it is, or was, produced, received and communicated. These theories bring literature down from the mountain top of aesthetic perfection where literature as "high culture" has resided since the Romantic period, to the valley of ordinary human life. Moreover, they show ordinary reality itself to be ambiguous, requiring interpretation like a literary text. Perhaps, in due time, these revisions of the relationship between fiction and reality, and between literary and ordinary language, can show historians how a language which is not straightforwardly descriptive but self-consciously literary can in its own way illuminate our understanding of reality, including those aspects that speak about its past. Then the silent majority of historians might slowly lose its realist distrust of literature.

26

"THE SECOND TIME AS FARCE": A BRIEF SURVEY OF

THE CONCEPT OF HISTORY UNDERSTOOD

AS FICTION AND FARCE

Margaret A. Rose

Aristotle and After

I would like to begin by citing Aristotle's distinction in the Poetics: "the difference between a poet and a historian is this: the historian related what has happened, the poet what could happen. Therefore, poetry is something more philosophic and of more serious import than history; for poetry tends to deal with the general, while history is concerned with delimited particular facts." It is also a fact of course that Marx's designation of history as farce in his 18th Brumaire of 1852 ironically if not paradoxically links these two areas of history and literature together--apparently to denigrate both. But this is a step preceded by and explicitly related to the step taken by Marx's object of derision, Hegel, before him, in attempting to equate not literature but history with the Universal. In doing this, Hegel was also juxtaposing those elements which Aristotle had made separate in distinguishing the particular and history from poetry and its ability to describe the universal. To Hegel, material history (as the objectification of Spirit and hence as a stage in the development of Absolute Spirit), had in fact represented the unity of Mind with Matter in the development of the Absolute, while the study of history (as the study of Spirit), was itself regarded as a necessary part of the creation of the Universal--a part, that is, of its self-fulfilment in "absolute" consciousness of itself. So-called "material" history was then to Hegel the unfolding of the Real itself in Nature where the Real was understood to be Reason or Spirit, and the latter both the subject and object of written history.

To Marx--whose 18th Brumaire opens with the remark that Hegel had forgotten to state that history repeats itself as farce when it repeats itself--Hegel's Idealist theory of history was a fictional unity--created by and in the human imagination and symptomatic of a division of mental and manual labour, the roots of which were (for Marx at least) economic and disparate. Yet despite its critical treatment of Hegel, Marx's 18th Brumaire was not just to attack the Idealist Hegelian concept of history, but also to attempt to use Hegel's description of the dialectical development of history for a new materialist analysis of human production. In this, Marx was also to go beyond the Idealist critiques of Hegel offered by Bruno Bauer and other Young Hegelians known to Marx in the 1840's, as also the work of another student of Hegel who was to speak of history as farce, the essayist and poet, Heinrich Heine.

In many of Heine's works of the 1830's, his adherence to Hegel's view of the history of Spirit had been evident. Not only in his "Zur Geschichte der Religion und Philosophie" but also in works such as his essay "Verschiedenartige Geschichtsauffassung," where the repetitive view of history of Ranke's historical school is compared with the "progressive" dialectical view of history of the Hegelian and Saint-Simonian Schools, Heine's statements of belief in the progress of Reason in history are supportive of Hegel. In 1822 Heine had moreover been a member of the "Verein für Kultur und Wissenschaft der Juden," together with Edward Gans and other Hegelians, and had at that time probably also attended Hegel's lectures on the philosophy of history and the philosophy of religion.

It had been in the Society for the study of Jewish Culture and Learning mentioned above that Heine had begun the study of the history of the Jewish people, of which he was to write in his Rabbi von Bacherach. While this study was originally to have described the emancipation of the Jews, and, in the sense of a Hegelian concept of history, the development of Reason toward its goal through that emancipation, the renewal of the persecution of the Jews in the Damascus pogrom of 1840 was to cause Heine to give up both his faith in his story of emancipation and the Hegelian faith in a rational development of history, and to turn his novel into farce. In 1824 when Heine began his novel Der Rabbi von Bacherach, his model had been the historical novels of Scott. In 1840 when, following the Damascus pogrom of that year, Heine took up his "Rabbi" again, he chose, however, as his model the parody of Cervantes' Don Quixote, and parodistically brought together the dialectical oppositions on which the historical novel had been based.

In an article in the Heine Jahrbuch of 1976 on the structural unity of Heine's Fragment,[1] I have attempted to show in greater detail how the parodistic figure of Don Isaak, who appears in the last chapter of 1840, incongruously juxtaposes the binary oppositions of the fairy tale (as outlined by Vladimir Propp)--of expectation for the helper and sacrifice, of flight and refuge--to parody their goal, and the goal of Heine's early chapters of the 1820's, of a new Messiah and new Land. Disraeli had also taken the subject of

---

[1] "Die strukturelle Einheit von Heines 'Rabbi von Bacherach,'" Heine Jahrbuch (Düsseldorf: Heine-Archiv, 1976), pp. 38-51.

the liberation of the Jews for his novel Alroy in 1833, a novel which was once called by Lewis Feuer "the first Jewish historical novel." Like Hegel, members of the "Verein für Kultur und Wissenschaft der Juden," which Heine joined in 1822, had looked to America as the land of the future, and for Heine it had appeared significant that its discovery in 1492 had taken place in exactly the same year as the expulsion of the Jews from Spain. Here utopian discovery had seemed to match a dystopian climax, and Heine's hero was to make his path through Italy to America--transforming dystopian into utopian reality in a similar reversal of history. The early chapters of the novel are, for this reason too, based on the principle of reversal--helpers reversing antagonists, flight superseding containment. But when history repeated itself as tragic farce in the Damascus pogrom of 1840, Heine too closed history as a circle--bringing Don Isaak back into the ghetto from which his hero had started and turning his historical novel into farce. In the late 1830's in France, Heine had already begun to describe developments in French politics as the expression of the idea that history could--in terms, for example, of a Restoration replacing Revolution--develop into farce. The use of farce in Der Rabbi, to cynically unite the oppositions of helper and foe, passivity and activity, implicitly comments both on the tragic circularity of history, as well as on the failure of Heine's belief in the ability of the dialectical, Hegelian view of history either to direct the course of history toward greater rationality, or to interpret the irrational in any positive, rationalistic manner.

Marx's Rejection of Hegel

To Hegel Reason had not only produced the apparent irrationalities in history, but was being brought to absolute self-consciousness of itself through them. History was hence essentially both rational and universal, and irrationality an antithetical moment in this movement, rather than the farcical prevention of progress. But to Marx the modern post-industrial society following Hegel's time had revealed not only an inherent and seemingly intransigent irrationality in human history, but also an increased division between mental and manual labour on which was based not only the division of Reason and Unreason in human history, but also the growth of both historical analysis and literature as entities separate from material production.

The very distinction made by Aristotle between the theoretical disciplines of history and literature could hence itself be seen to be based in a division of mental labour reflecting that between material labour and mental labour, while both history and literature could be seen as having served to reproduce the social and ideological relations of society. To Marx, Hegel's attempt to show History to be the material objectification of "God" in the world had not overcome this split but reduced the material to the mental--reflecting the character of its own activity while apparently ignoring the material basis of its existence. To the young Marx in 1844/5 material history was moreover not merely the objectification of human labour but an economic reality, in which, under capitalism, the objectifications of human labour were being exchanged for abstract monetary value and made alien to their owners.[2]

Marx had in 1845/6, in The German Ideology, also described Hegel's Philosophy of History as the last attempt at a holistic "theological" history, and the dangers of holistic, universal theories are also implicitly warned against in Marx's famous opening sentence in his 18th Brumaire of 1852, where Hegel is accused of having forgotten that history repeats itself as farce--but is also accused of having obscured this by his idealist concept of history as the objectification of an expressive totality in the world. Here too, however, Marx was also to attempt to give up the literary parody he had used in The German Ideology and which had remained popular with the young Hegelian "critical critics" still entrenched in Hegel's Idealist concept of history as the expression of a consciousness growing toward absolute unity with itself and its material objectifications. For them parody was a means both to escaping censorship and to achieving that self-conscious criticism of their objects which would achieve critical criticism's aim of a totally radical and rational self-consciousness. To Marx after 1845 parody was however but a further temptation to eschew both the criticism of material history, and social action. To Marx history--empirically observed--was neither consistently rational nor continuous. But neither was literature as "the expression of the Universal" superior to the "Idealist" study of history because of this--but akin to it as fiction, as a product of both the Imagination and false consciousness. The use of literary parody to escape censorship was therefore also for Marx no longer a sufficient form of criticism.

History repeated as farce is to Marx moreover not only the expression of the falsity of the concept of an ideal expressive totality but of the material domination of the forces of history by a class which had appropriated for itself the intellectual power thought by Hegel to be the motor of all material events. The writing of both history and literature were also alike for Marx in being interpellated by and in the ideological apparatuses of those controlling the forces

---

[2]   In this century the social philosopher Alfred Sohn-Rethel was able to argue from this point that it was from the process of abstract commodity exchange itself that the intellectual realms of science, literature, and philosophy had ensured their own abstract autonomy from material production. See Alfred Sohn-Rethel, Intellectual and Manual Labour. A Critique of Epistemology (London: Humanities Press, 1978).

of material production--although material determinants on the division of labour, such as that of increased productivity needs--were thought by Marx to determine in the last instance their ideological interpellation.

Marx's use of the metaphor of repetitious history as farce served then to introduce concepts of historical materialism foreign to both Heine and Hegel. But it had also (as seen) to function to free Marx himself from the Young Hegelian use of parody as a method of criticism.[3]

The Next Stage: Meta-history

Modern structuralist thought has, in general, re-introduced Idealist categories rejected by Marx. Foucault--though recognizing the role of censorship in the construction of discourse and denying alliance with structuralism--has for example restated Kant's idealist belief in parody as a positive force in the changing of intellectual reality. It is also interesting to note here that one of Foucault's earliest publications was his translation of Kant's Anthropologie, in which that belief is expressed, and that to Foucault as interpreter of Nietzsche's genealogy, it is the discontinuity characteristic of parody which is characteristic of our present episteme.

Hence Foucault writes in the 7th section of his essay on "Nietzsche, Genealogy, History,"[4] for instance, that in being critical of "identity-making" discourse, parody sets itself up against history as the description of continuity or tradition, and that in doing so, it makes sense of the repetitions Nietzsche saw as constitutive of the eternal recurrence.

It is also parody's ability to satirize and analyze identities which Foucault--having taken Cervantes, Beckett and Borges for

[3] Engendered and preserved as such by the ideological apparatus of censorship, parody, as used by Marx in e.g. The German Ideology and The Holy Family, had both served to extend publications to the statutory 320 pages needed to escape the pre-censorship used to control small or cheap publications, and to cover criticism with irony and satire. In his Preface to the second edition of the 18th Brumaire Marx explicitly condemned, moreover, the satire of Hugo as ineffectual against the material forces of history it would decipher.
[4] Michel Foucault, "Nietzsche, Genealogy, History," in Language, Counter-Memory, Practice: Selected Essays and Interviews, ed. with an introduction by Donald F. Bouchard, tr. Donald F. Bouchard and Sherry Simon (Ithaca: Cornell University Press, 1977).

his "authorities" in Les mots et les choses[5]--had chosen as characteristic of the modern episteme. In Madness and Civilization[6] too, the concept of a rational society making history in its own image is--as in Adorno's and Horkheimer's Dialectics of the Enlightenment[7]--shown up as a repressive mask, concealing the discontinuous and the irrational within the confines of a "panoptical" vision.

Returning to section 7 of Foucault's essay on Nietzsche and genealogy, we find Foucault claiming there that the "good historian," the "genealogist," is one who practices parody because it is he who understands the reality of the decentered subject to exist in the play of masking and unmasking. Foucault now gives Marx's example of the French Revolution as a form of masking, but implies that history can also be positively "deconstructed" by being understood as parody. For Foucault, who is concerned with epistemological history, parody is, in short (as it was for Kant) self-critical and deconstructive. Parody is this for Foucault moreover because it is able to describe itself as a process of repetitive masking, and to present itself as both subject and object of its deconstruction of this process of masking. More importantly, Foucault also speaks here of the parodist's ability to make a "counter-memory" to history which will free it from existing metaphysical and anthropological concepts of memory, claiming this to be necessary in order to allow a new and different kind of time to unfold in history. The need for a new time, and the need for a new understanding of time, seems, however, to be the central concern for Foucault, who criticizes the relegation of the imagination in recent (post-Rankean) history to the literary, and who demands of the imagination that it should help history break with the past. For Foucault parody is one way for the imagination to help liberate history from its past or arche. While Foucault had followed Nietzsche in arguing that history is best understood as discontinous rather than as rational (Nietzsche had written in par. 123 of his "Morgenröthe," "How did reason come into the world? As is fitting, in an irrational manner, by accident"[8])--and had thus, like Marx, rejected the Hegelian claim that History could be seen to be the

[5]   Michel Foucault, Les Mots et les choses (Paris: Gallimard, 1966).
[6]   Michel Foucault, Historie de la folie à l'age classique (Paris: Plon, 1961).
[7]   Theodor W. Adorno and Max Horkheimer, Dialektik der Aufklärung. Philosophische Fragmente. (Frankfurt: Fischer, 1969).
[8]   Karl Schlechta, ed., Friedrich Nietzsche: Werke in drei Bänden (Munich: Hanser, 1966), I, 1097: "Vernunft.--Wie die Vernunft in die Welt gekommen ist? Wie billig auf eine unvernünftige Weise, durch den Zufall. Man wird ihn erraten müssen wie ein Rätsel."

unfolding of Reason--he had not followed Marx in demanding a more scientific, materialist analysis of historical irrationality. Rather than giving up parody as a method of analysis, as Marx had attempted to do in the 1850's, Foucault has revived it, arguing moreover that history, though not conceived of as a study of the Universal, should itself be studied by literary and imaginative means.

While rejecting the study of history as the study of a continuous rational development, Foucault has, however, also raised the concept of history as the study of particular discontinuous moments to a new status. Through making these particular discontinuous moments the subject of a history which is related by method to the poetic imagination, and even to farce, Foucault has in fact given those particular moments the status of the universal understanding ascribed by Aristotle to poetry in opposition to history as understood as the study of particular facts.

While literature has ironically found a new authority for itself as history through such developments, the historian as parodist--as that is, a self-critical archeologist of his own text[9]--has today also taken on new authority and fame in the world of literary texts and structuralist historiography, where archeology has become a metaphor for the modernist self-reflexivity of a subject determined and formed by many particular words and events seemingly often beyond its own comprehension or Reason. To the historian aware of his or her role as parodist the texts of history must moreover take on the form of prefigured literary or fictional texts to be deconstructed as such.

Some years ago Jean-Pierre Faye's critique of history as text even argued for uniting a semiotic study of history as text with a Marxist analysis of the role of the language of commodities in the control of recent European history by specifically totalitarian languages. Where Faye had begun his "Totalitarian Languages"[10] with a reference to Hegel's Phenomenology of Spirit and its expressivist theory of the objectification of Spirit in the words of history, the erstwhile Althusserian and then nouveau-philosopher André Glucks-

---

[9] I have discussed the function of modern parody as an archeology of the text in Parody/Meta-Fiction (London: Croom Helm, 1979), and have argued there that the Structuralist obsession with the discontinuous and intertextual nature of texts is to some extent dependent on the parody character of the texts initially looked at by Formalists such as Shklovsky, and still chosen for analysis by Structuralists today.
[10] Jean-Pierre Faye, Langages totalitaires (Paris: Hermann, 1977).

mann has, however, claimed in his Maîtres penseurs,[11] that Hegel himself must be attributed some blame for the elimination of freedom from history, and for its totalitarian moments. Put briefly, the concept of history as the expression of Reason is seen by Glucksmann to be a deterministic "sentence," which writes unfreedom into what appears to be the celebration of freedom. Hegel himself is, for Glucksmann, a totalitarian--but also irrational--writer.

One symptom of the power of history as text over material history given by Andre Glucksmann in his Les maîtres penseurs--The Master Thinkers--is moreover the paradigmatic role taken on by the Revolution of 1789 for all other revolutions, from Hegel to Marx and Lenin. And yet Glucksmann both fails to acknowledge Marx's rejection of this paradigm because of its fictionality, and takes for his historic paradigm Solzhenitsyn's fictional account of the "Gulag." Glucksmann's own chosen role of theatre director--we find him quoting finally from that most paradigmatic account of the world as stage, from Prospero's departing words in The Tempest--also gives little hope of release from the metaphor of history as text, and shows how structuralist history can hold on to that image when either rejecting or condoning Hegel's universalization of Reason in history. Similarly, Lacanian analysis has appeared Hegelian to some in its reduction of the problem of the subject and its history to that of language. There is, however, a "negative Hegelianism" implied in Lacan's description of the formation of the subject (contemporaneous with Adorno's "Negative Dialectics" and with his rejection of the Enlightenment dialectic as the transformation of Reason into Unreason) which cannot be ignored here.[12] For, whereas to Hegel Mind had objectified itself in a development into Absolute Self-Consciousness of itself as both the Subject and Object of history, the Lacanian subject is created first in its "misrecognition" of its autonomy and then in its entry into the Symbolic Order of the father, in which it first sees itself defined in terms of absence and lack rather than presence and unity. The most appropriate literary metaphor for the history of subjects created according to these laws may moreover well be irony rather than farce.

For Hegel irony could be compared to that stage in the dialectic of history where absolute self-consciousness was preceded by the self-negation of the subject's consciousness. In the Lacanian system irony would, however, have to describe the absence of the Absolute and Ideal-Ego as a real goal from history. Here too, however, irony itself could become a goal and hence a norm of history,

[11] André Glucksmann, Les maîtres penseurs (Paris: B. Grasset, 1977).
[12] See Jacques Lacan, "Le stade du miroir comme formateur de la fonction du Je," in Ecrits (Paris: Editions du Seuil, 1966).

as does parody in Foucault's genealogy. But how helpful are these complicated literary historiographies? On the negative side, although Althusser's "Structuralist" account of history does not assume history to be the expression of a totality but constituted by various overdetermined structures, his and other Structuralist accounts of history as a discourse in which the subject is absent or determined by other structures, have often come dangerously close to "canonizing" the absence of real material conflict in history, as his own "Auto-Critiques" of 1974 have admitted.[13] On the positive side, such accounts have, however, pointed to the limitations of rational and intellectual analysis in comprehending itself or its material objects, and warned us that our intellectual understanding of historical analysis must also be subjected to a reading which will recognize the importance of its absence from those material forces for its own conclusions.

Given all this, Aristotle was nevertheless perhaps right in distinguishing between particularizing history and universalizing literature in his day--not only because he thereby avoided the dangers of legitimating history as a "totalitarian" text, but because it also enabled him to justify (further to his justification of the economic divisions of labour in his society) divisions of labour in a theoretical field, which would, theoretically at least, preserve history from becoming the site of either mythology or farce. Despite--or perhaps because of--recent attempts to merge history with literature, it is clear that we must continue to work toward a real communication between historical and literary research, which will make our knowledge of the particular facts of history more universal, but thereby also more open to a self-critical understanding, such as Foucault attempted to describe when he spoke of the good genealogist, but which he and others have in fact made more difficult by their insistence on the reading of history as "text," and by the denigration of a clear and traditionally historical explanation of the particular and empirical facts which have, in the past, after all provided the substance of both good history and good literature.

[13]   Louis Althusser, Eléments d'autocritique, (Paris: Gallimard, 1974).

TRANSFORMATION AND STORAGE OF

SCIENTIFIC TRADITIONS IN LITERATURE

Wolf Lepenies

This essay was written while I was a member at the School of Social Science of the Institute for Advanced Study in Princeton, N.J., during the Academic Year 1979-80. It is more a program for future research than the presentation of results. I have developed and slightly changed some ideas of the essay in the following article: Wolf Lepenies, "'Schön und korrekt.' Die Literatur als Bezugs-gruppe wissenschaftlicher Außenseiter," in: Soziologie in weltbürgerlicher Absicht. Festschrift fur René König zum 75. Geburtstag. Herausgege-ben von Heine von Alemann und Hans Peter Thurn (Opladen: Westdeutscher Verlag, 1981), pp. 90-100.

Case I:
From Natural History to Sociology

Balzac's <u>La Peau de Chagrin</u>, first published in book form in 1831, contains a detailed account of a visit of Professor Porriquet to his former student Raphaël. Porriquet, assuming that Raphaël is engaged in a work of creative literature, admonishes him to write in a clean style, and above all to refrain from imitating Ronsard. Raphaël reassures Porriquet, telling him that what he is writing is of a purely scientific nature: "Oh, then there is no more to be said," the schoolmaster answered. "Grammar must yield to the exigencies of discovery. Nonetheless, young man, a lucid and harmonious style, the diction of Massillon, of M. de Buffon, of the great Racine, a classical style, in short, can never spoil anything."

The following remarks aim at a refutation of Professor Porriquet's conjecture: I want to show that under certain circumstances too much concern for style and literature can indeed spoil something, not least scientific reputation. Buffon's fate will serve as a first example for this assertion. At the same time, I want to show that literature can play an eminent and hitherto somewhat neglected role in its precarious relationship to academic disciplines, a relationship which I would provisionally describe as the transformation and storage of scientific traditions or theoretical alternatives.[1]

By considering the author of the Histoire naturelle first, it is possible to elucidate the difficulties in which the scientist became increasingly involved, already in the eighteenth century, if he still conceived himself to be an author and considered the form in which he presented his scientific findings not to be incidental, but rather of great importance.

The original success of the Histoire naturelle which, although he was not too fond of Buffon, Condorcet said everybody had read and nearly everybody admired, was related to the opinion that its author was equally great as a naturalist and as a writer. Therefore it came as no surprise when Buffon chose, of all things, style as the topic of his discourse before the Acadēmie Française in August 1753. The lecture was regarded as one of the best "discours" since the Academy was founded; even in the nineteenth century it was published in at least sixty editions. Writers like Flaubert and Baudelaire mentioned it with praise. Others went so far as to claim that this was the only inaugural lecture that posterity would not forget.

When Flourens was asked, in the middle of the nineteenth century, to edit selections of Buffon's literary works, he first chose the Discours in order to then finally offer a cross-section from the complete Histoire naturelle. Literature and science could not, in other words, be separated from each other in Buffon because there everything was science and literature at the same time, and the literary character of his works was not least responsible for Buffon's reputation.

Yet the so-called "style-Buffon" was not uncontroversial even during the lifetime of the great naturalist. Criticisms like that of d'Alembert, who spoke unhesitatingly of him as the king of phrase-makers, hurt Buffon less than those ruinous expressions of agreement that praised the author at the expense of the scholar. Diderot preferred Buffon's style to Rousseau's and even the latter spoke of the "best pen of the age," but only after he had emphasized in no uncertain terms that Buffon was most certainly not the epoch's greatest scientist. Most striking of all, Condorcet's panegyric to Buffon comes very close to being a denunciation. While he admits that Buffon's verbosity, which occurs at the expense of pre-

[1] For earlier versions of the following argument, see Wolf Lepenies, Das Ende der Naturgeschichte (Munich: Hanser, 1976); also see Wolf Lepenies, "Der Wissenschaftler als Autor. Über konservierende Funktionen der Literatur," Akzente 2 (1978), pp. 129-147.

cision, is perhaps rooted more in the things themselves than in the words with which he describes them, he also points out, however, that Buffon employed the greatness of his ideas and the brilliance of his style in order to undermine the authority of other scientists and not to recognize obvious facts. In the nineteenth century, the German poet and reluctant admirer of Buffon, Jean Paul, gave an exact expression to the opinion that for Buffon the pleasant ring of his sentences was more important than their correctness:

> Thus the French, whom we should admire less for their language than for their love of their language, listen to their writers so closely...that Madame Necker even claims Rousseau had incorrectly called the Roman senate 'cette assemblée de <u>deux</u> cents rois' instead of the correct <u>trois</u> merely in order to avoid the sound of rhyme. And in this way Buffon's eulogy to Condamine, the Académician, referred to him as a "confrère de trente ans' instead of 'vingt-sept ans' which would not have sounded well. But that Rousseau deletes a <u>hundred</u> and Buffon omits <u>three</u> just for the sake of sounding well does not satisfy me or the truth. (<u>Vorschule der Aesthetik</u>, par. 86)

Sounding well instead of simply telling the truth--this is one of the many sentences in which the author Buffon was praised and the scientist Buffon was condemned. There is no better expression for this devastating praise than the pregnant phrase which the supporters of Linnaeus used to describe the merits of his French rival: <u>Stilo primus, doctrina ultimus</u>.

The condemnation of the science of the Ancien Régime very soon added new political and chauvinistic undertones to this critique. Since the time of Goethe German scientists were only too glad to recognize the stylistic rank of their French colleagues. As long as the French placed such value on the manner of presentation in their scientific publications, they could hardly be taken seriously as scientific competitors. It was clear that German scholars, if only they wanted to, could also write well--if the French, extraordinary stylists, of course, could also attain such scientific achievements was left an open question. In 1851, the German materialist Carl Vogt maliciously claimed that the Comte de Buffon now just belonged to the history of literature as a French writer, but that he no longer had any place in the cosmopolitan history of science.

Buffon is probably the last natural scientist whose recognition also could be traced to his achievement as an author. And he is perhaps the first whose literary capacities finally became a misfortune.

One of the unique characteristics of the reception of the tradition of natural history, however, is that it survived the nineteenth
century in literature, while the author of the Histoire naturelle was
dismissed as a writer and Buffon's so-called "novels" were no longer counted as contributions to science.

In the preface to the Comédie Humaine from 1842, Balzac
described his starting point as the comparison of the animal world
and society. There would always be social as well as animal
species, and Balzac would accomplish for human society what Buffon
had once done for zoology. Nonetheless, the Comédie Humaine is no
mere copy of the Histoire naturelle. Balzac does not slavishly imitate the method of natural history but rather adjusts it to the
particularities which distinguish the history of nature from the history of customs and morals. The social sphere is influenced by
chance in a way that is unknown in nature: it is both natural and
social at the same time. Since in the history of customs, unlike in
natural history, it is necessary to pay attention to the differences
between the sexes, the description of social species is twice as complex as that of zoological ones. In addition, mobility within society
is incomparably greater than in the animal kingdom. A shopkeeper
can become a peer of France; nobles can descend to the lowest
social rank. Although natural investigation had shown how interesting the kinds of behavior in animals are, a comparison with
human customs is hardly possible. These differ for every social
rank and, in addition, for every civilization, whereas those of animals, especially in our eyes, are similar to each other and remain
the same at all times. Taking all these differences into account, the
method of natural history remains valid for the analysis of society,
and even democratization will not result in its obsolescence; since
equality creates vast shadings, social analysis will be confronted
with the same problems natural history originally faced.

I regard this as an example of the transformation and storage
of scientific traditions in literature. But it may seem as if this con-
servation of obviously outlived and overcome forms of scientific
thought can be of only minor interest for the history of academic
disciplines and exclusively belongs in literary history. Not quite
so, however, for the story does not end here. After all, Balzac
first entitled the Comédie Humaine "études sociales" and it is well
known that Engels, in his famous letter to Miss Harkness for
instance, said that he, even in economic details, had learned more
from Balzac than "from all the professional historians, economists
and statisticians of the period together."[2] And Marx, who compared himself with the hero of the Chef d'oeuvre inconnu, admitted
openly how much had had profited by reading Balzac and that he

[2] Karl Marx and Friedrich Engels, Selected Correspondence
(London: Lawrence and Wishart, 1956), p. 479.

planned to write about the Comédie Humaine as soon as he should have finished his economic studies.[3] Of course, one need not rely only on these programmatic statements by Marx and Engels in the attempt to retrace Balzac's influence in the nascent social science of the nineteenth century: there is Hippolyte Taine, "fils de Balzac," as he was called (M. Leroy), who deeply influenced early sociologists like Mosca and Pareto, Tarde, Sorel and, maybe even Durkheim.[4]

How far and where Taine was influenced by Balzac is a difficult question which I cannot even try to answer here. But I think there is enough evidence to assume that Balzac was of greater importance for Taine than Comte for instance and that we can take the final and pathetic words of the essay on Balzac seriously: "With Shakespeare and Saint-Simon, Balzac is the greatest storehouse ("magasin") of documents on human nature that we possess."[5] It is through Balzac that Taine detects and develops a specific view of what the social sciences can and cannot do: "Nous aurons dépassé, d'ici à un demisiècle, la période descriptive; en biologie elle a duré jusqu'à Bichat et Cuvier, en sociologie, nous y sommes encore; tâchons de nous y tenir, avec application et intelligence, sans ambitions excessives, sans conclusions précipitées, sans théories hasardées et preconçues, pour entrer bientôt dans la

[3] Of course, Stendhal, Flaubert and especially Zola play an important part in this development. But Zola's theory of the experimental novel is little more than the imitation of natural scientific methods with the means of literature. This methodology remains a fiasco; it is close to ridiculous to claim that one only needs to replace the term "physician" with "novelist" in Claude Bernard's Introduction to the Study of Experimental Medicine (tr. Henry Copley Greene; New York: Schuman, 1949) in order to have the experimental literary method. Although Zola took Darwin, Balzac, Buffon as his models, Balzac's attempt seems more up-to-date, at least for me. The Comédie Humaine is the literary adoption of a scientific method, the Rougon-Macquart are merely its imitation. Zola's attempt to make the novel scientific had to fail because it was based on a premature harmonizing of literary and scientific procedure. His program is thus not too far removed from Remy de Gourmont's naive call for the introduction of more science into literature and more literature into science, in order to eliminate the schism between the two. I think Engels made a good point in saying that he regarded Balzac "a far greater master of realism than all the Zolas passés, présents et à venir" (Marx and Engels, Correspondence, p. 479).
[4] See Carlo Mongardini, Storia e sociologia nell'opera di H. Taine (Milan: Guiffrè, 1965).
[5] Hippolyte Taine, Balzac. A Critical Study, tr. by Lorenzo O'Rourke (New York: Haskell House, 1973), p. 240.

période des classifications naturelles et définitives...." (Letter to A. Delaire, April 19, 1890). Written in 1890, more than thirty years after Comte's death (1857) this is an astonishing document. It resembles Buffon's device to regard natural history, above all, as "description exacte" and when Taine says, in the History of English Literature, that first of all we have to find rich documents and know how to interpret them, this choice of modest description instead of premature systematization corresponds as well to the sociological monographs of the nineteenth century as it recalls the natural history of the eighteenth.

I know that Taine was not always so cautious, indeed all this may represent a program which he did not follow himself in all respects. But the idea of an asynchronism in the development of disciplines--e.g. systematic biology and descriptive sociology-- certainly represents one aspect of his work which has been neglected so far.

Case II:
From Literary to Experimental Psychology

Let me now--before I try to characterize the concepts of transformation and storage more generally--give you another and, I hope, more familiar example of what I have in mind when using these terms. I take my case from the history of psychology--in Germany, since it was there that psychology was first institutionalized and won a place in the university.

My argument runs as follows: At the turn from the eighteenth to the nineteenth century, prescientific psychology, the discussion of psychological problems that was conducted in philosophy and literature long before the institutionalization of psychology as an academic discipline, dealt with three outstanding topics that lost their importance rather completely with the emergence of experimental psychology and then were even almost bracketed out of scientific discussion. These are the topics of the unconscious, the abnormal, and early childhood experience and development. In contrast to this, the academically established experimental psychology was, to use a perhaps somewhat too pointed but pregnant formula, the analysis of the consciousness of the healthy and normal adult. The unconscious, the abnormal and early childhood became, if accepted at all, topics of minor importance. They reappeared later however, at the end of the nineteenth century, when an alternative orientation to experimental psychology was developed in the form of Freudian psychoanalysis, which, although never accepted by it, deeply influenced mainstream psychology. The institutionalization of psychology in the university system was connected with the repression of certain areas of inquiry, which had been prominent in prescientific psychology. These areas of inquiry, however, continued to play an important part in literature, where they were stored in the so-called literary psychology as part of the romantic discourse and reentered scientific discussion, when an alternative to the newly established and academically respectable experimental psychology was formulated in the form of psychoanalysis.

Let me now elaborate this argument in more detail.

I will be rather brief in regard to prescientific psychology. To maintain that around 1800 writers like Hoffmann, Tieck, Novalis, Hölderlin, Chamisso and Jean Paul, and philosophers like Schlegel and Schelling, to name but a few, developed a psychological discourse that concentrated on the unconscious and on relations between the normal and the abnormal, paying considerable attention to early childhood and problems of development, is nothing but a commonplace. I shall confine myself to but one example not only for the propagation but also for the broad acceptance of this set of problems as valuable and important questions in literary and philosophical discourse.

In 1783 the first journal of psychology was founded: Karl Philipp Moritz's "Magazin für Erfahrungsseelenkunde," which from a romantic German might be translated into a rather uninspired English as "Magazine for Empirical Psychology." Moritz was 27 years old when he founded the very successful magazine, which appeared thrice yearly and was published for ten years until the death of its founder in 1793. Moritz was also the author of the first psychological novel, Anton Reiser, extracts of which were published in the journal. Its "contributions ranged from the anecdotal to the carefully described and discussed case report, covering the entire gamut of psychological and psychiatric defects as noted in individual instances: psychoses, neurotic disturbances, character disorders, amnesias, somnambulism, deaf-mutism, etc. An especially marked attention was regularly given to both early childhood memories and to dreams. A related and recurrent interest as stated in the second volume of the year 1785, was 'action without consciousness of motives, or the power of obscure ideas'."[6]

Here we see most clearly that the unconscious, the abnormal, and early childhood represent preferred areas of inquiry.

In 1786 Moritz took a leave, went to Italy for three years and left another editor in charge. This editor, C.F. Pockels, tried to change the content of the journal considerably, shifting it into the

[6] Erling Eng, "Karl Philip Moritz' Magazin für Erfahrungsseelenkunde (Magazine for Empirical Psychology) 1783-1793," in Journal of the History of the Behavioral Sciences 9 (1973), pp. 300-305.

direction "of rational schemata and logical analysis."[7] Moritz however, after his return, was able to remove Pockels from the journal and to continue with its original editorial policy.[8] Literary or prescientific psychology had undergone a first, though somewhat premature, attack. Only a few decades later, new attacks were launched which did not encounter an equally strong resistance.

I have not the time to tell, however briefly, the complicated story of the institutionalization of psychology, by which I mean the process of its gradual acceptance as a reputable discipline in the university. I can only refer to decisive turning-points, the year 1873, for instance, when Wilhelm Wundt, its founding father, who already had taught courses on "Psychology as a Natural Science" for eleven years in Heidelberg, published the first volume of his Principles of Physiological Psychology (Grundzüge der physiologischen Psychologie), or to the year 1879, when the first psychological institute was opened in Leipzig and gave organizational stability to the new paradigm of experimental psychology.[9]

In Wundt's eyes this stability could only be maintained if psychology borrowed its analytic framework and its working practice from already acknowledged scientific disciplines. It was taken for granted that only the attributes of our consciousness were of significance for psychological analysis and that assumptions as to the state of the unconscious were entirely unproductive for psychology. If the notion of the unconscious had to be used at all--as Wundt did in his debate with Lipps--it was slyly defined as the "dimly perceived conscious" and psychopathology was regarded as the "science of the events of the diseased conscious."[10] Equally dismissed from the true, that is, scientific discourse of psychology

---

[7]   Ibid., p. 304.

[8]   Of course, the role of Maimon, whom Moritz after his return appointed as co-editor, has to be taken into account: "If Moritz's nature was on the side of the poetic, and Pockels' on the side of a dry rationalism, Salomon Maimon had something of both, without compromising either" (Eng, Magazin für Erfahrungsseelenkunde, p. 479). For the sake of my argument I have had to simplify the role of the Magazin: for a detailed analysis of it see Werner Obermeit, Das unsichtbare Ding, das Seele heißt. Die Entdeckung der Psyche im bürgerlichen Zeitalter (Frankfurt: Syndikat, 1980).

[9]   Lack of space has prevented me from discussing at all the role of Herbart in the history of psychology. For me Wundt's critique of him is equally as important as the attempt of some authors to prove the compatibility of Herbart's views with those of psychoanalysis. See Oskar Robert Pfister, The Psychoanalytic Method, tr. Charles Rockwell Payne (New York: Moffat, Yard and Co., 1917).

[10]   See Willy Hellpach, Grundgedanken zur Wissenschaftslehre der Psychopathologie (Leipzig: Engelmann, 1906).

were the abnormal and the child: one of Wundt's most influential disciples, Külpe, expressed his doubts that the study of mental diseases would afford any material aid to the student of psychology, and established the creed of the polarity between health and sickness. Inquiries into the psychology of childhood were regarded as equally uncertain if not useless, as was the psychological study of animals; problems of psychogenesis were disparaged in general.[11]

Thus, the unconscious, the abnormal, and the child were displaced, banned from established psychological discourse, while they had played such an eminent role at the beginning and still in the first half of the nineteenth century. The reasons for this expulsion are manifold--they range from the attempt to establish a cognitive identity for psychology first in, then outside of, philosophy, to political motives which had their origin in a contempt of romanticism. Another important motive, however, was the rejection of psychology's literary past, and I think that the history of this discipline and its academic breakthrough in the nineteenth century could also be written in this perspective. Let me give just two examples for this.

In the middle of the nineteenth century, two conceptions of medical psychology competed with one another in the German-speaking world: Griesinger's Mental Pathology and Therapeutics (Die Pathologie und Therapie der psychischen Krankheiten) and von Feuchtersleben's Principles of Medical Psychology (Lehrbuch der ärztlichen Seelenkunde) which both appeared in 1845. Although it seems today as if the latter's conceptions and conclusions were much more sophisticated than Griesinger's, Griesinger, who regarded "all nonmedical, particularly all poetical...conceptions of insanity as useless,"[12] scored an easy victory over his opponent, who was no less than Dean of the Medical Faculty at the University of Vienna, but at the same time a poet and well known for his literary predilections: to the students "Griesinger represented science, Feuchtersleben literature. The former was diligently read; the latter was scanned for enjoyment and perhaps was not taken quite seriously."[13] Only a few years ago, a psychologist had to admit that he remembered Feuchtersleben's name well from his high school days in Vienna, when he had to learn his

---

[11] See Oswald Külpe, Grundriß der Psychologie, auf experimenteller Grundlage dargestellt (Leipzig: W. Engelmann, 1893; tr. Outlines of Psychology: Based upon the Results of Experimental Investigations, New York: MacMillan, 1909).
[12] Hannah Decker, Freud in Germany. Revolution and Reaction in Science, 1893-1907 (New York: International Universities Press, 1977).
[13] I. Veith, Hysteria: The History of a Disease (Chicago: University of Chicago Press, 1965).

but that he had only realized after his retirement that this poet had been a kind of psychologist too, and the first ever to teach psychiatry in the Viennese Medical School.[14]

But even those authors who strove against mainstream psychology were cautious enough not to rouse the dangerous impression of complicity with psychology's literary past. Thus, Eduard von Hartmann, for instance, whose Philosophy of the Unconscious (Philosophie des Unbewußten, 1869) represented a serious attempt to establish psychology as science of the unconscious, was very well aware that many poets of the eighteenth and nineteenth century had described phenomena of the unconscious in most illuminating ways, yet his references to those writers remained of a purely ornamental sort and were not granted the privilege of discussion.[15]

With Freud, all this changes.

It is hardly necessary to prove in detail that psychoanalysis may indeed be regarded as an attempt to install the unconscious, the abnormal and early childhood experience as main areas of psychological inquiry.[16] There is abundant proof that the refusal to

[14]   Otto F. Ehrenteil, "The almost forgotten Feuchtersleben: Poet, Essayist, Popular Philosopher and Psychiatrist," in Journal of the History of the Behavioral Sciences 9 (1975), pp. 82-86.
[15]   For instance, after having discussed at length Schelling's notion of the unconscious and the deplorable fact that it all too quickly retreated into the background, von Hartmann claims that "far better did the divining poet-mind of Jean Paul (Friedrich Richter) know how to appreciate Schelling's Unconscious..." (Eduard von Hartmann, Philosophie des Unbewußten). He then quotes a wonderful passage from Jean Paul's Selina--without discussing it at all.
    The future treatment of such literary insights could be expected. In a "historico-critical monograph" on The Unconscious and Eduard von Hartmann Jean Paul, one of Germany's greatest poets, has become "a somewhat obscure 'theologian' of myths, who places his faith and anchors his hopes in the unconscious." See Dennis N. Kenedy Darnoi, The Unconscious and Eduard von Hartmann. A Historico-Critical Approach (The Hague: Martinus Nijhoff, 1967), p. 77.
[16]   In 1881, W. Preyer's The Mind of the Child (tr. H.W. Brown; New York: Arno Press, 1890) appeared; ten years later Stanley Hall founded the Pedagogical Seminary. In 1893 the British Association for Child Study held its first meeting; Witmer organized the first psychological clinic for maladjusted children in Philadelphia. In 1899 the German Association for Child Research (Allgemeiner Deutscher Verein für Kinderforschung) and the Berlin Association

accept a sharp dividing line between sickness and health, between the normal and the abnormal, ran counter to a central premise of experimental psychology, and Freud was well aware, as he said in the Introductory Lectures (1916-17), that any contradiction of the idea that psychology had to be the study of the content of consciousness would be regarded by academic psychologists as obvious nonsense. Here again, Freud, who disdainfully called the mainstream psychology of his time "surface psychology"[17] showed a remarkable talent for self-fulfilling prophecy.

Types of Storage

Let me now present some general remarks concerning the notion of "storage" and its place in current studies of science. Being above all interested in problems of the formation and development of disciplines, I have found it useful, instead of following the development of a single discipline over long periods, to look at broader, interconnected complexes of disciplines in a shorter period. The aim of this procedure is something like a general description of interdisciplinary relations; no isolated science is

for Child Psychology (Verein für Kinderpsychologie in Berlin) were founded; numerous journals began to appear, among them since 1896 Die Kinderseele, a yearly journal devoted to the character disorders of children.

The political impact of educational reform and the effect of Darwinism and Social Darwinism may equally have been responsible for a renewed interest in problems of childhood and development. Before arriving at his psychoanalytic insights, Freud had already published several monographs on cerebral palsy in children and had even been promised by a well known Vienna pediatrician, Max Kassowitz, to be put in charge of a department for the nervous diseases of children (Sigmund Freud, An Autobiographical Study, in Standard Edition XX; London: Hogarth Press, 1975; p. 14). But his discoveries as to the sexuality of children were made through the analysis of adults (ibid., p. 39) and Freud later never analyzed a child personally (see Stephen Kern, "Freud and the Birth of Child Psychology," in Journal of the History of the Behaviorial Sciences 9 (1973), pp. 360-368). I think it will be much more difficult to prove that in regard to problems of early childhood, Freud's literary experience was of equal or only comparably great importance, as it certainly was for his views of the unconscious and the abnormal. At the least, we can assume that literary knowledge was helpful here, by suggesting metaphors like that of the Oedipus complex, to attain greater conceptual clarity.

[17] H.C. Abraham and C.L. Freud, ed., A Psycho-Analytic Dialogue: The Letters of Sigmund Freud and Karl Abraham, 1907-1926 (New York: Basic Books, 1965), p. 12.

investigated but rather its historically changing relationships to other disciplines. Especially interesting are the moments when specific theoretical (methodological, conceptual) alternatives are selected and others rejected by the scientific community.

The most important questions in present studies of science are directed to problems concerning the origin and the selection of scientific alternatives. It is my conviction that the problem of storage is equally important. From the history of science we know well that alternatives to prevalent theories may be weeded out at a certain time but do not disappear completely, rather are retained and taken up again at later times into scientific discourse and, indeed, in some cases then decisively influence its development.

Further clarification of the storage concept is necessary. At this moment I find it particularly useful to distinguish between inner- and extra-scientific and between intra- and inter-disciplinary storage. Let me use a simple illustration of what I have in mind. I am thinking of science as one storehouse and of literature and art as two others, buildings which did not always exist apart but had to be constructed when certain professional activities of the residents required further differentiation.[18]

Concentrating on the storehouse of science, I speak of inner-scientific storage to describe a process which takes place only in one specific building, and of extra-scientific storage when another building is involved. All these storehouses have many and different floors which might be regarded as scientific disciplines, literary genres and branches of art, respectively. Of course, all storehouses are rebuilt again and again, and change their appearance as well as their internal structure. If storage takes place (and again I speak only of the storehouse of science) on just one floor, we might regard this as an intra-disciplinary storage, and we might speak of inter-disciplinary storage when more floors are involved.

Where things come from and where they are stored is of utmost importance. Of course, not each floor enjoys the same reputation: there is always a basement, a bel étage and a lofty penthouse--and of course, following Popper's remark about surpassed but memorable theories, a granny-flat for the grey-haired....

---

[18] The origin of modern science, especially in regard to the professional roles involved, has to be described as a process of un-differentiation, as Edgar Zilsel has shown very clearly. Its institutionalization however, either in the Royal Society or in the Académie Royale des Sciences, must be described as a differentiation process on many levels.

The number of rooms, specialties we might call them, is important too--the chances for intra-disciplinary storage increase with the number of rooms available, i.e., with the internal differentiation of a discipline. Additionally, each culture is provided with all three of these storehouses, and cross-cultural storage is a most interesting case: for instance when German philosophical phenomenology is stored and transformed into American sociology and then is reintroduced in Germany as an American tradition, or when Renan, as Taine said, transforms into a French style all the findings on myth, religion and language which the Germans had stored ("emmagaziné") beyond the Rhine.

I could go on for a while in this vein, but I will stop here. Let me just repeat what I regard as crucial for the concept of "storage." First, it is a three-part phenomenon. There is always a place of origin, a storage-place, and the new environment. Second, storage is most likely combined with the transformation of the original concept, idea, metaphor, theory, tradition, etc. Third, I deliberately chose the concept of storage to describe and analyze relationships between disciplines. Fourth, remembrance and oblivion are part of the storage-process. Fifth, this implies for the perspective I have chosen that storage, transformation, and revival are most important for periods in which disciplines are forced or inclined to "remember, to recover or to invent" their disciplinary past, to use Bernard Lewis's expression.[19]

When Freud used the notion "storehouse of science" in his Autobiographical Study,[20] he praised Charcot's findings--evoking thereby, as he called it, "a permanent place," where the scientific valuables are kept. The picture I have in mind is more that of a place where things which are no longer fashionable are kept in one house or on one floor but which might become, with alterations, fashionable again on another floor, in another house, in another environment.

So far I have presented to you two examples of extra-scientific storage. I will now use the second case in order to discuss specific problems of the storage and transformation of scientific traditions in literature, and I will especially ask what impact the remembrance of their literary past had for some disciplines in the nineteenth and at the beginning of the twentieth century.

[19] Bernard Lewis, History. Remembered, Recovered, Invented (Princeton: Princeton University Press, 1975).
[20] Freud, An Autobiographical Study, p. 13.

Case III:
The Rejection of Psychoanalysis (Freud)

Throughout the nineteenth century romantic literature represented a mode of discourse on the unconscious and the abnormal which was very well known to Freud. He borrowed concepts and metaphors from other authors as well, but it was the tradition of literary psychology in which the mood of psychoanalytic inquiry seemed to be anticipated.[21] Freud's predilection for literature and his carefulness in matters of style were not just an expression of personal preference, but had their roots in theoretical conceptions and practical experiences. I am interested in the question how the institutional fate of psychoanalysis, which may be regarded as an alternative theory program in psychology, was affected by its relationship to literature and by Freud's willingness to accept, to say the least, the creative writer as "the precursor of science, and so too of scientific psychology."[22]

[21] Arguments for and against the connection of romantic psychology and psychoanalysis are listed in Schrey (see note 29). Whether or not the "rationalism" of psychoanalysis is compatible with the "irrationality" of the romantics (see Albert Béguin's L'âme romantique et le rêve, Paris: J. Corti, 1956, as a negative answer to this question)--I would like to argue that Freud took romantic literature as seriously as any literature and, maybe, tried to rationalize literary insights.

[22] If--which may sound fantastic today--one had to found a college of psycho-analysis, much would have to be taught in it, which is also taught by the medical faculty.... On the other hand, analytic instruction would include branches of knowledge which are remote from medicine and which the doctor does not come across in his practice: the history of civilization, mythology, the psychology of religion and the science of literature. Unless he is well at home in these subjects, an analyst can make nothing of a large amount of his material. By way of compensation, the great mass of what is taught in medical schools is of no use to him for his purposes. (Freud, The Question of Lay Analysis, Standard Edition XX, p. 246.)

The question of how much Freud wanted psychoanalysis to become a regular part of a university curriculum is not easy to answer. When, in 1918, Freud discussed "The Teaching of Psycho-Analysis in Universities," in Standard Edition XVII, pp. 171-173, he said: "The inclusion of psycho-analysis in the University curriculum would no doubt be regarded with satisfaction by every psychoanalyst. At the same time it is clear that the psychoanalyst can dispense entirely with the University without any loss to himself." I

To say that the work of analysis involved an "art of interpretation"[23] was more than a metaphor for a method, it was a methodological choice in itself. Already in the Studies on Hysteria (1893-5), which are usually regarded as the starting point of psychoanalysis, Freud made this perfectly clear:

> I have not always been a psychotherapist. Like other neuropathologists, I was trained to employ local diagnoses and electro-prognosis, and it still strikes me myself as strange that the case histories I write should read like short stories and that, as one might say, they lack the serious stamp of science. I must console myself with the reflection that the nature of the subject is evidently responsible for this, rather than any preference of my own. The fact is that local diagnosis and electrical reactions lead nowhere in the study of hysteria, whereas a detailed description of mental processes such as we are accustomed to find in the works of imaginative writers enables me, with the use of a few psychological formulas, to obtain at least some kind of insight into the course of that affection (my emphasis).[24]

Ten years later, Freud admitted that he originally had not looked for a confirmation of his findings in imaginative writings (Delusions and Dreams in Jensen's "Gradiva," 1906), but that he was almost forced to accept, as he ironically put it, that writers are on the same side "as the ancients, as the superstitious public and as the author of The Interpretation of Dreams." For, imaginative writers had taken as the basis of their creations the very things that Freud believed he had freshly discovered from the sources of

find it hard not to take this last sentence as a reaction out of spite. The paper I just mentioned was first published in a Budapest medical periodical in 1919. "It is likely that Freud wrote it in the autumn of 1918, at about the time of the Fifth International Psycho-Analytical Congress in Budapest. There was then a considerable agitation among the medical students at Budapest for the inclusion of psycho-analysis in their curriculum. In March 1919, when a Bolshevik government took temporary control in Hungary, Ferenczi was in fact installed as Professor of Psycho-Analysis at the University." See Standard Edition XVII, p. 170.

[23] Freud, An Autobiographical Study, p. 41.
[24] Freud, Studies on Hysteria, Standard Edition II, pp. 160-161.

his medical experience. All of a sudden, literary imagination could match scientific insight.[25]

> Let us ask whether this imaginative representation of the genesis of a delusion can hold its own before the judgment of science. And here we must give what will perhaps be an unexpected answer. In fact the situation is quite the reverse: <u>it is science that cannot hold its own before the achievement of the author</u> (my emphasis).

Twenty years later, when Freud dreamed about a college of psychoanalysis, he described the science of literature as an essential part of its curriculum.[26]

Whereas Freud and Ernest Jones always proclaimed that psychoanalysis was totally ignored or rejected at its beginning, we know today--especially since the publication of Hannah Decker's book on <u>Freud in Germany</u>--that the story was much more complicated. Of course, "sexual prejudice, anti-semitism, and the critic's personal neurosis"[27] played an important part in the negative reception of psychoanalysis, but a specific positive reaction may have been equally injurious. It was not least the recognition of nonprofessional observers, amateur psychologists and literati which helped the newly established experimental psychology to counter all psychoanalytic attacks on its central assumptions.

The first positive review,[28] to give but one example, of the

---

[25] It may have been most disturbing to established scientists that Freud challenged the newly acquired cognitive and institutional identities of psychology in many ways--for instance by sticking to its literary affinities, while at the same time sounding exactly like one of the serious arch-enemies of psychoanalysis, Karl R. Popper, two years later: "We put forward conjectures, we construct hypotheses, which we withdraw if they are not confirmed" reads one passage in the <u>New Introductory Lectures</u>, Standard Edition XXII, pp. 5-182.

[26] Freud, <u>The Question of Lay Analysis</u>, pp. 183-258.

[27] Decker, <u>Freud in Germany</u>, p. 1.

[28] Also responsible for the long professional neglect of psychoanalysis was the fact that the emerging behavioral sciences did not yet dispose of an institutional "infra-structure" which corresponded to their cognitive identity. <u>The Interpretation of Dreams</u>, for instance, was therefore "reviewed in nonmedical journals because the topic was not suitable for the medical review literature." See Ilse Bry and Alfred H. Rifkin, in <u>Science and Psychoanalysis</u>, ed. Jules H. Masserman (New York/London: Grune and Stratton, 1962), Vol. 5, pp. 22-23.

Studies on Hysteria was, significantly enough, written by a literary historian, Alfred von Berger. The honorable director of the Vienna Burgtheater certainly came to praise Freud, but perhaps he only buried his academic reputation like others who were hardly able to judge Freud's scientific findings and concentrated instead on talking about his masterly prose.[29]

Psychologists took immediate advantage of this and have continued to do so. Already German psychiatrists and neurologists who had labeled Charcot's demonstrations as unscientific and "theatrical"[30]--only to be pleased at the same time by the extent of French decadence which the large number of his hysterical patients indicated[31]--could regard Freud's un-Germanic consorting with Charcot as another proof for the literary and therefore unscientific character of psychoanalysis. Later, when psychoanalysis had become fashionable, destructive praise[32] replaced open contempt:

> Models and dramatic language are useful in ramming
> home psychological insights to patients and to a

[29] In 1906, for instance, S. Mehring, a Berlin poet and feuilletoniste, called Freud "a physician equipped not only with the expert knowledge of his profession, but also with the fortunate talent of a writer who has a sense for wit and probably can lay claim to the adjective 'ingenious'." See Hannah S. Decker, "The Interpretation of Dreams: Early Reception by the Educated German Public," in Journal of the History of the Behavioral Sciences XI (1975), pp. 129-141. Numerous other examples can be found in Decker's book as well as in Gisela Schrey, Literaturaesthetik der Psychoanalyse und ihre Rezeption in der deutschen Germanistik vor 1933 (Frankfurt am Main: Athenaion, 1975), and already in Wolfgang Schönau, Sigmund Freuds Prosa (Stuttgart: Metzlersche Verlagsbuchhandlung, 1968). See also William G. Niederland, "Freud's Literary Style: Some Observations," in American Imago 28 (1971), pp. 17-23.

[30] In this regard it is significant to note that Freud wrote to Martha Bernays in 1885 about Charcot: "...he exhausts me; when I come away from him I no longer have any desire to work, and I have no feelings of guilt. My brain is sated as after an evening in the theater."

[31] Decker, Freud in Germany, p. 56.

[32] The characteristic "scientific misunderstanding" of Freud can be found in Skinner: "Freud recognized that damage must be put up with." See B.F. Skinner, "Critique of Psychoanalytic Concepts and Theories," in The Foundations of Science and the Concepts of Psychology and Psychoanalysis, ed. Herbert Feigl and Michael Scriven (Minneapolis: University of Minnesota Press, 1956), p. 79. See also S.E. Hyman, The Tangled Bank. Darwin, Marx, Frazer and Freud as Imaginative Writers (New York: Atheneum, 1962).

wide public in a suffering civilization. Parents, nursery teachers, mild neurotics and social workers would not be touched by the mathematical constructs of Hull or the topological jargon of Lewin.[33]

Ironically enough, its literary character, which had also been responsible for the failure to find a niche in the university, helped psychoanalysis not only to survive but also to build up strong though extra-universitarian institutions: the second generation of Freudians, young doctors and laymen who became psychoanalysts in the 1920s, always emphasized their interest in literature and reportedly were attracted above all by the nonmedical and literary aspects of psychoanalysis.[34] One cannot but speculate that its initial academic failure was responsible for the tremendous influence psychoanalysis has had on modern culture.

Institutionalization, Storage and Reputation

The circumstances of and the reasons for the rejection of psychoanalysis by mainstream, i.e., experimental psychology are not unique at all, they are in many respects characteristic of the institutionalization of other disciplines in the nineteenth century.

Let me make some general remarks about processes of institutionalization before coming back to this point.

Any theory program can only survive when it is able to claim a cognitive identity, uniqueness and coherence of "its intellectual orientations, conceptual schemes, paradigms, problematics, and tools for inquiry." At the same time it has to find a social identity "in the form of its major institutional arrangements."[35] In addition, I regard the acquisition of a historical identity as equally important, the reconstitution of disciplinary past to which in principle all members of a scientific community would agree to belong.[36] The proof of cognitive identity serves a theory program foremost in distinguishing it from established or competing programs; its social

---

[33] R.S. Peters, ed., Brett's History of Psychology (London: Allen and Unwin, 1953), p. 682.

[34] Decker, " The Interpretation of Dreams: Early Reception," p. 141.

[35] Robert K. Merton, The Sociology of Science. An Episodic Memoir (Carbondale: Southern Illinois University Press, 1979), p. 5.

[36] Wolf Lepenies, "Anthropological Perspectives in the Sociology of Science," in Cognitive and Historical Sociology of Scientific Knowledge, eds. Y. Elkana and E. Mendelsohn (Dordrecht: Riedel, 1980).

identity is achieved through organizational stability which makes it more fit to survive the academic struggle; claims for a historical identity distinguish it from competitors too, but at the same time prevent premature differentiation in the discipline.

I would strongly emphasize that processes of institutionalization imply acts of refusal: a nascent discipline acquires a stable identity not only through affirmation but through negation as well. It must not only declare whom it wants to follow but also whom to abandon. For these strategies of intrusion and avoidance the reputation of academic disciplines is of utmost importance: cognitive, social and historical identities usually are formed after the model of some discipline of higher reputation, whereas the claim for uniqueness or the copying of the lower ranks remains the exception to the rule.[37]

I am interested in the analysis of such an exception. To look at the transformation and storage of scientific traditions in literature inevitably brings up the question which role literature and literary, or in a broader sense, aesthetic orientations play in the assessment of a discipline's reputation and acceptance in the academic community. As an example of what I have in mind, I quote a nearby physicist who declared that for insights into human affairs he turned "to stories and poems rather than to sociology,"[38] thereby disturbing, and rightly I think, at least the universe of some sociologists.

While, in the nineteenth century, the use of classical metaphors and the demonstration of literary knowledge is still part of scientific discourse, the departure from literary attitudes becomes for some disciplines a prerequisite for the acquisition of academic reputation. It is my conjecture that in the nineteenth century disciplines like psychology, sociology and anthropology imitate disciplines of higher reputation, especially the natural sciences, and reject their own literary past--and thereby gain academic respectability. Wherever literature is regarded as a storehouse from which one can borrow more than just metaphors and stylistic

[37] I would suggest that we distinguish between the "adoption" and the mere "imitation" of disciplines of higher reputation. By "adoption" I understand the ability to transform theoretical insights, conceptual tools, etc.; by "imitation" the echoing of a prestige-laden language.
Lamprecht's attempt for instance to establish cultural history as a new paradigm for German historiography also consisted in the imitation of certain natural sciences, but he was never able to show that he really could adopt their methods and techniques.
[38] Freeman Dyson, Disturbing the Universe (New York: Harper and Row, 1979), p. 5.

advice, attempts to institutionalize a theory program are doomed to fail.

Paced by the methodological rigor of Neo-Kantianism,[39] young disciplines, once they had acquired a cognitive, social and historical identity, became the most orthodox members of the academic community. One has, for instance, to take into account that experimental psychology was a young discipline when it was challenged by psychoanalysis and that it had not yet overcome the birth trauma of its separation from philosophy. The youthful heroics which the then nineteen-year-old student and later psychologist William Stern displayed in his diary in 1871, are most significant for this distraction:

> All bridges are broken, there is no retreat. In philosophy, I must find my salvation, or perish. One consolation there is, namely that a philosophical discipline is open to me as my special field, psychology....[40]

Eight years later, the new experimental psychology had established itself. But the danger of falling back on a literary past was not yet over, as a French psychologist, Ribot, pointed out in his book on German psychology. There was still the danger that the psychologist might again become a romancer, "a poet of an especial kind..., psychology...a kind of literary criticism, very penetrating and acute, but nothing more.... In this refinement of subtleties, always increasing, we reach at most symbols only: all reality has disappeared."[41]

Freud challenged the newly acquired identity of academic psychology in many ways. To use literature as a storehouse in order to reintroduce the unconscious, the abnormal, and early childhood into the psychological discourse was an act of rebellion, similar to Engels' preference of Balzac over all possible professional col-

---

[39] It might be useful to analyze to what extent the social and the human sciences in nineteenth-century Germany really imitated the natural sciences or only an image of them which was to be found in the neo-Kantian gallery. I am grateful to Hans-Peter Dreitzel for having made this suggestion in reaction to some of the ideas developed here.

[40] William Stern, "Autobiography," in A History of Psychology in Autobiography, ed. Carl Murchison (Worcester, Mass.: Clark University Press, 1930), vol. 1, p. 340.

[41] Théodule Armand Ribot, La psychologie allemande. Ecole expérimentale (Paris: F. Alcan, 1879), trans. as German Psychology of Today: The Empirical School (New York: Scribner, 1885), pp. 3-5.

leagues, "Guizot e tutti quanti" as he flatly declared. In their classic paper on the origin of psychology in Germany, Ben-David and Collins[42] explained that a specific disciplinary constellation in the German universities of the nineteenth century was responsible for the formation of the new discipline. Physiologists and physiologically oriented physicians, finding no positions in their own overcrowded fields of study, emigrated into philosophy, where they pursued their psychological interests by using concepts and tools from their original and more highly regarded discipline, i.e. physiology. When by 1860 natural scientists were near to extinguishing the academic reputation of philosophy (Paulsen), more and more philosophers went over to the enemy, and the way was open for the institutionalization of experimental psychology as an academic discipline. That Freud "attempted to maintain his status by trying to raise medical practice into a form of scientific research"[43] however, is only part of the story: at the same time, his literary orientations threatened the seemingly successful imitation of physiology, a discipline of high reputation, by experimental psychology.

Freud's divergence from mainstream psychology was perhaps most dramatic in regard to its historical identity. That psychology had "a long past, but only a short history," as one of its leading figures, Hermann Ebbinghaus, put it, was not just a description, but a prescription as well. After all, at least in German, disciplines are female, and psychology--die Psychologie--was better off not remembering its long and sometimes notorious past if it wanted to become a respectable member of the scientific community.

That Freud refused to repress the literary past of psychology and instead tried to remember it constantly cluttered up his access to the university. Therefore, it was only appropriate that the first organization of the psychoanalytic movement--the so-called "Committee," founded in 1913--resembled more closely a romantic literary circle than a research institute,[44] following, as Ernest Jones admitted, "stories of Charlemagne's paladins from boyhood and many secret societies from literature."[45]

[42]   Joseph Ben-David and Randall Collins, "Social Factors in the Origin of a New Science: The Case of Psychology," in American Sociological Review 31, No. 4 (1966), pp. 451-465
[43]   Ibid., p. 459.
[44]   On the sectarian character of the psychoanalytic movement see George Weisz, "Scientists and Sectarians: The Case of Psychoanalysis," in Journal of the History of the Behavioral Sciences XI (1975), pp. 350-364.
[45]   Ernest Jones, The Life and Work of Sigmund Freud (New York: Basic Books, 1955). In vol. 2, Years of Maturity, p. 152.

Case IV:
The Rejection of Aesthetic Sociology (Simmel)

Let me now return to the history of sociology before I conclude with a glance at history.

The history of sociology could be written as the story of its separation from art and literature, and it would indeed, as Robert Nisbet proposed, be useful to reflect "how different things would be...if the social sciences at the time of their systematic formation...had taken the arts in the same degree they took the physical sciences as models."[46]

When Comte was once criticized for his style, the founding father of sociology angrily countered that he commanded the scientific style appropriate to his subject and that for the rest he would gladly be compared to all those whom the rhetoricians did not regard as particularly great writers. Writing clearly not in the tradition of the Histoire naturelle, he finished by quoting Buffon's famous "le style est l'homme même," by which he meant that he could not change his style anyway. Writing in 1840 to Valat about his cerebral hygiene, his "régimen philosophique," he made perfectly clear that his aesthetic taste, especially his love for great poetry, only distracted and relaxed him, but had nothing to do with his work proper.[47]

At the end of the century, a literary attitude had become dangerous for anyone who had professional interests as a sociologist. In 1893 for instance, K. Bleibtreu wrote in Die Gesellschaft that all too soon Taine would only be regarded as a writer but not as someone who had contributed substantially to the development of sociology. Simmel, who always remained a stranger in the academy, is a particular case in point.

A glance at Simmel's publications reveals this strangeness most clearly: "Of the 180 articles published in his lifetime...only 64 were published in scholarly journals, while 116 appeared in non-scholarly publications destined for a wider cultivated public such as liberal newspapers, art magazines, and literary monthlies."[48] Yet I think it is somewhat superficial to regard this, as Lewis Coser and others have done, as a reaction of Simmel against the lack of aca-

[46] Robert Nisbet, Sociology as an Art Form, 2nd ed. (London: Oxford University Press, 1976), p. 16.
[47] Auguste Comte, Corréspondance générale et confessions, ed. Paulo E. de Berredo Carneiro and Pierre Arnaud (Paris/The Hague: Mouton, 1973), p. 130. See his letter to Valat in 1824.
[48] Lewis A. Coser, ed., Georg Simmel (Englewood Cliffs, N.J.: Prentice-Hall, 1965), p. 34.

demic recognition which he had to live with. It is true that Simmel, who was finally called to Strasbourg as a full professor in 1914, when he was 56 years old, after having been a non-paid professor extraordinary in Berlin for fourteen years, suffered from the fact that he belonged to the ranks of the "unsuccessful," to quote Max Weber. His literary and aesthetic attitude, however, was not a consequence of this, but rather a basis of his sociological theory. Simmel, who wanted to prove the right of sociology to exist, did so in a peculiar and dangerous way. Sociology was conceived as a method by which societal <u>forms</u> could be described like objects of art. The aesthetic viewpoint was most appropriate to the analysis of the beautiful, but it could in principle be applied to sociology and other disciplines as well, as Simmel tried to explain in his <u>Sociology of Money</u>.

It was this theoretical choice which also prevented Simmel's sociology from being fully accepted by his fellow sociologists, let alone other members of the academic community. Of course, as in the case of psychoanalysis, anti-Semitism again played an important role, but anti-Semitism certainly was not responsible for the fact that colleagues of Simmel--Durkheim, Sorokin and Max Weber among them--deplored his lack of discipline and methodology (Vierkandt) and regarded his writings as a sociology for the salon (v. Wiese). Like Freud, Simmel was first admired by the wrong audience, literary men and artists who gladly acknowledged that Simmel's theory resembled more closely an art collection than a scientific system.[49] Who, today, would not like to be called the "true philosopher of impressionism," the philosophical Monet whom no Cézanne succeeded? Marxists like Trotzki and Lukács, with slightly different intentions, used these expressions more to criticize Simmel than to praise him. Having compared him to the composer Strauss and the poet Rilke, no positivist had to fear Simmel's proximity. And when, in 1908, the historian Dietrich Schaefer was requested to evaluate Simmel's work for the cultural ministry in Baden, he could easily concentrate on Simmel's performance and alleged Semitism without mentioning his intellectual competence or his writings at all in his letter of non-recommendation:

> He speaks exceedingly slowly, by dribs and drabs, and thus offers only little material, although it is

[49] "The Simmelian order resembles the interrelations in the collection of a real friend of the arts, who has always bought only what excited him and was an experience to him.... And yet, the collection has a compelling unity, because all its pieces were chosen on the basis of a unique attitude toward art, of a unique view of life and world." Emil Utitz, "Simmel und die Philosophie der Kunst" in <u>Zeitschrift für Aesthetik und allgemeine Kunstwissenschaft</u> XIV (1920), pp. 1-41.

well-rounded, succinct, and polished. These features are very much appreciated by certain categories of students who are very numerous here in
Berlin. In addition, he spices his words with clever sayings. And the audience he recruits is composed accordingly. The ladies constitute a very
large portion--even for Berlin.[50]

In his merciless critique of the Philosophy of Money, Durkheim
certainly did not do justice to Simmel, but he anticipated his future
image with prophetic clarity, speaking of "ce genre de spéculation
bâtard, (qui) ne serait nous donner des choses ni les sensations
vives et fraiches qu'éveille l'artiste ni les notions distinctes que
recherche le savant."[51]

Of course, Simmel's relationship to sociology is of another sort
than that of Freud to psychology. Freud's theory was rejected by
an experimental psychology which proudly claimed to belong to the
natural sciences. Simmel remained an outsider even for his reluctant admirers because he threatened the compromise sociology finally had reached between the nomothetic and the idiographic.
Therefore it might be especially useful to compare Simmel to Max
Weber, who was equally torn between the narrative and the analytic
mode, but who managed to work up his key metaphors--like the
"elective affinities" which he took from Goethe--into decent concepts. Economy and Society reflects, in its orgy of formal
definitions, classifications and typologies (Marcuse) and in its
attempt to combine interpretive understanding with causal explanation, a compromise that succeeded.[52] That Simmel originally was
almost kept out of the university but in the last few decades has
become a sociological classic, is a result of the increasing impor-

---

[50] Ibid., p. 38.
[51] Emile Durkheim, Review of G. Simmel, Philosophie des Geldes,
in L'année sociologique V (1900-1), pp. 140-145.
[52] See Richard H. Howe, "Max Weber's Elective Affinities: Sociology within the Bounds of Pure Reason" in American Journal of
Sociology 84 (1978), pp. 366-385, and Frederic Jameson, "The Vanishing Mediator: Narrative Structures in Max Weber" in New German Critique I (1974), pp. 52-89. Here again the "minimal"
differences, as Mannheim would have called them, are the most
important, especially those which Max Weber tried to formulate in
his critique of Simmel's sociology but which he never
finished--probably because he was well aware that its publication
would further diminish Simmel's tiny chances to get a position in the
university. See Weber, Economy and Society. An Outline of Interpretive Sociology, ed. Günther Roth and Claus Wittich (New York:
Bedminster Press, 1968). See also Donald N. Levine's introduction.

tance which interpretive understanding has won at the cost of causal explanation in the social sciences.

Final Remarks

Let me finish with some remarks on history which in many respects might be regarded as a counter-example for what I have said so far. To regard history as art and as science[53] is more a commonplace than an original insight, and to speak of the poetry of history[54] or to confirm the revival of the narrative[55] will do no harm to any professional historian in his own guild or in the academy in general. And even if one has to admit that not all historians write well and some don't care, a poet, after all, has been a professor of history (Schiller as extra-ordinarius at the University of Jena from 1789 on) and is still regarded, although reluctantly, as part of its professional past. And whereas the theory-programmes which were rejected by psychology and the social sciences at the turn of the century--psychoanalysis and Simmel's sociology--were also rejected because of their aesthetic attitudes, German historiography successfully expelled a paradigm-candidate which tried to imitate the natural sciences: Lamprecht's and Breysig's cultural history (Kulturgeschichte).

One of the reasons for this rejection was the confidence history as a discipline had won in the nineteenth century by developing a critical method, distinguishing it from the social sciences and providing an alternative to the nomothetic orientation of the natural sciences. Yet the formative years of history, and especially German history in the nineteenth century, display a conflict which is similar to that in sociology and psychology much later. When the Historische Zeitschrift was founded in 1859, the editor, Heinrich von Sybel, and other contributors stressed the scientific character of the journal, which should represent the true method of historical research ("historische Forschung") and mark all deviations from it with restless zeal.[56] It should be of a truly national character,

[53] H. Stuart Hughes, History as Art and as Science (Chicago: University of Chicago Press, 1975).
[54] Emery Neff, The Poetry of History (New York: Columbia University Press, 1947).
[55] Lawrence Stone, "The Revival of Narrative: Reflections on a New Old History," in Past and Present 85 (1979), pp. 3-24.
[56] The first issue of the Historische Zeitschrift is a good example of the significance of "negation" in the institutionalization of a new discipline: already its second article, by Waltz, is called "Wrong Directions" (Falsche Richtungen). I give but one example of the harshness of this negation, which I deliberately choose to quote in the Teutonic original: "Es gibt überhaupt auf dem Gebiet der

distinguished especially from French historians who probably disposed of a better style of writing but were not able to match the thoroughness of their German counterparts.[57] Eight years later, Heinrich Ritter, in a somewhat unusual open letter to Ranke, criticized that he had not distinguished clearly enough between the writing of history, which was of artistic character and therefore could take on a different style in the various European schools of history, and historical research proper, which was scientific and universal.[58]

Nevertheless, it is my assumption that above all the distinction and even the opposition between writing and research has endowed history with a flexibility that has helped to institutionalize the discipline and today still proves useful for its survival under changing organizational structures and extra-scientific demands.

Characteristic of the still remaining disciplinary differences in this respect is that a book on the Historical Imagination in Nineteenth-Century Europe[59] could be written within the historical profession, whereas The Dialectical Imagination[60] is the book of an historian about an oppositional sociological school and The Sociological Imagination[61] the creed of an outsider and rebel in sociology. Following Mills, the sociological imagination demands qualities typi-

Geschichte, ja mehr fast auf diesem als auf dem irgend einer andern Disciplin, Strebungen, die krankhaft und verderblich in hohem Grade sind, die in der Anwendung, die sie auf das Leben suchen, und in dem, was sie in der Wissenschaft selber thun, großen Schaden stiften. Diese muß unsere Zeitschrift bekämpfen, offen, entschieden, rücksichtslos. Da darf sie sich nicht scheuen, mit dem Schwerte dreinzuschlagen, darf sich nicht für zu gut halten, Unkraut auszujäten, und wenn sie einen ordentlichen Haufen beieinander hat, ein lustiges Feuer davon zu machen." See Georg Waltz, "Falsche Richtungen. Schreiben an den Herausgeber," in Historische Zeitschrift I (1859), p. 19.

[57] Wilhelm Giesebrecht, "Zur Charakteristik der heutigen Geschichtsschreibung in Deutschland," in Historische Zeitschrift I (1859), pp. 1-17.

[58] Heinrich Ritter, An Leopold von Ranke über deutsche Geschichtsschreibung. Ein offener Brief (Leipzig: Fues's Verlag, 1867).

[59] Hayden V. White, Metahistory. The Historical Imagination in Nineteenth-Century Europe (Baltimore: Johns Hopkins University Press, 1973).

[60] Martin Jay, The Dialectical Imagination. A History of the Frankfurt School and the Institute of Social Research 1923-1950 (London: Heinemann, 1973).

[61] C. Wright Mills, The Sociological Imagination (New York: Oxford University Press, 1959).

cal, among others, of political analysis and literary work. The writers of the nineteenth century had been its true sociologists; the sociologists of the twentieth in turn, without imitating them, should try to be their legitimate successors in dealing with "private troubles and public issues."

Following this advice, it might be useful, and not only for the sociological imagination, to remember a literary past for the better understanding of a sometimes illiterate present.

POETRY, HISTORY, TRUTH, AND REDEMPTION

Louis Mackey

I love to tell the story,
Because I know 'tis true;
It satisfies my longing
As nothing else can do.
Gospel Hymn

You can go home again..., so long as you
understand that home is a place where you
have never been.
Ursula Le Guin,
The Dispossessed

In 1957 an English solicitor named Owen Barfield published a book entitled Saving the Appearances: A Study in Idolatry. In his Introduction he describes the book as "a sort of outline sketch...for a history of human [mainly Western] consciousness."[1] In the body of the work he traces the evolution of consciousness from an edenic state of union with itself and nature (which he calls Original Participation), through a state of diremption and fragmentation (which he calls Idolatry), toward a state of eventual reunification (which he calls Final Participation). The book, which narrates the history of consciousness as a redemptive history, is itself a myth of redemption in which the redemptive agent, the power that saves the appearances, is the iconoclastic imagination.

A lot of theologians and literary people have found the book interesting. I know a few philosophers and one political scientist who have studied it. Whether historians have ever taken it seriously I do not know. Perhaps they should. For thereby hangs a tale.

Once upon a time, everyone knows, Aristotle declared poetry more philosophical than history. Everyone also knows, though not everyone agrees about, why he thought so. What Aristotle says on this head is said in the Poetics, early in his discussion of the tragic

---

[1] Owen Barfield, Saving the Appearances: A Study in Idolatry (London: Faber and Faber, 1957), p. 13.

plot, that <u>mythos</u> which, as <u>mimesis praxeos</u>, is the <u>arche</u> and as it were the <u>psyche</u> of the tragedy. (Exceptionally rich cluster of words in this region of the text):

> It is evident...that it is not the function of the poet to relate what has happened but what can happen according to the law of probability or necessity. Whether the writer is a historian or a poet is not to be determined by whether he uses metre or prose.... The difference between a poet and a historian is this: the historian relates what has happened, the poet what could happen. Therefore, poetry is something more philosophic and of more serious import than history; for poetry tends to deal with the general, while history is concerned with delimited particular facts.[2]

Philosophy is concerned to discover and state general truths: truths about genera and species, about the kinds of things of which, fundamentally, the universe consists. For in spite of his opposition to the Platonic <u>chorismos</u>, Aristotle like his master is inclined to ascribe more reality to kinds than to the singulars that instantiate them. At least these are the subjects of knowledge and the topics of demonstration.

The historian relates particular events, the things done by or to particular people. Matters of fact. But the poet tells of things in general: what persons of a certain sort might do, could do, would do, should do, or would be bound to do in circumstances of a certain sort. And for this reason, that his subject-matter is universal rather than particular, the poet's work is more philosophical and therefore of more gravity than that of the historian.. He gets closer to the structures of being and the sources of cognition, while the historian only skims the surface of truth and reality.

I have made it sound as if (and most of Aristotle's commentators have made it sound as if) the difference between history and poetry were a difference between their respective subject-matters: the one deals with singulars, the other with universals. That certainly makes the distinction clear. It also makes the superior philosophicity of poetry easy to understand. Aristotle's language, however, suggests another reading. It may be that the difference between history and poetry is a difference between the modalities of their discourses. History is written in the indicative mode, the mode of assertion and matter of fact. But poetry, at its most philosophical, is in the mode of necessity, and, at its least

---

[2] Aristotle, <u>Poetics</u>, tr. Preston H. Epps (Chapel Hill: University of North Carolina Press, 1942), p. 18.

philosophical, in the mode of probability and possibility. When its discourse is not necessitarian (at which point it almost merges with philosophical science), the language of poetry is subjunctive or optative. On this view of the matter one might regard both philosophy, ideally a system of necessary truths, and history, never more than a relation of facts, as modally constricted forms of poetry, which has all of possibility, including the actual and the necessary, as its domain.

But it is unlikely that Aristotle, stalwart champion of poetry though he was, would agree to this privileging of poetry over both history and philosophy. He was after all a philosopher defending poetry, and it is clear where authority hangs its hat.

Here's another way to think of it. History tells (merely) true stories. Poetry tells likely stories. (I intend the full ambiguity of the English idiom: bards do tell many a lie.) But philosophy trumps them both: it offers essential truth, a vision of the structures of being as such. If we plot the hierarchy this way (and overlook the wobbling of "likelihood"), then poetry is more philosophical than history only on the condition that possibility (fiction in the "what if" sense of imaginative hypothesis: likelihood poised in stable equilibrium between probability and dissemblance) is closer to necessity than actuality is. Not all, maybe not many, philosophers would go for that. Appropriately, poetry has got short shrift from the philosophy department, while history has been accorded at least the lip service due a semi-science. Aristotle, however, might subscribe to the notion that possibility is higher than actuality and closer to necessity. He knew a bit about the modality of modalities. And he did regard poetry as more philosophical than (read: superior to) history.

Of course not many historians have been willing to accept Aristotle's description of their activity. Historians have not been content merely to tell true stories, in the mode of indication, about matters of particular fact. That, as any historian knows, is only chronicle, not yet elevated to the level of authentic history. Historians--a lot of them since the nineteenth century--have insisted that history is or ought to be or soon will be a science that enunciates the necessary laws of the development of the human race (sometimes spirit) through time. That view too has had its philosophers (often the historian and his philosopher are conveniently the same person), who have offered to formulate for the historian his method of inquiry, the nature of historical explanation, the arguments by which historians may legitimately defend their claims, and even the mode of that necessary historical truth to which the historian may aspire.

One might go on in this vein, unprofitably enough, for a long time. But one thing is clear even from this timid shuffling of the counters. And that is: however poetry and history may decide to arrange themselves at the foot of the table, philosophy is not about to be displaced as master of the revels. One thing traditional philosophers have always agreed on (almost the only thing they have agreed on) is that philosophy is the custodian of the norms of truth, keeper of the master representations by which all (purported) lesser representations of reality (e.g., poetry and history) are to be judged. I think most philosophers still believe that, though nowadays they tend to whisper it apologetically among themselves rather than proclaim it with authority at interdisciplinary congresses. Once queen of the sciences, philosophy is scarcely even a lady any more. Discretion is the better part of a monarch in exile.

Meanwhile, down at the foot of the table. In recent years Hayden White, to the consternation of orthodox historians but to the delight of the heterodox in many departments, has suggested (I do not say argued, but I will say that his suggestion is massively documented, rigorously sustained, and convincing) that history is more poetical than scientific. More poetical even than anything previously conceived as historical.[3] Historians tell tales. They dispose their information along familiar lines of emplotment, valorize their fictions by means of standard tropologies, and narrate them in obedience to conventions of traditional rhetoric. With the help of categories drawn from the works of critics like Northrop Frye and Kenneth Burke, White has persuasively shown that, for all their commitment to fact and truth, historians, just like novelists, epic poets, and tragedians, shape their narratives. And the shapes they give their stories are neither facts nor necessary implicates of fact nor scientific strategies of explanation demanded by the facts. But rather: formative principles of a different order derived from an altogether different source.

To what order do these principles belong? From what source do they derive? Rather than try to answer these questions directly, I recur to the observation made earlier, that philosophers, with few exceptions, have always thought philosophy the inventor and guardian of truth. Whether from the edicts of pure reason or the deliverances of brute experience or some combination of these, the philosopher garners a basket of basic truths (an exhaustive list of the predicaments of being qua being, a principled system of the categories of any possible experience, etc.) and protects them

[3]   Hayden White, Metahistory: The Historical Imagination in Nineteenth-Century Europe (Baltimore: Johns Hopkins University Press, 1973), especially Part One, but also passim. Elements of the argument of Metahistory are restated in some of the essays in Hayden White, Tropics of Discourse. Essays in Cultural Criticism (Baltimore: Johns Hopkins University Press, 1978).

against assault with all the weapons in his arsenal of invincible logic. Or something like that. It has always been clear to the philosopher that philosophy is neither poetry nor history, but the keeper of the norms of verity. A kind of universal ontological bureau of standards and a court of epistemological last resort. Philosophy sits upon the rock of Truth Itself, on which all other discourses, truth-telling or fictive, are either founded or foundering. Or something like that.

What interests me, however, is not these extravagant ironies, but another altogether. This: the history of philosophical theories, including theories of truth, plots a curve that coincides with the cycle of fictional modes proposed by Northrop Frye in his Anatomy of Criticism[4]. The same circuit that Hayden White has traced in the modes of nineteenth-century historiography. That is, philosophy's purported custody of truth sub specie aeternitatis is interrupted by the intrusion into its own discourse of the (purportedly secondary and derivative) discourses of the poet and the historian. Philosophy is written, and it has a history: it is inscribed in history, just as history is inscribed in the forms of fiction.

This poltergeist of deconstruction inhabiting the structure of philosophy recommends an irony over the philosophical enterprise as such. An irony not unlike that recursiveness which, in the texts of Kenneth Burke, appears to be the trope of ultimacy.[5] An irony more extravagant even than Hayden White's ironies over historiography: more extragavant because the radical of self-distrust undermines the foundations of a discourse that has always already had to regard itself as fundamental. An extravagant irony, more ironical yet its extravagance.[6]

---

[4] Northrop Frye, Anatomy of Criticism (New York: Atheneum, 1967), First Essay. For Frye's explanation of displacement, see Anatomy of Criticism, pp. 136-137, 365. See also Northrop Frye, Fables of Identity: Studies in Poetic Mythology (New York: Harcourt, Brace and World, 1963), pp. 21-38.

[5] See Kenneth Burke, A Grammar of Motives (Berkeley: University of California Press, 1969), pp. 503-517, for a major theoretical discussion of irony. But irony is not only a theme that is discussed throughout Burke's corpus; it is also the dominant trope of his texts themselves.

[6] I invoke Frye and Burke in this essay partly in order to suggest a congruence between what I like to do with philosophy and what Hayden White has already done with historiography; partly because it was White who, among others, suggested to me this approach to philosophy; and partly because I think it works.

According to Frye the principle of all narrative is myth. Both genetically and structurally, myth is the primordial mode of discourse. Prior to the distinction between truth and falsity, the language of myth is an undisplaced metaphoric identification of opposites: Jupiter is the thunder, in Christ the divine is the human. But chiefly the identification of the radicals of representation: the myth, both the telling and the ritual enactment, is reality.

Every other (i.e., subsequent) mode of discourse is a displacement of myth: a distribution of the unities of myth into the distinctions prescribed by increasingly strict demands for plausibility, verisimilitude, rationality, and moral responsibility. Romance, at one remove from myth, changes metaphoric identity into the concrete universal or the Coleridgean symbol. The romantic narrative itself is synecdoche of the structure of reality. Another step down the ladder of displacements, high mimesis (the home of tragic heroes) rewrites metaphor as an analogy of proportionality. The high mimetic work (e.g., Oedipos Tyrannos) is an analogy of fate or a proportional representation of the rational order of nature. At the next remove, low mimesis (the scene of comedy) reduces metaphor to simile: disparate terms linked with each other and with the world they describe by external relations of similarity. The characters and events of the naturalistic novel are (we say, in low mimetic admiration) just like real life. At the bottom of the scale, in the mode of irony, the metaphoric bonds that hold the mythic narrative together and confuse it with reality are completely relaxed. The terms of ironic discourse are juxtaposed (to each other and to the things they seem to represent) without commitment to, or even allegation of, any determinate mode of relationship. Irony is, as we say, detached. Ironic poems don't mean. They just be (and not much of that) in hermetic purity.

Mythic narrative celebrates the exploits of gods and heroes. Ironic discourse, by contrast, victimizes both its characters and its themes. The sequence of the modes becomes a self-iterating cycle by virtue of the fact that ironic discourse, taken to the end of the line, reconverts to myth. If the victimization of the anti-hero is sufficiently brutal, he ceases to be merely ridiculous and becomes (at first) pathetic and (eventually) a divine scapegoat who suffers for our sins. It is not far from the church of The Hippopotamus to the Church of The Rock. And when Hume says that the Christian faith was not only attended at the first by miracles but to this day cannot be believed by any reasonable person without one, it is not clear whether he is mocking or genuflecting; just as Kierkegaard presented Christianity with such sublime indirection that his readers (and occasionally himself) could not tell if he was friend or foe.[7]

Thus irony, pursuing its own reductive purposes and faithful to its own diremptive logic, returns to myth. Or perhaps we should call it--in view of the sophistication picked up in the first go-round--mythopoeia. Naiveté forever behind it, the cycle repeats itself sentimentally (if not farcically) the second time around.

In order to protect the autonomy of literature (imaginative writing) and criticism (the systematic study of literature) Frye classifies philosophy as assertive discourse. This suggests that philosophy, centrifugally opened on the world rather than centripetally withdrawn into itself, escapes the categories of literature and exempts itself from the canons of criticism. But Frye knows better and on occasion will permit himself a remark aparte that gives it all away. For example, this one:

> All verbal structures with meaning are verbal imi-
> tations of that elusive psychological and physiolog-
> ical process known as thought.... Anyone who
> imagines that philosophy is not a verbal imitation of
> this process, but the process itself, clearly has not
> done much thinking.[8]

Encouraged by this and by many other such obiter dicta systematically disseminated throughout the Anatomy, I can imagine how a philosophical notion might trace its path along the sequence of Frye's historical modes. I take, not quite at random, the notion of truth.

The notion of truth most favored by philosophers--almost the only notion of truth that is even discussed by recent Anglo-American philosophers--is the notion that truth is the correspondence of symbols (mental or verbal) with reality (matters of fact or states of affairs). Whatever its intrinsic merits, it is fairly clear that the correspondence theory of truth reflects a commitment to low mimetic conventions of writing. Truth means the representation of things just as they are, where "things as they are" means nature and society as directly given to our awareness.

---

[7] David Hume, An Inquiry Concerning Human Understanding (Indianapolis: Bobbs-Merrill, 1955), pp. 140-141. Søren Kierkegaard, Training in Christianity, tr. Walter Lowrie (London: H. Milford, 1944), pp. 132-133.
[8] Frye, Anatomy of Criticism, p. 83. For other "asides" of this sort, see pp. 326-337, 352-353, 12.

The second most popular theory of truth (in the West, at least) is the coherence theory. On this view truth is the coherence of all propositions in a systematic totality, and a true proposition is one that coheres within such a totality. The coherence theory is often adopted because of an apparently insuperable difficulty in the correspondence view. The trouble with correspondence is that we can never distinguish things themselves from our ways of symbolizing them, since we only have access to things as already symbolized. There is no meaningful sense in which indistinguishables can be said to correspond. Reality cannot be distinguished from knowledge; therefore, truth is not the correlation of symbols with unsymbolized reality, but simply the coherence of all symbols (= realities) in a totality.

Since, on this view, reality itself is taken to be an ideal structure, the coherence theory of truth reflects a commitment to the conventions of the high mimetic mode. Truth is the conformity of thought and language, not to the facts of quotidian experience, but to a higher and (of course) more rational order of things. As the correspondence theory is commonly held by empiricists, so the coherence view is almost universally favored by idealists.

These are only the most widely held and generally debated theories of truth in recent Western philosophy. There are other theories of truth adapted to other conventions of representation. For example, all classical theologians will affirm the proposition, "God is truth." Theologians of different times and persuasions qualify this statement in different ways. But at bottom the "is" of "God is truth" is the "is" of identity, and "God is truth" is a proposition in the mythic code.

Opposite the metaphoric identification of God and truth is the skeptical doctrine that truth is unattainable or the nihilistic doctrine that there is no such thing as truth. Views of this sort are patently ironic. As is also Nietzsche's suggestion that truth is a woman who will not allow herself to be possessed--or violated--by dogmatic philosophers; or his other suggestion that truth is no more than the system of conventional lies (he calls them metaphors) honored by a society and necessary to its survival.[9] Romantic theories of truth are a bit harder to track down, lurking as they do in the crannies of the tradition. There is an element of romance in any philosophy (usually it's a form of idealism) in which truth is offered as the term of a heroic intellectual quest. For example, in

[9]   Friedrich Nietzsche, Beyond Good and Evil, tr. Walter Kaufmann (New York: Random House, 1966), pp. 2, 148-149; and Friedrich Nietzsche, "Truth and Falsity in an Ultramoral Sense," in Geoffrey Clive, ed., The Philosophy of Nietzsche (New York: New American Library, 1965), pp. 503-515.

Hegel's Phenomenology, where truth an und für sich is achieved only at the cost of the struggles, the sufferings, and the eventual triumph of the Absolute Spirit. In the more high-minded kinds of pragmatism, where truth is the goal of inquiry, and in the more pragmatic forms of idealism--e.g., the philosophy of Josiah Royce, in which the ultimate value is "loyalty to loyalty"--truth is conceived in accord with the conventions of romance.[10] (Ordinary forms of pragmatism, or the low-minded part of any pragmatism, tend to rewrite the coherence theory in terms of low-mimetic conventions--and to insist that it is really a version of correspondence. Pragmatism after all is just idealism naturalized and brought down to earth: transcendentalism for the preterite.)

Kierkegaard's proclamation that "subjectivity is truth" is romantic in one of its meanings but ironic in others.[11] Likewise romantic is the exhortation to seek truth not in the conformity of one's propositions to fact but in the fidelity of one's life to the sources and powers of one's own being, or to some paradigm of humanity. Truth in the sense of authenticity is perhaps the most recent attempt to rehabilitate romance, a reconstruction already under attack by the forces of deconstruction.

One could rewrite the history of philosophy from this perspective by incongruity. But even this all-too-brief review indicates that one can find, several times over in the course of Western thought, theories of truth answering to all the modes of fiction. And (though I have not tried to show this, I think it could be shown) they arrange themselves in historical sequences, with a historicity at least as precise as Frye's. This should not be surprising, in view of the fact that the philosophical presentation of truth and the literary production of narrative are both ways of representing reality. In the case of literature, Frye says that life and thought are only the content of the work, whereas its form is wholly a product of the conventions of representation. But surely the same is true (whatever that means) of philosophy, insofar as philosophy is not just thought but the verbal imitation of thought. "Nothing built out of words can transcend the nature and conditions of words, and...the nature and conditions of ratio, so far as ratio is verbal, are contained by oratio"[12] Philosophical and literary techniques of mimesis are alike verbal and therefore alike subjected to the modalities of representation and the law of their sequentiality.

[10] Josiah Royce, The Philosophy of Loyalty (New York: MacMillan, 1924), pp. 101-146.
[11] Søren Kierkegaard, Concluding Unscientific Postscript, tr. David F. Swenson, ed. Walter Lowrie (Princeton: Princeton University Press, 1941), pp. 169-224.
[12] Frye, Anatomy of Criticism, p. 337.

In the formula of St. Hilary of Poitiers, quoted throughout the Middle Ages, truth is "declarative being."[13] For all philosophers, including the skeptic, truth as the manifestation of reality is something to be acknowledged, lived by, and revered. That is almost a definition of philosophy. And for that reason the primordial designation of truth would be the mythic identity, "God is truth." Or, since identity converts simpliciter, "truth is God." All other accounts of truth--romantic, high mimetic, low mimetic, and ironic--would be, Fryewise, displacements of his original metaphor in the interests of greater credibility, rationality, and responsibility. It is also worth noting that just as irony among the literary modes turns back into myth, bending the sequence into a circle, so there is a cycle in theories of truth. Skepticism has flourished during at least two periods in the history of Western philosophy: once at the end of the ancient world, and once again at the end of the Middle Ages. In both cases the victimization of truth by skepticism was associated with a reassertion (more or less ironic in tone) of the rights of religious faith. In Fathers like Tertullian and Augustine, and in philosophers like Hume and Kierkegaard. Even in Nietzsche, though the myth that is resurrected out of Nietzsche's vision of nihilism is no more pure Christian than it is pure Dionysian.

The appearance in this list of a belated thinker like Nietzsche betrays the fact (which I could scarcely conceal) that skepticism has visited Western philosophy a third time: at the end of the modern world, among those upon whom (as we so often feel) the ends of the world itself are come. This third advent of skepticism--represented perhaps by this discussion--seems to argue for another and more devastating kind of irony. An irony that may not be the unwitting agent of the cunning of myth. An irony more Burkean than Northropian, because it is an irony over the whole project of philosophy.

What am I doing in this text if not standing back in ironic detachment from the whole history of philosophy (to which I am at the same time a miniscule amendment) and suggesting (ironically indeed, in view of the passion for truth by which philosophers have always been driven) that we regard the story of the philosophical search for truth as a merry-go-round of the modes of intellectual mimesis? A merry-go-round, perhaps, without a brass ring. A Burkean dialogue in which everyone gets to speak his piece, but in which no one has the last word. In which there is no last word, just more words. The final and apparently unredeemable irony

---

[13] St. Hilary of Poitiers, De Trinitate, Book V, No. 14, in vol. II of Opera Omnia, ed. J.-P. Migne (Paris: Vrayet, 1844-45); cited at, among many other places, St. Thomas Aquinas, Summa Theologiae, Ia, q. 16, a. 1, corpus (Turin: Marietti, 1952-53).

would be to detach the question of the philosophy of truth from the question of the truth of philosophy.

Of course it might be argued (I am again following a clue from Frye) that my view of philosophy is guilty of a fatal perspectival fault. I may be taken to have suggested that philosophy is nothing but a kind of poetry. But that, it will be objected, is absolutely the wrong slant on this thing. Frye points out that every literary work in whatever mode projects a metaphysic appropriate to that mode.[14] For example, myth projects a theological world view as its mise en scène, high mimesis projects a form of Platonic idealism, low mimesis naturalism, romance a world of fantasy, and irony something like existentialism. But these are only functions of particular literary forms. If you're writing a low mimetic novel, you need to locate the action in a naturalistic world, whereas tragedy requires something like the rational order of nature for its setting. And so on. It would be a fallacy--Frye calls it the fallacy of existential projection--to infer from this that every poet has a philosophy to impart. This is a fallacy even if the poet himself is taken in by it. The world view of the poet is part of his formal achievement, not a philosophical content recommended for our belief.

Frye's argument is easily converted. Every philosophy (it might be said) discovers a literary form appropriate to its statement. Plato wrote dialogues for the same reason that Descartes wrote meditations, Hume essays, and Nietzsche aphorisms. The form matched the content and served the purpose. But it would be a non sequitur to conclude from this that philosophy is poetry. Perhaps we should call this the fallacy of hypothetical retrojection or aesthetic subjection. A whole clutch of mouth-filling neologisms rise in the throat.

However, it is not my intention to argue that philosophy is only (or really) poetry, any more than I suppose poetry to be philosophy. On the contrary, what I mean to do is blur all such distinctions, compromise all such discriminations, and thereby evacuate all facile identifications. My point is to suggest that categories like "philosophy" and "poetry" are essentially metastable, just as Hayden White has shown that the category "history" is pretty shifty. More to the point, I think that "philosophy" (as the custodian of necessary truth) and "poetry" (as the superintendent of possibility and/or the purveyor of lying fables) are not baskets into which all verbal objects may be dropped, but the terms of an uncertain and restless dialectic. A dialectic which we have reason

---

[14] Frye, Anatomy of Criticism, pp. 63-65. On the fallacy involved in arguing that philosophy is nothing but poetry, see also, p. 353.

to think constitutes the nature of language itself. If language is the house of being, it is also a house of mirrors.

Be that as it may (to quote one of my favorite disclaimers), it might still be protested that my ironizing over philosophy is superfluously pretentious or at least belatedly valedictorian. For as we all know, nobody--not even the philosophers themselves--any longer thinks of philosophy as the bastion of truth.

That may be the case. I doubt it, but it may be the case anyway. But if it is the case, it is not so for the reason that is usually alleged. Namely, that truth has passed from the keeping of Dame Philosophy, who was far too casual and compromised a guardian, into the hands of her more responsible children, the sciences. The natural sciences, first of all, but also those behavioral sciences which with diligence, hard work, good behavior, and a bit of luck may some day become natural. The hard sciences, and those that are doing their best to stiffen up.

This, I think, will not do. Because, to cite only one reason, too many remnants of myth are already at work forming those theories in which the sciences presume to enshrine the truth. The truth of science itself is shaped around a fiction or two, including the fiction of its own truthfulness.

A single gross instance will suggest the sort of thing I have in mind. Evolutionary theory, though it may be supported by factual evidence, is motivated by the need for a myth of origins. At its first emergence and beyond, the theory of evolution, like the speculative cosmologies occasionally perpetrated by theoretical physicists, told a tale of beginnings designed (more or less consciously) to replace the discredited story in Genesis. (It is true that the theory of evolution helped to discredit the creation myth, but it is also the case that the theory of evolution was attractive because a lot of people no longer wanted to believe the Bible. More of this duplicity later.) Theological opponents of evolution argued that the facts adduced by evolutionists as evidence for their theory--all those bones and fossils and strange survivors--had been planted by the devil to expose unbelievers and trap the unwary. The theologians' claim was mocked by the advocates of natural selection. But their raillery was not justified by any fault in the fundamentalists' logic. The theologians' reasoning, given their premises, was flawless. The target of the evolutionists' attack was the whole theological story about man and the world, a story that had become ridiculously implausible to right-thinking (i.e., scientifically minded) people long before evolution provided them with an alternate account of the arche. The theory of evolution did not simply replace a theological fiction with a scientific truth. It substituted for the relatively pure religious myth of beginnings a low-mimetically displaced form of that same narrative. The question of the "truth" of evolution vs. the "truth" of Genesis can be raised, if at all, only in the context of a consciousness of their common mythic motive. (I almost said "their common mythic origin.")

The point of all this is not to badmouth any scientific theory nor to resuscitate fundamentalism, but only to suggest that if philosophy is no longer the guardian of truth, it is not because her care and feeding have been taken over by the sciences, who know how to treat her right. For the sciences themselves are entangled in the same dialectic of displacements--the same uneasy cohabitation of truth and fiction--as philosophy, poetry, and history. And if neither philosophy nor science any longer has secure dominion over truth, it is not because these disciplines have forfeited their right to such dominion by philandering with myth and fable. Rather, the notion of truth itself has become questionable. If the parents and guardians are corrupt, it may be a corruption owed to the delinquency of their child and ward.

It is useful to ask ourselves what we mean by truth. More exactly, what is the significance of our desire for truth? What is it we want when we want truth? St. Anselm of Canterbury, in one of the most spectacular tours de force in Western philosophy, his Dialogus de Veritate, begins with the correspondence theory of truth, which all of us accept as a rule of thumb in daily life, and tries to translate it by a series of equipollent substitutions into the proposition Christians hold by faith, "God is truth."[15] In this way he both finds necessary reasons for an article of faith (his theological program) and returns a low mimetic displacement to metaphoric identity with its mythic Origin. The nerve of his argument is the contention that truth, even in the low mimetic sense of correspondence, has gerundive force. A proposition, whether or not it conforms to fact, is still a proposition: a genuine predication, hence a real proposition, truly a proposition, and in that sense a true proposition. But in fact we call a proposition true in the fullest sense only if it represents things as they are. "Elephants are a species of fish," though truly a proposition, is not what we would call a true proposition.

Propositions, Anselm says, are under obligation to tell the truth in the sense of correspondence. Truth is to be told. It is, in the pale vocable of modern logic, a "value." Verbal symbols are bound by their nature to faithful representation. To use symbols so as not to tell the truth is an abuse of discourse. Frustrating the

---

[15] Anselm of Canterbury, Truth, Freedom, and Evil: Three Philosophical Dialogues, ed. and tr. Jasper Hopkins and Herbert Richardson (New York: Harper and Row, 1967), pp. 91-120.

purpose for which speech was created, failure of correspondence is a moral fault and an offense against God.

The interesting and perhaps unique feature of Anselm's dialogue is that it raises and tries to resolve a question not even imagined by most of those who profess a passion for truth. The question, namely, Why do we care about truth? Why do we care if our symbols correspond to reality? Anselm defines truth as the rectitude of the mind (it is the intellectual counterpart of justice, the rectitude of the will) and implies that what we seek when we seek truth is an uprightness in our relationship to God. In a word: righteousness.

However one judges Anselm's claim, it is a fact that philosophers have always had an almost religious horror of skepticism. St. Augustine, whose capacity for religious horror was boundless, confronted the skeptic with the following reductio. If the proposition "there is no truth" is true, then there is truth. That one at least. So there. If you say you have discovered that truth cannot be discovered, then you are saying you have discovered a truth[16]. Similar discomforts attend other notions of truth. The coherence theory, which drops the question of reality altogether or sublates it without remainder into the web of belief, has always seemed a bit like cheating. And the pragmatist who never ceases to tell us, Wait just a little longer, appears to be temporizing in matters that demand decision.

The passion for truth, like the passion for mimesis, is a passion for reality. All definitions of truth, as Aquinas observes, invoke the name of correspondence.[17] Every truth is an allegory of adaequatio. But our concern to make words correspond to reality is, I believe, a soteriological impulse. The passion for correspondence is, more or less displaced, a passion for salvation. That is: a desire for the reunion of verbal signs with that being of which their being is the alienation.

Perhaps we should call this desire to reappropriate the alienated a rhetorical passion, since rhetoric, according to Burke, is the attempt to achieve in language the consubstantialization of terms (radically language and being) which are originally, in and by language, transsubstantiated.[18] But whatever we call it, the passion

---

[16] St. Augustine, Contra Academicos, Book II; Soliloquia, Book II; De Vera Religione, xxix, 73; and many other places. See Vol. I of Opera Omnia, ed. J.-P. Migne (Paris: Garnier, 1841-1902).
[17] St. Thomas Aquinas, Summa Theologiae, Ia, q. 16, especially a. 2.
[18] Kenneth Burke, A Rhetoric of Motives (Berkeley: University of California Press, 1969), especially pp. 174-189, 267-294.

for truth is plainly a paradoxical passion. For (this too in the name of Burke) at the same time that it desires a reunion of signs with reality, it presupposes a distinction between being and the signs by which we purport to represent it. The sign can be sign only as and by virtue of its difference from reality. Perhaps I should have written "differance." For it is also the case that reality is not the reality desired by the desire for truth unless it is a reality not already alienated in the sign. The passion for truth--this is the source of its intensity and its poignancy--at once presumes the diremption of word and thing and longs to repair it. Therefore the acquisition of truth (in the sense of correspondence) would frustrate the desire for truth (for the reunion of sign and reality) in the very act of gratifying it: the truth of correspondence iterates the difference that the passion for union craves to obliterate. And conversely, the achievement (sit venia verbo) of a real union of sign and being would efface the difference between them that motivates the search for truth and makes it possible in the first place: the solution would destroy the problem. The original differance (the silent "a" is now a necessity) of sign and signified both generates the passion for recuperation and indefinitely defers its satisfaction.

Therefore skepticism, which tries to quell the desire for truth rather than gratify it, only outrages the passion and prompts refutations of the sort Augustine offered: an epistemological return of the repressed, in which the reality of truth returns as the truth of the assertion that there is no truth. The achievement of truth in the sense of coherence, which abrogates any distinction of sign and reality, also annuls (this is why coherence has always seemed too facile to be true) the difference of (self)consciousness by which the notion of truth is constituted and truth itself made desirable. Truth as the object of a romantic quest postpones gratification so perfectly that it never comes at all. Pragmatism, whatever its other virtues, doesn't work.

It is the paradoxical essence of the passion for truth itself, not the historical fact of the supercession of philosophy by the sciences, that calls into question the claim of philosophy (or any other discipline) to be the inventor and purveyor of truth. Truth, it appears, does not subsist, but only stands--or rather: perpetually recedes--as the term of a desire that can never be satisfied and never quenched. The impasse, we have been led to believe, lies in the nature of the linguistic sign and its relation to extra-linguistic reality. Unless the sign in some way participates the reality it signifies, it cannot do its job, which is to mediate cognition of the thing signified. But sign and thing signified cannot be identical, for in that case there would be no sign distinct from the thing signified and so, once again, no cognition of the thing mediated by the sign. In order to do what it is supposed to do the sign must be both the same as and different from the thing it stands for. The signified is both implicated in the sign (to be a sign is to signify the signified) and ontically-epistemically distinct from it (so that no sign is sufficiently motivated by its signified). These are the conditions which must, impossibly, be met in order for truth to occur.

Therefore, when we are offered truth, we are asked to accept either a symbolic representation of reality so fragile and precarious that it does not quiet our desire (the contingent truths fostered by low mimetic correspondence) or an identity of symbol and reality so faultless that it severs the root of our desire (the necessary truths enunciated by high mimetic coherence) or an indefinite postponement of the advent of truth that sets us on pins and needles forever (the romance of pragmatism) or a divorce of symbol and reality so final that it bids us be satisfied with frustration as a matter of principle (the ironic renunciations and jejune abstentions of skepticism). What we really want is the metaphoric confusion of identity and difference: God, who is Truth Itself because his intellect and his essence, rationally distinct, are ontologically one (differunt ratione, subjecto idem). But that, it appears, is a myth.

I have suggested that the many theories of truth advocated by philosophers may be conceived as displacements, in Frye's sense, of an original mythic identity of sign and signified. But of course myth--and its equivalent opposite, irony--are never actually given in their putative purity. The most primitive and unitive kind of discourse is no longer myth, and the most sophisticated and fragmented specimen of language is not yet irony. All actual discourse converges toward romance, high mimesis, and low mimesis, in all of which the distinction of symbol and reality is preserved, and in all of which truth is sought as a relation of the two. How we conceive of truth and truthful discourse depends on how we imagine the human condition. But in any estimate of our situation the distinction of symbol and reality is presumed. That is the condition of estimation. And imagination. For pure myth (identity without difference) and pure irony (difference without identity) would be wordless, and therefore beyond the distinction of truth and falsity. Mysticism and a world perfectly deconstructed would, equivalently and equivocally, solve the problem of truth by eliminating it. They would be, if they were possible at all, not solutions but dissolutions.

Implicit in the passion for truth in all its forms is the nostalgia for a mythical Eden in which symbol and reality were not yet disconnected, a prelapsarian state in which the symbol-using animal had not yet fallen out of harmony with being and with itself, but was still one and at one with all that is. Every religion postulates such a paradise lost and nurtures the expectation of paradise regained. Religion itself, which is close to the (alleged) mythic sources of human thought and feeling, is the soteriological trajectory from paradise lost to paradise regained along some revealed axis of redemption. Our closest approximation to the purity of myth itself, religion, is, mythopoetically and mythomorphically, the myth of myth.

That is why I propose that we regard the passion for truth as a displacement of the soteriological impulse natural to religion and originating in myth. Truth is salvation removed from the quasi-mythic categories of religion into the alienated categories of historical humanity. As the quest for salvation is an attempt to recover original righteousness, so the search for truth (in Burke's sense of the word, a rhetorical project) is an attempt to recover being, to reinstate reality in our alienated symbols. A projection from myth to myth, nostalgia protended as apocalypse, philosophy, which originates (historically) as a critique of myth (the religion promulgated by the old Greek poets), is a strategy of salvation: a displaced redemption myth.

But not philosophy only. Any discourse that aims at the discovery of truth, or for that matter any discourse that disavows this purpose, falls under the same judgment. It may be appropriate here to return to Aristotle's distinction of philosophy, poetry, and history. From what has been said we might extrapolate that philosophy, poetry, and history are the conceptual, imaginative, and narrative forms, respectively, of a single myth of redemption. Philosophy essays the recuperation of being conceptually and in the mode of necessity. Poetry, always the most disillusioned of these enchantments, endeavors to redeem the symbol imaginatively and in the mode of possibility. (Poetry is "most disillusioned" because it is always conscious of and so never convinced by its own fabrications.) And history, speaking narratively in the mode of actuality, has always contended (in one way or another) that the story of the world is the justification of the world. Otherwise, why write it? Derrida has observed, laconically but astutely, that history "has always been conceived as the movement of a resumption of history, a diversion between two presences."[19] Or even more pointedly, apropos of my argument here, "History and knowledge, istoria and episteme have always been determined...as detours for the purpose of the reappropriation of presence."[20] Western historiography, from The City of God down to Hegel and beyond, has always been the most direct transcription of the prototypical Western redemption myth. Every version of Western history is a

[19] Jacques Derrida, "Structure, Sign, and Play in the Discourse of the Human Sciences," in Richard Macksey and Eugenio Donato, eds., The Structuralist Controversy (Baltimore: Johns Hopkins University Press, 1970), p. 262.
[20] Jacques Derrida, Of Grammatology, tr. Gayatri C. Spivak (Baltimore: Johns Hopkins University Press, 1977), p. 10.

revisionary displacement of the story told in the Old and New Testaments: the original, total, and final story of the world, from its beginning at the creation, through its redemption in the fullness of time, to its ultimate restoration in the last day.

Unfortunately, there's a catch to all this. When I say that the desire for truth is a displaced soteriological passion and the definition of truth a transportation of the metaphor of redemption into the categories of diremption, I iterate the displacement in reverse. Having drawn the signifieds of philosophy, poetry, and history into the play of signifiers, I reinvest these (my "own") signifiers with the authority of a transcendental signified. I valorize my "own" miniscule amendment. That is, I have (once more with feeling) posited myth itself as the transcendent origin and the inner substance of both truth and (my "own" contribution) the truth about truth. I might now try to displace <u>that</u> move. But what would be--what has always already been--the source of the displacement? Either it comes from within the myth that is proposed as the undisplaced origin, or it comes from a source outside of myth. If it comes from within, then myth itself is always already fractured, tending to diaspora, and not the seamless unity demanded by the use of "displacement" as a category of explanation. If it comes from without, then the supposed mythic unity is not the comprehensive origin it must be in order for the explanatory strategy of displacement to work. In either case, myth is (must be, in order for displacement to "occur" at all) aboriginally displaced from/within the cause of its own displacement.[21]

Is displacement something that happens to an original myth? Or is myth something that happens in and by reason of the original non-originality of displacement? Is myth itself a myth? Is the origin an origin, or is origin itself a retrojection from an always already prior "condition" of ab-originality? Is the center a fiction of the periphery? And is our nostalgia a sign of paradisal beginnings, or only a symptom of our always already alienation?

Philosophy is, historically, a dialectical critique of religion which proposes to restate the content of myth in the form of truth. But the "content of myth" is a piece of philosophical mythopoeia and the "form of truth" a philosophical mythomorph. The philosophical critique deconstructs its attempt to reconstruct a viable redemption myth. As the prophetic bard knows that his vatic insights are also lying fables, and as the historian, perpetually recasting <u>Heils-</u>

---

[21] For a different, but related, critique of the idea of displacement, to which I am much indebted, see Geoffrey H. Hartman, "Ghostlier Demarcations: The Sweet Science of Northrop Frye," in Hartman's <u>Beyond Formalism</u> (New Haven: Yale University Press, 1970), especially p. 37.

geschichte as Weltgeschichte, is also always profaning the shrines at which he worships, so the philosopher's fictions undermine the truth they sustain. Philosophers, poets, and historians are all language-users (or in the more accurate phrase of James Branch Cabell, "used by language"[22]), and for that reason they are and can only be their own worst enemies. That is part of what it means to be (one last Aristotelian tag) zoon logon echon. The unexamined life is not worth living...and barely viable.

A paragraph back I asked a lot of embarrassing questions. The point of this excursion is just to make these questions questionable. As Derrida observes in an essay from which I have already quoted, it is not possible--or even meaningful--to align oneself with either of the alternatives apparently opposed by such questions.[23] For the language in which we are destined to think these options also requires that we embrace, ambiguously, both of them.

At the beginning of this paper I have placed two mottoes. Both of them are, I think, necessarily true. Or if you will, matters of fact. At the very least...worth pretending. There is no question of a choice between them.

---

[22] James Branch Cabell, Figures of Earth. A Comedy of Appearances (New York: McBride, 1921), p. 126.
[23] Derrida, "Structure, Sign, and Play in the Discourse of the Human Sciences," p. 265.

II.

LITERATURE IN HISTORY AND HISTORY IN LITERATURE:

CASE STUDIES

TACITUS ON GERMANY:

ROMAN HISTORY OR LATIN LITERATURE?*

M. Gwyn Morgan

Since the concern of this volume is the interrelationship between history and literature, there is excellent reason to consider Roman views on the subject: where we see a problem, they saw none. In fact, they would probably have been baffled by the title of this paper, unless they dismissed it as another example of Helle-nophile logic-chopping. To explain this situation and, I hope, to give some insight into the problems we face by contrasting them with a very different way of thinking, I shall use as my illustration the greatest of the Roman historians, Cornelius Tacitus, while the context requires that we focus on the Germania. Outside Germany it is a treatise to which scant attention is paid,[1] but that neglect is more than counterbalanced by the consideration it has received within the country. There it is unquestionably the best known and

*I would like to express my thanks to the University Research Institute of the University of Texas for a leave of absence which greatly facilitated the research on which this article is based.
Because the bibliography on Tacitus and the Germania is moun-tainous, I have tried (not very successfully) to limit annotation, and for ease of reference the following works will be cited by author's or editor's name and page number(s) only:

John G.C. Anderson, ed., Corneli Taciti de origine et situ Germanorum (Oxford: Clarendon Press, 1938).

Stefan Borzsák, "P. Cornelius Tacitus," Pauly-Wissowas Real-encyclopädie der classischen Altertumswissenschaft (Stuttgart: J.B. Metzler, 1894ff), Supb. XI, cols. 373-512.

Rudolf Much, ed., Die Germania des Tacitus. 3rd ed. (Hei-delberg: Carl Winter, 1967).

Eduard Norden, Die germanische Urgeschichte in Tacitus Ger-mania (Leipzig: B.G. Teubner, 1923).

Karl Trüdinger, Studien zur Geschichte der griechisch-römischen Ethnographie (Basel: Emil Birkhäuser, 1918).

[1] So Alain Michel, Tacite et le destin de l'empire (Paris: Arthaud, 1966), pp. 63-64; Tom Alan Dorey, ed., Tacitus (London: Routledge and Kegan Paul, 1969), p. 12.

the most widely read work of any classical author. Indeed, it is a work which has inspired and haunted Germans, if not from the moment it was published in A.D. 98, at least from its rediscovery in the first half of the fifteenth century.[2] Ever since, it has proved a work to live up to and a work to live down. Yet much of the uproar to which it has contributed stems from a refusal to understand the Germania on its own terms, as a treatise in which literary and historical elements coexist, in an uneasy balance perhaps, but a balance nonetheless. Even classical scholars tend to divide into literary and historical factions and, between them, to rend Tacitus asunder. For the one group he is preeminently a literary artist, a sincere and truthful reporter to the others. So we are all, it seems, victims of a dichotomy the Romans contrived somehow to avoid.

It will be best to begin with a few remarks about Tacitus the man and his work.[3] A Roman from a wealthy family of Northern Italy or Southern Gaul, Cornelius Tacitus made his career in politics and reached the highest office, the consulship, in A.D. 97. He chose that same year to launch his career as a writer, publishing as his first work what is normally described as a biography of his father-in-law, Cn. Iulius Agricola, sometime governor of Britain.[4] The Germania followed a year later, in A.D. 98, and thereafter Tacitus went on to write his Dialogus de oratoribus, designed to show that political oratory must decline under an emperor,[5] and his

---

[2] For the date of publication see Borzsák, p. 416. The manuscript's rediscovery is discussed by Clarence W. Mendell, Tacitus: the Man and his Work (New Haven: Yale University Press, 1957), pp. 241-255, and Kenneth C. Schellhase, Tacitus in Renaissance Political Thought (Chicago: University of Chicago Press, 1975), pp. 32-35.

[3] Many details remain highly controversial: see Borzsák, pp. 373-399.

[4] Although the Agricola is primarily a biography, it is difficult to see it solely as such: hence the continuing need for extensive discussions of the monograph's purpose, e.g., by W. Steidle, "Tacitusprobleme," Museum Helveticum 22 (1965) 81-114 at pp. 96-104; Borzsák, pp. 399-416; and Robert M. Ogilvie and Sir Ian Richmond, ed., Corneli Taciti de vita Agricolae (Oxford: Clarendon Press, 1967), pp. 11-20.

[5] On the Dialogus see Borzsák, pp. 428-442 and Gordon Williams, Change and Decline: Roman Literature in the Early Empire (Berkeley: University of California Press, 1978), pp. 26-51. However, as was long ago noticed by Gaston Boissier, Tacitus and Other Roman Studies, tr. W.G. Hutchison (London: A. Constable, 1906), p. 72, political oratory may have lost its power under the Principate, "but it preserved all its prestige. An Emperor incapable of eloquence seemed scarce worthy to reign."

two major historical works, the Histories covering the years of the Flavian emperors (A.D. 69-96), and the Annals devoted to the period from the accession of Tiberius in A.D. 14 through the suicide of Nero in A.D. 68. The Annals is generally, and rightly, considered his masterpiece, but different people see different things in the work. We shall have to consider in detail a passage in which he discusses the historian's role, but in German eyes it is another section altogether which has always stood out, the section dealing with Arminius, the German chieftain who destroyed three Roman legions in A.D. 9 and ended Rome's chances of conquering territory east of the Rhine and north of the Danube.[6]

The Germania itself is a relatively short work which appears to fall naturally into two halves of almost equal length. The first half (chapters 1-27) constitutes a general account of the land, the people, their customs and their institutions. Hence reports on their mythical ancestors, the nature of the terrain, their public life (mostly warfare), their religion, and their private life, including details on their clothing, their marriage customs, their diet and amusements (mostly drinking), and their burial customs. In the second half of the work (chapters 28-46) we have a catalogue of all the tribes, starting with those nearest to the Roman frontiers and ending with the Hellusii and Oxiones, who--says Tacitus (Germ. 46. 6)--"are reported to have the faces and features of men, the bodies and limbs of wild animals. Since I cannot verify such accounts, I leave them an open question."

If description of the Germania is relatively easy, it has proved rather more difficult to establish the treatise's purpose.[7] It was thought once that Tacitus aimed to contrast noble, uncorrupted Germans with degenerate, effete Romans,[8] but that motif runs

---

[6]   Tacitus, Ann. 4. 32-33 contains his views on historiography, 2. 88. 3-4 his tribute to Arminius. The story of the clades Variana was known in Germany during the Middle Ages, primarily through Orosius 6. 2. 26-27, but the rediscovery of Tacitus' account created a sensation: see Schellhase (above, note 2), pp. 12 and 45-49.

[7]   Borzsák, p. 424: "Die Germ(ania), deren literarische Gattung sich genauso wie diejenige des Agr. nicht leicht definieren läßt bereitete den Forschern fast mit jedem Kapitel (ja jedem Satz) immer viel Kopfzerbrechen." The lack of prooemium and/or epilogue certainly does not help.

[8]   This view apparently originated with Voltaire: see Jürgen von Stackelberg, Tacitus in der Romania. Studien zur literarischen Rezeption des Tacitus in Italien und Frankreich (Tübingen: Max Niemeyer, 1960), pp. 224-225. There have been several variations on this theme, all alike unconvincing. Borzsák, pp. 418-422, for example, reissues it after substituting "political" for "moral"

through only the first half of the work, and even there lapses from view fairly frequently. Another theory held that Tacitus was trying to frighten the Romans, either into attacking these formidable adversaries or into not attacking them, but both variations founder on the fact that this theme does not stand out clearly and consistently in the work as a whole.[9] Which leaves the current interpretation, best argued by Karl Trüdinger and Eduard Norden,[10] that Tacitus was simply writing an ethnographical treatise, a type of work long traditional in the Greco-Roman world, and a type of work fashionable in the first century A.D., if we are to judge by Seneca's having written such essays, de situ Indiae and de situ et sacris Aegyptiorum, some forty years earlier.[11] I am not sure that this explains very much, since it fails adequately to account for Tacitus' wanting to write an ethnographical treatise at all, or for his choosing the German tribes as his particular subject. These, however, are questions to which we may return later in the discussion.

Our next step must be to set the scene, the background against which Tacitus wrote, and the background against which Roman attitudes to history and literature ought to become comprehensible. In essence, Rome was a highly structured society run by a small elite, the governing class. That governing class might be of different composition at different times, but it was always pre-eminent, not only dictating the social values of the community as a whole but also insisting that its own function--governing--was

throughout. E. Wolff, "Das geschichtliche Verstehen in Tacitus Germania," Hermes 69 (1934), pp. 121-166 is a long-winded attempt to maintain that Tacitus aimed to compare current Germanic virtues with those of antique Romans. Karl Büchner, P. Cornelius Tacitus: die historischen Versuche (Stuttgart: A. Kröner, 1955), pp. 141-148, adapting the views of Friedrich Klingner, saw the Germania as a monument to uirtus, a uirtus to be found only beyond the Roman frontiers. And Anton D. Leeman, Orationis Ratio I (Amsterdam: A.M. Hakkert, 1963), p. 341, offered the anachronistic view that Tacitus wrote of Germanic mores to gain a better insight into Roman mores.

[9] So Karl V. Müllenhoff, Deutsche Altertumskunde (Berlin: Weidemann, 1887-1900), Vol. IV, pp. 13-17; see also Friedrich Pfister, "Tacitus and die Germanen," Studien zu Tacitus Carl Hosius dargebracht, ed. Pfister et al. (Stuttgart: W. Kohlhammer, 1936), pp. 82-88; H. Drexler, "Die Germania des Tacitus," Gymnasium 59 (1952), pp. 52-70. This view is adequately refuted by Jacques Perret (ed.), Tacite, La Germanie (Paris: Belles Lettres, 1962), pp. 6-8.

[10] Trüdinger, pp. 146-170; Norden, pp. 8-41.

[11] Servius on Vergil, Aen. 6. 154 and 9. 30; Pliny, N.H. 6. 60; see Norden, pp. 27-28.

the one truly honorable profession.[12] It is important to recognize, furthermore, that this situation existed long before the Romans developed any worthwhile kinds of literature. For the first five hundred years of their existence the Romans farmed and fought, cultivated and conquered territory; and five centuries of such conditioning sufficed to convince them that literature buttered no parsnips and conquered no worlds. Having won control of the Western Mediterranean, however, the Romans came into contact with the Greeks and discovered that civilized peoples considered the liberal arts the sine que non of culture. It was not a welcome discovery, nor was Cato the Elder alone in thinking that literature, poetry especially, would corrupt the Romans.[13] It is a commonplace to remark that most of the great Roman writers did not come from Rome itself, the implication being that Rome was not the true home of Roman values, that the city--like an antique London--revived itself by draining the strength from outlying regions. Geographical determinism may be acceptable in moderation, but it is absurd to maintain that being born in Rome robbed a man of literary genes. Few Roman writers came from the elite in Rome itself, because that elite recognized but one truly honorable profession, politicking.[14] In fact, this is one of the best illustrations we have of Roman values and Roman priorities.

It should be noted next that this elite, whether it wrote itself or paid others to write in its behalf, established almost as much control over the various branches of literature as it exerted over the bulk of the citizenry. Literacy in Rome was always restricted,[15] and as if that were not enough, the price of books

---

[12] Donald C. Earl, The Moral and Political Tradition of Rome (Ithaca: Cornell University Press, 1967), pp. 11-43 and 80-95.

[13] Cato, Libri ad Marcum filium, frag. 1 Jordan = Pliny, N.H. 29. 14. He was a good deal more savage about poetry in particular: poeticae artis honos non erat. si quis in ea re studebat aut sese ad conuiuia adplicabat, grassator uocabatur (Carmen de moribus, frag. 2 Jordan = Gellius, N.A. 11. 2. 5); see also Ovid, Tristia 4. 10. 15-26 and Gordon Williams, Tradition and Originality in Roman Poetry (Oxford: Clarendon Press, 1968), pp. 31-51.

[14] Note Sallust, Cat. 3. 1-2 and Jug. 3. 1-4. 4. Over the years, of course, this outward hostility to literature moderated considerably, and the writing of history became virtually a senatorial preserve. But even in the first century A.D. a leading orator could safely represent himself as ignorant and contemptuous of literature (Tacitus, Dial. 2. 6).

[15] See Williams (above, note 5), pp. 275-280. Latin literature at all periods evinces the characteristics of a society in which the bulk of the population is at best semi-literate, "the tendency towards preciosity, antiquarianism, and other forms of literary exclusiveness."

was exorbitant.[16] For practical purposes, therefore, the elite was the readership, and its members--pragmatists themselves--knew exactly what they wanted, literature to serve a useful purpose, literature to instruct and to uplift. They had no pressing need for poetry of whatever sort, or for fiction, or for philosophy--least of all for philosophy. What the elite could use were basic handbooks, on practical arts like warfare or medicine or agriculture.[17] In history they could find instruction and uplift simultaneously. On the one hand, it made them aware of their heritage and the grandeur of Rome's achievements, besides satisfying their passion for precedents for any action they might contemplate.[18] On the other, it told of great heroes and great villains, models of conduct to inspire or terrify the reader.[19] But above all else there was oratory, the art of public speaking, and in the ancient world it was an art. For a Roman aristocrat the need to persuade (or dissuade) was constant, be it in open senate or ill-lit backroom, on the battlefield or in the imperial palace. No Roman politician wittingly delivered a poor speech.

This love of oratory is one of the keys, perhaps the key, to any understanding of the Roman mind. For oratory meant drama.[20] When Romans began writing erotic poetry, therefore, the tone might be defensive or defiant, but the results were sensational. Oratory meant style. So when Romans took to writing novels, as did Petronius in Nero's reign, they wrote about low life in the style of an elite gone slumming. There has been much discussion of the amount of Vulgar Latin in the Satyricon, but whatever the percentage may be, the Satyricon itself must have been well-nigh incomprehensible to the vulgar. And finally, oratory meant inconsistency because, as we are so often told, circumstances alter cases. This is one reason why Romans had so little tolerance for philosophy, why Tacitus could report with relief that his father-in-law Agricola had not tak-

---

[16] Alexander Scobie, Aspects of the Ancient Romance and its Heritage (Meisenheim a. Glan: Hain, 1969), pp. 16-20.

[17] Cato himself wrote handbooks de medicina, de agri cultura, de rhetorica and de re militari. Nor were Roman poets slow to exploit the didactic mode as a means of expressing themselves acceptably (in theory or reality) to their hard-headed audience: see Williams (above, note 13), p. 357.

[18] Livy, Praef. 4-5 offers a variation on this theme. See further E. Badian's valuable remarks on the Origines of Cato in Tom Alan Dorey, ed., Latin Historians (London: Routledge and Kegan Paul, 1966), pp. 7-11.

[19] Livy, Praef. 9-11; Tacitus, Agr. 1. 1 and Ann. 3. 65. 1.

[20] V. Pöschl, "Zur Einbeziehung anwesender Personen und sichtbarer Objekte in Ciceros Reden," pp. 206-226 in Alain Michel and R. Verdière, ed., Ciceroniana. Hommages à Kazimierz Kumaniecki (Leiden: E.J. Brill, 1975).

en philosophy "more seriously than is appropriate for a Roman and a senator."[21] For the same reason, dissertations on Tacitus' Weltanschauung uncover no Weltanschauung, while in the Germania, as Sherwin-White has pointed out, there is no consistent theoretical attitude toward the barbarians.[22] What Romans wanted, it may reasonably be said, was a maxim for every occasion, a style for every theme, and a drama as often as possible.

Against this background it becomes clear, I think, that to a Roman history would be inevitably both history and story, both fact and (in some measure) fiction. Facts, obviously, were essential. As the orator M. Antonius is made to remark, "surely everybody knows that the first law of history is to venture to say nothing untrue, the second not to avoid mentioning anything true."[23] But a suitable style was just as essential, inasmuch as poor or inept writing would take away from the impact--and thus from the truth--of the narrative; stylistic considerations, indeed, might even be allowed to override the purely factual.[24] The results we can see in the famous passage from the Annals (4. 32-33) where Tacitus bemoans his plight as an historian of the principate:

> I realize that many of the events I have described
> and shall describe hereafter are perhaps minor mat-
> ters, trifles too slight for record; but nobody will
> compare my account with the works of the men who
> wrote the history of ancient Rome. Gigantic wars,
> cities stormed, the rout and capture of kings
> or--when they turned to domestic politics--the dis-
> sension between consuls and tribunes, land-laws
> and grain-laws, the struggles between nobles and

[21] Tacitus, Agr. 4. 3. The hostility to philosophy and philoso-phers, more or less constant in Latin literature, rested on (a) an antithesis between the man of action and the man of words--see Quintilian, Inst. Orat. 11. 1. 35 and 12. 2. 6-7; and (b) a distaste for cosmic schemes so great that even the philosophers of the first century A.D. eschewed a systematic approach--see Williams (above, note 5), pp. 175-177.

[22] Adrian N. Sherwin-White, Racial Prejudice in Imperial Rome (Cambridge: Cambridge University Press, 1967), p. 40.

[23] Cicero, de orat. 2. 62: nam quis nescit primam esse historiae legem, ne quid falsi dicere audeat? deinde ne quid ueri non audeat?

[24] Thus history is declared to be opus oratorium maxime at Cice-ro, de leg. 1. 5, and the early annalists are condemned for their poor style, while at Brut. 42 we find the rhetoricians allowed to distort history in order to sharpen up their narrative (concessum est rhetoribus ementiri in historiis, ut aliquid dicere possint argu-tius).

common people--such were the themes on which they dwelt or digressed. Mine is inglorious labor in a restricted compass. For this was an age of peace, unbroken or half-heartedly challenged, of tragedy in Rome itself, of an emperor unconcerned with expanding the empire. And yet it may not be unprofitable to look beneath the surface of these episodes, at first sight trivial, since it is from them that major events often take their departure.... These themes may be useful; pleasing they are not. Descriptions of countries, the uncertainties of battles, commanders dying valiantly in the field, these are the episodes which arrest and spur the reader's attention. I, however, must tell of savage edicts, constant accusations, traitorous friendships, and the ruin of the innocent, everywhere sameness and to excess.

The passage spells out clearly what Romans thought the subject-matter of history to be, the public actions of public men, preferably actions on a grand scale by men from the governing class, in short, actions worthy of record.[25] Not for Romans social history with its concentration on the poor or the peasantry. Roman writers might idealize peasant virtues, but the reality is better captured in the anecdote about P. Scipio Nasica. Running for the aedileship around 145 B.C., he was soliciting votes and shook hands with a peasant in the crowd. Impressed by the hardness of the man's hands, Scipio asked him whether he walked on them![26] Not for Romans economic history and its fixation with budgets and revenues. Often enough it is difficult to find any motives behind an emperor's issuance of coinage save a wish to advertise his own virtues or to display his own munificence.[27] To a Roman history meant politics, law-making and warfare as conducted by the members of the governing class. What Tacitus is bewailing, therefore, is the substitution of palace intrigue for politicking in the open marketplace, the replacement of disagreement over laws by unanswerable edicts from the throne and, worst of all, a search for peace instead of war.

Although most senators would have found these lamentations justified, they still reflect the dominance of oratory. There is need

---

[25] See also Tacitus, Ann. 13. 31.
[26] Valerius Maximus 7. 5. 2. The various handbooks on agriculture, perhaps needless to say, were not intended for peasants.
[27] For what little evidence there is, and a valiant attempt to make sense of it, see C.H.V. Sutherland, The Emperor and the Coinage: Julio-Claudian Studies (London: Spink, 1976), pp. 78-95.

for drama, says Tacitus, for deeds of derring-do to "arrest and spur the reader's attention." Yet even as he emphasizes his own lack of suitable material, he shows himself able--as no previous writer had been--to exploit "all the devices which had been used in Greek tragedy, so far as those can be used in the medium of prose."[28] There is need for style, too, to convey the drama to the reader. To write dramatically of trivial matters, Tacitus implies, would be incongruous, and yet he proceeds to write in a highly dramatic style.[29] And above all, there is inconsistency here. Tacitus no doubt was being ironic, but he self-evidently did not believe that his material was trivial at any level of perception; he strained every nerve to ensure that his style matched his theme; and far from regarding the Annals as an inglorious labor, he knew that this was in every sense his masterpiece, able to stand comparison with any previous work on the history of Rome.

Today such procedures are deprecated, but attitudes to history and historiography have changed. In the nineteenth century, when rationalism (if not reason) appeared to reign supreme, and men thought that all knowledge lay within their grasp, Ranke could develop the thesis that the facts speak for themselves, and the concomitant notion that history could--and should--be written wie es eigentlich gewesen. The events of the twentieth century have served to demonstrate that neither rationalism nor reason reigns supreme in human affairs, while the inability of the facts to speak for themselves is evidenced by the successes of the image-maker. "Presidential candidates may be sold to the American public like cigarettes. The difference is that only the latter have to be marked as a health hazard."[30] Yet many people, not a few practicing historians among them, cling to the belief that history is still to be written wie es eigentlich gewesen; and if it is written in as graceless a manner as Ranke himself achieved, so much the better. Apparently a constipated style guarantees sincerity, honesty and accuracy, whereas the least whiff of oratory arouses immediate sus-

---

[28] Bessie Walker, The Annals of Tacitus: a Study in the Writing of History (Manchester: Manchester University Press, 1960), p. 44; as she also notes (p. 36), "his frequent complaints over the monotony of his subject strengthen...the impression of continual, unremitting tyranny" which he credits to Tiberius. See also Gerold Walser, Rom, das Reich und die fremden Völker in der Geschichtsschreibung der frühen Kaiserzeit. Studien zur Glaubwürdigkeit des Tacitus (Baden-Baden: Verlag für Kunst und Wissenschaft, 1951), p. 53.

[29] See, e.g., Leeman (above, note 8) I, pp. 348-360 or Uwe Rademacher, Die Bildkunst des Tacitus (Hildesheim, New York: G. Olms, 1975).

[30] See B. Baldwin, "Rulers and Ruled at Rome: A.D. 14-192." Ancient Society 3 (1972), pp. 149-164, esp. p. 157.

picions of devious maneuvering and double standards. Clearly we stand worlds apart from the Romans.[31]

To reject the views of Ranke's disciples, to deny the possibility of writing history wie es eigentlich gewesen, as historiographers seem progressively more willing to do,[32] is not to endorse the structuralists' approach. For of them it might be said that they believe nothing, especially not a concrete fact, since concrete can be poured in any shape.[33] There are definitely such things as historical facts. Carr made the point neatly, when he remarked that it is a fact that millions of people have crossed the Rubicon, whereas it is an historical fact that Caesar crossed it.[34] The real problem lies in the identification and utilization of these historical facts, and our sole recourse is interpretation.[35] But interpretation requires imagination, and if we leave aside the matter of focus and field, the crucial difference between a Roman historian like Tacitus and a modern historian of Rankean or post-Rankean cast lies precisely in the amount of play legitimately to be accorded to the imagination.

The modern viewpoint is well defined by the remarks Robertson Davies attributes to one of his characters, aptly enough an attorney: "imagination is a good horse to carry you over the ground, not a flying carpet to set you free from probability."[36] With their love of oratory, Romans frequently allowed good horses to metamorphose into flying carpets. Not that they felt any compulsion to suppress or distort the facts as such. Even a writer as wilful as Tacitus would have accepted Housman's dictum that "accu-

---

[31] This is not to deny that Romans could feel distrust for orators [see R. Gungerich, Classical Philology 46 (1951) pp. 159-160]; in the classical period, however, distrust was triggered by bad oratory, since that caused the audience to wonder about the good faith (fides) of the orator; see Quintilian, Inst. Orat. 4. 1. 8 and 12; A.W. Allen, "Sunt qui Propertium malint," pp. 107-148 in John P. Sullivan, ed., Critical Essays on Roman Literature: Elegy and Lyric (Cambridge: Harvard University Press, 1962).
[32] See, for example, Edward H. Carr, What is History? (London: MacMillan; New York: St. Martin's Press, 1961); David H. Fischer, Historians' Fallacies (New York: Harper and Row, 1970).
[33] This formulation I owe, with apologies, to Charles McCarry, The Secret Lovers (New York: E.P. Dutton, 1977), p. 72.
[34] Carr, pp. 5-6.
[35] According to Sempronius Asellio, frag. 1 Peter = Gellius, N.A. 5. 18. 8, writing around 120 B.C., "it is not enough to make known what has been done...one should also show with what purpose and for what reason things were done." See Tacitus, Ann. 4. 32. 3; Hist. 1. 4. 1.
[36] William Robertson Davies, The Manticore (New York: Viking, 1972), p. 227.

96

racy is a duty and not a virtue."[37] Did he not insist, on more than one occasion, that he wrote without bias or partiality?[38] And did he not refuse, on more than one occasion, to believe the fabulosum, what he judged to be neither true nor likely to be true?[39] Nevertheless, Tacitus was a master of the interpretation which flies in the face of the facts, the kind of interpretation a trial lawyer might manufacture in a hopeless case. Thus he reports the situation, gives briefly the explanation most likely to be correct, and then he launches into the interpretation he prefers, often described--no doubt correctly--as an erroneous rumor circulating at the time; but by dwelling on the rumor and by positioning it last, he clearly intends for the reader to be left with the impression that this is the true version of events.[40]

It may be urged by way of extenuation that Tacitus' Roman audience was no less educated than he, no less aware of oratory and its possibilities, and presumably no less able to dissect his account than he had been to construct it.[41] Moreover, just as Cicero in his Philippics appealed constantly to a higher legality than

[37] Alfred E. Housman, ed., M. Manilii Astronomicon Liber Primus, 2nd ed. (Cambridge: Cambridge University Press, 1937), p. 87.

[38] Tacitus, Ann. 1. 1. 5; Hist. 1. 1. 4. Any such claim is difficult to evaluate, of course, since it was both unavoidable and conventional: Joseph Vogt, Orbis: ausgewählte Schriften zur Geschichte des Altertums, ed. Fritz Taeger and Karl Christ (Freiburg: Herder, 1960), pp. 113-115.

[39] Tacitus, Hist. 2. 50. 2; Ann. 4. 11. 2-3; 11. 27. For full discussion see K. Barwick, "Die Gliederung der Narratio in der rhetorischen Theorie und ihre Bedeutung für die Geschichte des antiken Romans," Hermes 63 (1928), pp. 261-287; Pfister (above, note 9), p. 90 n. 3. Tacitus, of course, exploits the marvelous or miraculous where he considers it plausible: see Williams (above, note 5), pp. 240-241 and 261. But there are remarkably few instances of this in the Germania, as is emphasized by Perret (above, note 9), p. 25 n. 1.

[40] See Inez Scott Ryberg, "Tacitus' Art of Innuendo," Transactions of the American Philological Association 73 (1942), pp. 383-404; also J. Cousin, "Rhétorique et psychologie chez Tacite," Revue des études latines 29 (1951), pp. 228-247; Walker (above, note 28), pp. 22-137.

[41] How much more care an orator had to employ in addressing the senate than he needed when speaking to the people was demonstrated in detail by Dietrich Mack, Senatsreden und Volksreden bei Cicero (Würzburg: K. Triltsch, 1937), but an educated audience was no less open to an emotional than to an intellectual appeal: see J. Lucas, "La relation de Cicéron à son public," pp. 150-159 in Michel and Verdière (above, note 20).

the mundane variety with which he had to contend when making his attacks on Marc Antony, so Tacitus claimed to be searching for a truth deeper than that vouchsafed by the known facts of any given situation, and strove to present it in the appropriate style.[42] Tacitus, that is, "aimed seriously at authoritative generalization, as Sallust had done, with...reference to the underlying causes in human behaviour."[43] Yet there are many novels of which the same could be said.

It has taken a long time to set the background for the Germania, too long perhaps for the purist, who can maintain that this is ethnography, not history. That this makes a decided difference in the subject-matter there can be no doubt. Here we find no great deeds by great Romans, but catalogues, of barbarian customs and barbarian tribes. During his narrative, moreover, Tacitus makes the remarks ethnographers are expected to produce: the Osi, for example, cannot be a Germanic tribe, because they speak Pannonian and pay tribute, a non-Germanic practice.[44] But the difference in subject-matter will not explain the basic inconsistency in Tacitus' attitude towards the tribesmen. There are numerous occasions in the first half of the work where he lavishes praise on the Germans, picturing them very much as noble savages: they are not greedy for gold, their marriage code is strict, they are uncorrupted by public shows and banquets, their hospitality is generous, and their funerals are unostentatious.[45] In the second half of the work there is as much to condemn. The Semnones practice human sacrifice, a "savage ritual." Among the tribes that worship the goddess Nerthus, there is a festival at the end of which the ceremonial "chariot, the vestments and (believe it if you will) the goddess herself are cleansed in a secluded lake. This office is performed by slaves who are drowned in the lake immediately thereafter." And

[42] For the claim see Tacitus, Ann. 4. 32. 4: non tamen sine usu fuerit introspicere illa primo aspectu leuia, ex quis magnarum saepe rerum motus oriuntur (translated above, pp. 93-94). This aspect of his style is discussed by W.-H. Friedrich, "Stilistische Symptome der Geschichtsauffassung des Tacitus," pp. 23-39 in Doris Ableitinger and Helmut Gugel, ed., Festschrift Karl Vretska (Heidelberg: Carl Winter, 1970).
[43] A.H. McDonald in Maurice Platnauer, ed., Fifty Years (and Twelve) of Classical Scholarship (New York: Barnes and Noble, 1968), p. 484; see also Leeman (above, note 8) I, pp. 341-342 and 344-345.
[44] Tacitus, Germ. 43. a, a remark which contradicts what he has said at 28. 3, unless the text there is interpolated.
[45] Tacitus, Germ. 5, 18, 19, 21, and 27 respectively.

finally, there are the tribes living in stone-age squalor.[46] To a Roman, we may be sure, all this was clearly savage and not in the least noble.

It is to explain this sort of thing--and to make up for the lack of a prologue or an epilogue to the Germania--that it has been necessary to discuss Tacitus' interest in style and his attitude toward historiography as evidenced by the Annals. For the one feature which makes sense of his ambivalent viewpoint on the Germans, as of so much else in the Germania, is oratory. "The idealization of the virtuous barbarian," as Sherwin-White has said, " is limited to aspects of Germanic life that provided a legitimate contrast with the contemporary vices of Roman society."[47] Conversely, the tales about human sacrifice or stone-age squalor could arrest and spur the reader's attention, not by horrifying him perhaps but by sending a delicious frisson up his aristocratic spine. Which leaves the material reported in neutral tones. It may be that, for the moment, the ethnographer in Tacitus gained the upper hand, but some evidence suggests that responsibility lay rather with the inability of the orator in Tacitus to think of a way of exploiting the material.

Any suggestion that Tacitus overdoes the rhetoric in the Germania, if not met with outright incredulity,[48] tends to elicit indignant responses based on the assertion that--so far as we can tell--Tacitus is nowhere inaccurate on purpose.[49] The existence of contradictions and mistakes must be conceded (however they are to be explained), together with instances of interpretatio Romana.[50] Nevertheless, archaeologists and historians seem generally to find

[46] Tacitus, Germ. 39, 40n and 46 respectively. See also Edgar Polomé, "A propos de la déesse Nerthus," Latomus 13 (1954), pp. 167-200.

[47] Sherwin-White (above, note 22), p. 40; so also Trüdinger, p. 166; Walser (above, note 28), pp. 80-85 and 154-160. The technique, in other words, is identical to that announced at Ann. 3. 65. 1.

[48] Witness the descriptions of the Germania's style to be found in Boissier (above, note 5), p. 31 or Mendell (above, note 2), pp. 86-87.

[49] Thus H. Heubner, "Sprache, Stil und Sache bei Tacitus," Interpretationen (Gymnasium, Beiheft 4: Heidelberg, 1964), pp. 133-148.

[50] Perret (above, note 9), pp. 22-24, 26-27 and 30-33 divides Tacitus' errors into those caused by ignorance and those caused by rhetoric; not every other scholar would concur. Interpretatio Romana is obvious when Tacitus discusses German gods (Germ. 9 especially); other instances include the suggestion that Germans built their houses far apart from fear of fire, a natural idea for anybody living in Rome (Germ. 16. 2; W. Beare, Greece & Rome 11

his account reliable where there is other evidence to act as a control.[51] Unfortunately, this is not adequate rebuttal, even if we ignore the possibility--and it is a very real possibility--that the archaeologists and historians have forced that other evidence into agreement with the Tacitean text.[52] Tacitus' rhetoric works in various ways its wonders to perform.

There are clear indications, for example, that rhetorical considerations led Tacitus to omit material from the Germania, to say much less than was known in his day,[53] and thus to break the rule that one should not avoid mentioning anything true. He gives practically no details about the geography of the country, none at all about its physical dimensions.[54] That he was interested in people rather than in real estate is undoubtedly true; it leads him even to personify geographical features--when he can be persuaded to mention them.[55] But this is no excuse for a man engaged in the composition of an ethnography. What makes sense of his attitude is Mela's comment that such topics produced an impeditum opus et facundiae minime capax.[56] Similarly, he makes but one comment

---

(1964), pp. 65-66), and the reference to arcana sacra at Germ. 18. 3, a confusion with the patrician ceremony of confarreatio.

[51] See, e.g., Müllenhoff (above, note 9) IV, pp. 17-29; K. Schumacher's excursus in Wilhelm Reeb, ed., Tacitus Germania (Leipzig: Teubner, 1930), pp. 110-134; Anderson xxvii-xxxvii; Borzsák, pp. 427-428. A more critical view is advanced by K. Tackenberg, "Die Germania des Tacitus und das Fach der Vorgeschichte," pp. 55-70 in Dieter Ahrens, ed., Festschrift Max Wegner (Münster: Aschendorff, 1962).

[52] The serious methodological problems, now recognized if not solved, are discussed by Gerold Walser, Caesar und die Germanen (Historia, Einzelschrift 1; Wiesbaden: 1956), pp. 45-51; Rolf Hachmann, Georg Kossack and Hans Kuhn, Völker zwischen Germanen und Kelten (Neumünster: K. Wachholtz, 1962), pp. 9-15; and Rolf Nierhaus, Das swebische Gräberfeld von Diersheim (Berlin: Walter de Gruyter, 1966), pp. 1-12 and 182-234.

[53] So Trüdinger, p. 147 and 168; Norden, p. 40; Friedrich (above, note 42), pp. 28-29.

[54] So Trüdinger, p. 149 and 158-159; Gerold Walser, (above, note 28), pp. 24-25; Büchner (above, note 8), p. 128.

[55] See Friedrich, pp. 27-29; Rademacher (above, note 29), pp. 83-88.

[56] Mela 1 Praef. 1, rightly adduced by Sir Ronald Syme, Tacitus (Oxford: Clarendon Press, 1958), Vol I, p. 126; see Trüdinger, p. 158 n. 1. Ironically, Tacitus, Agr. 10. 1, avers that whereas earlier writers had hidden their ignorance of Britain's geography under fine words, he will give an accurate account; the results, impeccable stylistically, remain vague and inaccurate: Ogilvie and Richmond (above, note 4), pp. 31-46.

about the fauna of Germany, referring to the flocks and herds in a
sentence simultaneously erudite, pointed and poetic, this when it
was customary to include a description of the animal life in the
briefest of ethnographical digressions.[57]

The most startling omission from the treatise, however, is
Arminius, the German chieftain who had wiped out Quintilius Varus
and his three legions in A.D. 9. To him Tacitus pays a magnificent
tribute in the Annals, describing him as undoubtedly the liberator
of Germany (liberator haud dubie Germaniae), a man who had
defeated Rome when she was at the height of her power, and one
who had received less than his due from Roman writers.[58] In the
Germania there is no mention of Arminius, and his tribe, the Cherusci, are quickly passed over; nor is it even the freedom-fighters
on whom Tacitus dwells here.[59] Instead, he picks out the Chatti
for extended comment (Germ. 30. 2): "for a Germanic people they
have plenty of judgement and discernment;...and a quality rare
save in a Roman organization, they place more confidence in their
general than in their troops." Rhetorical considerations explain the
difference. In the early books of the Annals the dominant figure is
an evil and despotic emperor, Tiberius; what is needed is a foil to
counterbalance him, be it a senator speaking out in Rome, a general
campaigning on the frontiers, or a barbarian chieftain struggling
for freedom. None of this obtains in the Germania. In that section
of the work where Cherusci and Chatti appear, Tacitus has
arranged his material in a sequence of antitheses which type the
Chatti as fierce warriors, the Cherusci as indolent peace-lovers.[60]
Besides, when a Germanic tribe possesses judgement, discernment
and some idea of organization, that can be held to be far more

[57] Tacitus, Germ. 5. 1-2, best analyzed by Norden, p. 53; the
omission is registered by Trüdinger, p. 158 and Büchner, p. 128.
More detail would have helped to explicate Germ. 9. 1, 17. 2, and
23. 1, but the Realien are given by Much, pp. 111-118.
[58] Tacitus, Ann. 2. 88. 3-4. The concluding remark about
Arminius' neglect by Roman writers is not to be construed as a
Tacitean apology for omitting him from the Germania; he is attacking writers like Livy.
[59] Tacitus, Germ. 36. 2; there is a brief reference to the clades
Variana at 37. 5, an oblique reference at 41. 2. It would not have
helped Tacitus' case that Arminius had served in the Roman auxilia:
see Dieter Timpe, Arminius-Studien (Heidelberg: Carl Winter,
1970), pp. 14-21. But the neglect of the libertas-motif, at least in
the form in which it appears in the Agricola, Histories and Annals,
led Sherwin-White (above, note 22), pp. 34ff. and 41ff., unneces-
sarily, to doubt Tacitus' authorship of the Germania.
[60] See below, note 66 and literature there cited.

frightening than an individual guerrilla leader like Arminius.[61] The Romans had made themselves masters of the world thanks to such qualities; it suits Tacitus now to suggest that the Chatti may follow their lead. Or, as he puts it just a little later (Germ. 33. 2): "long, I pray, may the tribes of Europe persist, if not in loving us, at least in hating one another; for destiny is driving our empire along its appointed path, and fortune can bestow on us no greater gift than discord amongst our enemies." Whether this is a prayer from the heart or, rather, a piece of posturing is a question which has been debated endlessly, and no doubt will long continue so. Whatever the truth, the sentiment certainly reminded the reader of the significance of the treatise, and presumably had a striking effect on him. For Tacitus that could have been sufficient.[62]

Closely allied with the matter of omissions is the extreme care Tacitus took in structuring his treatise. As Tacitus himself makes clear (Germ. 27. 3), the work falls into two main sections, cataloguing Germanic customs (chapters 1-27) and Germanic tribes (chapters 28-46). It could be coincidence that these sections are of almost equal length, were it not that the correspondence goes deeper, perhaps much deeper. Different scholars excogitate different schemes, but even the economical version by Perret demonstrates the artistry involved.[63] Tacitus, that is, provides an introduction on landscape and origins (chapters 1-5), to which answers a conclusion on the tribes practically beyond human ken (chapter 46). In between there are four sub-sections in two pairs: public life (chapters 6-15) is balanced with private life (chapters 16-27), non-Suebic peoples (chapters 28-37) with Suebic peoples (chapters 38-45), and each of these four sub-sections contains almost exactly the same number of lines. Which is no accident: to achieve his effect, Tacitus extended the definition of the Suebi far beyond the

[61] The idea was not new: Seneca, de ira 1. 11. 4; Tacitus, Agr. 12. 2.
[62] I have no wish to add to the huge mass of literature on this passage, but it is worth remembering that Tacitus was using a traditional line of thought (Steidle [above, note 4], pp. 90-91), and that in antiquity the sincerity of the author was determined primarily by the audience's perceptions (see above, note 31).
[63] Perret (above, note 9), pp. 37-38; see Pfister (above, note 9), pp. 88-89. For other schemes see Büchner (above, note 8), pp. 126-127; G. Bielefeld, "Der kompositorische Aufbau der Germania des Tacitus," pp. 44-54 in Ahrens (above, note 51); Francesco Giancotti, Strutture delle Monografie di Sallustio e di Tacito (Messina and Florence: G. D'Anna, 1971), pp. 426-471.

limits recognized before or after his day.[64] At the same time, he displays great skill in linking each chapter to the next, working in the first half of the treatise through association of word or thought,[65] in the second half relying on antithetical groupings of tribes and a vague geographical scheme anchored on the Rhine and the Danube.[66] It is extravagant to set the Germania almost on a par with Vergil's Georgics as "eines der schönsten Zeugnisse für den baumeisterlichen Sinn der Römer,"[67] but it would be perverse to deny the existence of this artistry. And whatever Tacitus' intentions qua ethnographer, this structuring must have affected the amount and type of material presented, and thus the overall accuracy of the treatise.

One reason Tacitus was able to exert so rigorous a control over his material, of course, lay in the fact that he was working entirely at second hand, mostly from literary sources; there is neither evidence nor reason to suggest that he personally had ever set foot in Germany.[68] Not that this was considered blameworthy in antiquity. It was seldom possible for ethnographers to visit the peoples they studied, especially those whose territories lay beyond the Roman frontiers, even had they wanted so to do.[69] It is no more surprising that Tacitus' information on occasion is several decades out of date; perfectly reputable treatises on India were

[64]   See Much, pp. 425-426; Anderson, p. 178; Perret, pp. 102-103; Hachmann, Kossack and Kuhn (above, note 52), p. 49; K. Peschel, "Die Sueben in Ethnographie und Archäologie," Klio 60 (1978), pp. 259-309.
[65]   Trüdinger, pp. 162-163; Norden, pp. 460ff.; A. Gunz, Die deklamatorische Rhetorik in der Germania des Tacitus (Lausanne: A. Bovard-Giddey, 1934), pp. 64-67; Drexler (above, note 9), pp. 53-55; Büchner, pp. 128ff.; Bielefeld, pp. 45-49; E. Kraggerud, "Verknüpfung in Tacitus' Germania," Symbolae Osloenses 47 (1972), pp. 7-35.
[66]   G. Kettner, "Die Composition des ethnographischen Teils der Germania des Tacitus," Zeitschrift für deutsche Philologie 19 (1887), pp. 257-274; Trüdinger, pp. 168-169; E. Wolff (above, note 8), pp. 147-154; Büchner, pp. 134-136; Bielefeld, pp. 49-53; Norden, pp. 39-40.
[67]   So Büchner, p. 126.
[68]   The only source Tacitus names is Caesar (Germ. 28. 1), but the relationship between their accounts is unclear (below, note 96). It is usually assumed that his main source was the twenty books of Bella Germaniae by the Elder Pliny (Norden, pp. 207-312). Livy, Book 104, is another possibility, but Perret (above, note 9), p. 14, plausibly suggests that Tacitus' debt was artistic rather than historical. Finally, some favor Posidonius, less plausibly: see Trüdinger, pp. 166-170; Steidle (above, note 4), pp. 81-8.
[69]   See M.G. Morgan, Historia 23 (1974), p. 201.

normally several centuries out of date.[70] But Tacitus' reliance on second-hand evidence, besides permitting the structuring of his treatise to which we have already drawn attention, seems also to have encouraged a tendency to sacrifice consistency, or material, or factual accuracy in order to score a rhetorical point. Indeed, there are grounds for believing that the most famous passage in the entire work, the section on the origo of the Germans (Germ. 2. 1 - 4. 1), was composed in the way it is primarily for rhetorical pur- poses--to justify and lend weight to his theme, and to support the essentially frivolous sententia that nobody but a German would choose to live in Germany.

It was a topos of ancient ethnography to discuss whether the people under study were indigenous, immigrants, or some mixture of natives and outsiders, and Tacitus adheres to this scheme. What needs emphasis, however, is that while ancient peoples regularly claimed to be both indigenous and free from foreign contacts, this being the most honorable status to possess,[71] the ethnographers were seldom willing to accept these claims at face value. As Seneca had remarked, uix denique inuenies ullam terram, quam etiam nunc indigenae colant; permixta omnia et insiticia sunt.[72] Yet Tacitus, having commented in the Agricola that one would not expect to find an answer to this question when dealing with a barbarian people,[73] now emerges triumphantly from the ruck with the Germans, accord- ing to him (Germ. 4. 1) a propria et sincera et tantum sui similis gens. It is entirely possible, of course, that he believed, or was able to persuade himself, that the Germans were indeed an auto- chthonous race, largely free from contact with outsiders, but nor should it be forgotten that only this conclusion would have justified the treatise, making of the Germans a people worthy of extended

[70] On Tacitus see especially Syme (above, note 56), I, pp. 127-128, to be modified--but not rejected--in the light of B. Melin, "Zum Eingangskapitel der Germania," Eranos 58 (1960), pp. 112-131, at pp. 121-131. India is discussed by A. Dihle, "The con- ception of India in Hellenistic and Roman Literature," Proceedings of the Cambridge Philological Society 10 (1964), pp. 15-23.
[71] See Diodorus 1. 9. 3-5; Josephus, contra Apionem 2. 152; E.J. Bickerman, "Origines Gentium," Classical Philology 47 (1952), pp. 65-81, at p. 76.
[72] Seneca, ad Helv. de cons. 7. 1-10 (quotation from §10), rightly emphasized by Trüdinger, p. 151.
[73] Tacitus, Agr. 11. 1: ceterum Britanniam qui mortales initio coluerint, indigenae an aducti, ut inter barbaros parum compertum. Caesar had maintained that the tribes living inland were indigenous (B.G. 5. 12. 1), Diodorus that no outsiders had visited the island and that the tribes were autochthonous (5. 21. 2 and 5). All this Tacitus ignores, going on to adduce the islanders' physique: habitus corporum uarii atque ex eo argumenta, etc.

study by author and reader alike.[74] Furthermore, this was not the only possible conclusion. The stories Tacitus repeats to the effect that Hercules and Ulysses had visited the country (Germ. 3) show clearly that at least some earlier writers had entertained very different ideas about Germanic origins. With a semblance of impartiality, Tacitus declares that he "will not argue for or against these stories; the reader must accept or reject them according to his temperament."[75] But he goes on immediately to restate in forceful terms his own opinion that the Germans were indigenous and largely untainted by outside contacts!

Wissowa long ago made the point that a comparison between what we know about the origins of the Jews and what Tacitus has to say on that subject "enthält...eine dringende Warnung vor Überschätzung des objektiven Quellenwertes der Germania, denn nichts berechtigt uns zu der Annahme, daß der Verfasser über die Germanen besser unterrichtet war und sein konnte als über die Juden."[76] But though archaeological discoveries in Germany have tended to bear out Wissowa's observation,[77] the question to be considered is not the historical accuracy of Tacitus' account here, so far as that can be established by other evidence. Nor is anything to be gained by attempts to establish Tacitus' sincerity or lack thereof in propounding his view, since there is no evidence which bears directly on that. What can--and should--be subjected to scrutiny is the internal logic, the construction of his argument for Germanic autochthony and purity; for careful analysis will show, I think, that it is rhetoric which determines the course he takes, in other words, that the entire section is built around the paradoxical proposition that nobody save a German would choose to live in Germany.

Having opened the section by indicating his readiness to believe the Germans an indigenous race, largely untainted by contact with outsiders, Tacitus offers a brace of reasons: "In the old days settlers used to travel not by land but by sea, and the boundless and--one might say--hostile Ocean beyond the coasts of Germa-

---

[74] See Büchner (above, note 8), pp. 127-128.

[75] Tacitus, Germ. 3. 4. Although it was common in ethnographical writing to announce a suspension of judgement on supposedly knotty problems (see Germ. 46. 4; Agr. 11. 1; Sallust, Jug. 17. 2), it is naive to maintain (as does Anderson, p. 52) that Tacitus here "will not force his opinion on his readers." The structuring of the passage guides the reader in the desired direction.

[76] G. Wissowa, reviewing A. Gudeman's edition of the Germania in Gött. Gel. Anz. 178 (1916), pp. 656-678, at p. 657. For the excursus on the Jews see Hist. 5. 2-3.

[77] Hachmann, Kossack and Kuhn (above, note 52), pp. 48-54 and 69-75; Tackenberg (above, note 51), pp. 55-70.

ny [i.e., the North Sea] is seldom visited by ships from our world. Besides, even if we ignore the dangers of this awful and unknown sea, who would quit Asia, or Africa, or Italy to make his way to Germany, unless it were his homeland? With its wild landscape and its dreadful climate, it is a grim plaçe to live in and to look on."[78] The insistence that immigrants in the old days (olim) must have traveled by ship results--so the commentators assure us--from the fact that only migrations by sea are reported in legendary times.[79] This is not quite correct: Hercules had no more journeyed around the Mediterranean by sea than Dionysus had sailed from India to Greece, and some held Hercules to be the Urvater of the Gauls.[80] When we remember, however, that Romans hated to sail the Mediterranean, and that their experiences on the outer Ocean had made it an object of fear and loathing,[81] we can see why Tacitus places so much emphasis on sea-travel: his readers would have found the prospect so repugnant that they would unhesitatingly have fallen in with his line of reasoning.

The proposition that the immigrants must come from the Mediterranean World, if they are to be accounted immigrants, is somewhat less specious. Like the stories of Hercules and Ulysses, it depends on a Hellenocentric view of the world, on the tenet that the only meaningful contact is contact with orbis noster.[82] And while this could be held to imply that all the northern barbarians are stamped out of more or less the same mold, it has the additional

---

[78] Tacitus, Germ. 2. 1-2: nec terra olim sed classibus aduehebantur qui mutare sedes quaerebant, et immensus ultra utque sic dixerim aduersus Oceanus raris ab orbe nostro nauibus aditur. quis porro, praeter periculum horridi et ignoti maris, Asia aut Africa aut Italia relicta Germaniam peteret, informem terris, asperam caelo, tristem cultu aspectuque, nisi si patria sit? The connotations of aduersus (I render it "hostile") are disputed, but even if it is translated "antipodal," that makes no real difference to my argument.

[79] See, for example, Müllenhoff (above, note 9), IV, p. 109; Anderson 38. More caution is shown by Much, p. 47.

[80] See W.H. Roscher, Ausführliches Lexicon der griechischen und römischen Mythologie, I (Leipzig: Teubner, 1884-1890), cols. 1029-1089 and 2253-2298. Hercules is declared the Urvater of the Gauls by Diodorus 5. 24, while his importance in origo-literature is emphasized by Trüdinger, p. 153.

[81] For Romans as land-lubbers see Johannes H. Thiel, Studies on the History of Roman Sea-Power in Republican Times (Amsterdam: North-Holland Publishing Co., 1946), pp. 1-31. As for the Outer Ocean Tacitus himself refers to its opposition to Roman plans at Germ. 34. 3 (see also 44. 3), and describes it as an adversary to be conquered at Agr. 25. 1.

[82] See Bickerman (above, note 71), pp. 70-71 and 77-78.

advantage of protecting Tacitus against any objections raised on the basis of such physical, temperamental or cultural variations as he will report in the sequel.[83] But that leaves the main problem: although adverse comments on the German climate and the German landscape were commonplace,[84] and although Tacitus undoubtedly shared the belief that climate and landscape affected a people's nature,[85] the core of his reasoning here is provided by a sardonic and biting witticism--that nobody but a German would choose to live in Germany. It is a clever variation on the more usual (and historically more accurate) portrayal of Germans as barbarians who invaded the territory of others because desperate to get away from their native heaths and swamps.[86] And it is a paradox, inasmuch as it tends to undercut the reader's acceptance of the raison d'être for the treatise, the proposition that Germans merit extended study because an autochthonous and pure race. If the reader presses on nevertheless, he will do so for the style and spirit of the work rather than for its content.

It is perhaps awareness of this which leads Tacitus immediately to adduce a third, seemingly more substantial reason for his view, the Germans' own belief in a god Tuisto, his son Mannus as the first German man, and his three sons, from whose names the tribes of Germany are known as the Ingaevones, Herminones, and Istaevones.[87] It is irrelevant that this represents, or at least contains material drawn from, a genuine Germanic tradition, albeit a tradition restricted to the tribes of Western Germany.[88] Nor is it

[83] Tacitus notes physical and temperamental variations at Germ. 30. 2, 36. 1-2, 45. 4, and 46. 1-3, variations in culture at 9. 1, 28. 3-4, 43. 1-2, and 45. 2.

[84] Horace, Odes 4. 5. 26-27; Seneca, de prov. 4. 14-15 and de ira 1. 11. 3; Mela 3. 26 and 29; Tacitus, Ann. 2. 24. 1; see also Caesar, B.G. 6. 24.

[85] Although this is denied for the Germania by Trüdinger, p. 157, Germ. 29. 3 is decisive; see Pfister (above, note 9), pp. 78-79.

[86] Tacitus himself advances this view at Hist. 4. 73. 3, but much the same had been said of Cimbri and Teutons (Florus 1. 38. 1), of the Belgae (Caesar, B.G. 2. 4. 1-2), and of Ariovistus' hordes (Caesar, B.G. 1. 31. 5 and 11).

[87] Tacitus, Germ. 2. 3: celebrant carminibus antiquis, quod unum apud illos memoriae et annalium genus est, Tuistonem deum terra editum. ei filium Mannum originem gentis conditoresque Manno tres filios adsignant, e quorum nominibus proximi Oceano Ingaeuones, medii Herminones, ceteri Istaeuones uocentur.

[88] See Müllenhoff (above, note 9), IV, pp. 117-124, especially p. 121; Much, pp. 52-55; Anderson, pp. 40-41; Perret (above, note 9), p. 102; Hachmann, Kossack and Kuhn (above, note 52), pp. 50-52; Tackenberg (above, note 47), p. 69. There is nothing

unduly significant that a Roman should have been willing to accept a native tradition in preference to the Hellenocentric view, which demanded that every foreign people be grafted somehow onto the family tree of Greek mythological heroes. When the Romans had themselves been the victims of this fixation, protesting that Romulus was their Urvater but finding Aeneas of Troy foisted on them too,[89] Tacitus could well have felt reluctant to inflict Hercules or Ulysses on the Germans--and yet there was acceptable evidence to support such connections.[90] The real problem now is that by granting credence to this native tradition he gets himself into a fearful tangle when he comes to the subsequent evolution of the Germanic tribes. He is forced to admit at once that there are tribes which cannot be included within the threefold division (Germ. 2. 4); in fact, he will never again mention the Ingaevones, Herminones and Istaevones, and no attempt will be made to establish a relationship between them and the tribes he catalogues in the second half of his work. He rescues himself from this difficulty with the observation that Germani began life as the name of a single tribe and grew to encompass all the other Germanic peoples, a convenient label to hide a multitude of sins.[91] It could be coincidence that the difficulties

to be gained by arguing that Tacitus viewed the West Germans as the main representatives of things Germanic, an idea urged by Wolff (above, note 8), p. 154, since that presumes differences between the tribes which Tacitus cannot afford to concede here.

[89] See Bickerman (above, note 71), pp. 65-68 and 75-76; also Walser (above, note 28), pp. 67-72.

[90] The evidence adduced in support of Ulysses' visiting Germany (Germ. 3. 3), it may be emphasized, was entirely acceptable by the standards of the time, nor was it absurd to maintain that he had traveled the Ocean (see Seneca, E.M. 88. 7); though Diodorus 5. 21. 2 held that no Greek hero had visited Britain, Solinus 22. 1 preserves a tradition that Ulysses had put in on the Scottish coast (see Norden, pp. 182-202). The case for Ulysses, however, was slighter than that for Hercules (which is probably why Tacitus concludes with Ulysses: it makes the whole line of argument look weaker). Besides the material recorded in this chapter (Germ. 3. 1-2), Tacitus will report that the Germans worshiped Hercules (Germ. 9. 1), and that there were pillars of Hercules on the northern coast (Germ. 34. 2).

[91] Tacitus, Germ. 2. 5. Tacitus' explanation of the name Germani is usually considered correct, but what needs examination is whether he was influenced by the Latin word germanus, meaning "brotherly" and then "real" or "true," an explanation for the tribal name which had been advanced explicitly by Strabo 7. 1. 2 (290 C). Tacitus argues in such a way that he cannot appeal to this etymology (so, rightly, Trüdinger, p. 154; contra, T. Pekkanen, "Tac. Germ. 2,3 and the name Germani," Arctos 7 [1972], pp. 107-138); but since he is ready to accept such simple derivations in his

of this Namensatz are notorious, but it could also be that the very obscurities (not to say obscurantism) of the passage serve to distract the reader from a certain breakdown in the logic of what has gone before.

Be that as it may, Tacitus reports next the stories of Hercules and Ulysses, restates his belief that the Germans were autochthonous and--more emphatically--that they were relatively untainted by contact with the outside world, and offers his fourth and final reason for holding this view: "So far as one can generalize from their vast numbers, all Germans alike have the same build: fierce blue eyes, reddish hair, and large frames good only for violent effort; they show less stamina for toil and hard work, are unaccustomed to endure thirst or heat, but they are inured to cold and hunger by their climate or their land."[92] Since ancient ethnographers regarded such racial stereotypes as their stock in trade and were expected to deploy them in their discussions, we can hardly fault Tacitus for retailing such material.[93] But there are still difficulties in the passage. First, as was noted by Trüdinger (p. 150), there is something odd about the way Tacitus moves from his statement of belief in German autochthony and purity to the matter of German physique and stamina. In fact, the material ought logically to be reversed, the evidence of physique being presented first and the statement of belief following as the conclusion. Second, there is the fact that what Tacitus says of the Germans Posidonius had held to be traits of all northern barbarians, other writers of the Gauls, Livy of the Galatians, and the Elder Pliny of the inhabitants of Ceylon![94] It cannot seriously be maintained that Tacitus was

excursus on the Jews (Hist. 5. 2), it is by no means implausible to suggest that this idea was lurking in the back of his mind, impelling him to accept Germanic claims of autochthony and purity.

[92] Tacitus, Germ. 4. 2: unde habitus quoque corporum, tamquam in tanto hominum numero, idem omnibus: truces et caerulei oculi, rutilae comae, magna corpora et tantum ad impetum ualida. laboris atque operum non eadem patientia, minimeque sitim aestumque tolerare, frigora atque inediam caelo soloue adsueuerunt. See also 20. 1.

[93] Trüdinger, pp. 154-155; Norden, p. 105ff.; Pfister (above, note 9), p. 78. For what it is worth, Tacitus shows an interest in the personal appearance of his human subjects in all his works: see Cousin (above, note 40), pp. 234-239.

[94] Posidonius' views are held to underlie Vitruvius 6. 1. 3-4 and 9-11. For the Gauls see Diodorus 5. 28. 1; Strabo 4. 4. 2 (195 C) and 5. 2 (200 C); Caesar, B.G. 1. 39. 1 and 2. 30. 4; see also Plutarch, Marius 11. 3 and 8; 26. 4-5. The Galatians: Livy 38. 17. 3-10. Ceylon: Pliny, N.H. 6. 88. The difficulties involved in separating peoples one from another on this kind of basis were, of

unaware of this,[95] nor is it in the least likely that Tacitus has chosen to show his disagreement with and contempt for the opinions of a whole series of earlier writers merely by setting down his own view so baldly.[96] Which appears to leave only the possibility that Tacitus has arranged his material to yield an argument that is simply bizarre.

If we view the whole passage as a piece of rhetoric, a more reasonable explanation emerges. Norden demonstrated that the origo is a very carefully structured episode, made up of four panels with numerous correspondences in detail.[97] With the two central panels, the disquisition on Tuisto and the Germanic tribes (Germ. 2. 3-5) and the tales of Hercules and Ulysses (Germ. 3. 1-4), we need not concern ourselves. The flanking panels are another matter. Each opens with a statement of Tacitus' belief in Germanic autochthony and purity (Germ. 2. 1 and 4. 1), and each closes with a hostile comment on the German landscape and climate (Germ. 2. 2 and 4. 3). But Tacitus arrives at his hostile comment in very different ways. In the initial panel the train of thought is logical (if also frivolous), based on the arguments that nobody could have traveled to Germany, and nobody would have done so unless a native. In the final panel the train of thought is back to front, the description of Germanic traits strangely brief and bland. Scholars who comment on this latter passage declare that the final reference to "climate or land" enables Tacitus to pass on smoothly to a

course, formidable; see Morgan (above, note 69), pp. 199-208 and literature there cited.
[95]   Contra, Anderson xxxiv. Syme (above, note 56), I, p. 126 tries to palliate the situation by implying that Tacitus subscribed to the "enhancement" of these traits, making the Germans "larger and fiercer, with redder hair." That view is found not in Tacitus, but in Strabo 7. 1. 2 (290 C) and Manilius 4. 715-716.
[96]   There are several passages in the Agricola and the Germania where Tacitus makes a flat statement which demonstrably contradicts views previously expressed by Caesar, and on this basis it has been argued that he was hostile to and contemptuous of the earlier writer: see P. Couissin, "Tacite et César," Revue de philologie 58 (1932), pp. 97-117; Perret (above, note 9), p. 14, n. 2. But even at Agr. 11. 1 (above, note 73) Tacitus provides some arguments to back up his view. Here there is no argumentation at all and--apparently--contradiction of many more writers. These are sufficient grounds, it seems to me, to warrant the search for a different kind of explanation altogether.
[97]   The best analysis is that of Norden, pp. 42-46, repeated by Gunz (above, note 65), pp. 54-56 and Pekkanen (above, note 91), pp. 107-112; see also Trüdinger, p. 150; Perret (above, note 9), p. 38; Kraggerud (above, note 65), pp. 11-12.

description of the landscape in the next chapter,[98] nor would I deny this--especially when Tacitus has little good to say of the land anyway. But nor is this the entire explanation. The passage is structured, I suggest, to keep the information on Germanic physique and stamina short and (on the face of it) uncontroversial. Thus the reader is brought, without delay or distraction, to the final comment, the comment which will remind him of the earlier bon mot.[99] For Tacitus that sardonic and biting witticism is the crucial consideration, the point he wants to drive home. Whatever Tacitus believed or found in his sources, in other words, the quality of the argumentation and the structuring of the passage suggest a definite frivolity in his approach to the origo of the Germans. One could well apply to this entire section a comment Norden made of Tacitean style: Tacitus, he remarked, "sucht das Ungewöhnliche, sagt nichts, was der Leser auch gesagt haben würde, jedenfalls nicht so, wie dieser es gesagt haben würde."[100]

Which brings us to the style employed in the Germania, one of Tacitus' most effective weapons in the struggle to make literature out of ethnography or history. The epigrammatic sententiae with which he peppers his narrative are justly famous, e.g., the jibe that "recently the Germans have given us more victory processions than victories."[101] His efforts go much further than this, however. As Anderson observed, when Tacitus "comes to describe customs and institutions which he believes to involve important principles or beliefs, his diction becomes elevated and he strives to engage the interest of his readers by the use of all manner of stylistic devices--anaphora...to give impassioned emphasis, antithesis, alliteration, asyndeton, poetical (especially Virgilian) colouring, epigrammatic phrase."[102] In fact, Tacitus serves notice on the reader that style will be a major consideration with the very first clause of his treatise: Germania omnis a Gallis Raetisque et Pannoniis Rheno et Danuuio fluminibus, a Sarmatis Dacisque mutuo metu aut montibus separatur.[103] In ancient ethnography it was standard

[98] So Müllenhoff (above, note 9), IV, p. 147; Norden, pp. 460f.; Trüdinger, p. 155; Melin (above, note 70), p. 120; Kraggerud, p. 12.
[99] Steidle (above, note 4), pp. 86-87, made precisely this point, but failed to realize its implications in his eagerness to defend the historicity of Tacitus' account.
[100] Eduard Norden, Die antike Kunstprosa (Leipzig: Teubner, 1915; rpt. Stuttgart: B.G. Teubner, 1958), I, p. 331.
[101] Tacitus, Germ. 37. 6: proximis temporibus triumphati magis quam uicti sunt. See further Gunz, pp. 73-78.
[102] Anderson xvi; see also Gunz, pp. 68-88; Rademacher (above, note 29), pp. 224-228.
[103] Maurice Hutton rendered this: "Undivided Germany is separated from the Gauls, Rhaetians and Pannonians by the rivers

practice to state the geographical limits of the territory whose occupants the writer was studying, and it was likewise standard practice to use rivers and mountain ranges as the dividing lines.[104] Hence it is possible to cite countless parallels for the phraseology employed here,[105] except for one detail, the expression mutuo metu. Editors comment that Tacitus often evinces a taste for linking a physical and a mental idea like mutuo metu aut montibus, and they remark on the alliteration with which Tacitus, again characteristically, draws attention to what he is doing.[106] The significant point, however, is that this is a highly unusual collocation for an ethnography, serving to warn the reader that this will be an ethnography with a difference, no dry, scholarly treatise but a self-conscious work of art written in a high and highly rhetorical style.

It is time to return to the questions we posed at the beginning, why Tacitus chose to write an ethnographical treatise or, at any rate, what purports to be an ethnographical treatise, and why he selected the Germans as a suitable subject for his endeavors. It may be said at once that, whether ethnography was or was not fashionable in the first century A.D., Tacitus clearly had a genuine interest in the subject. He had included an ethnographical digression on the Britons in the Agricola, he would include another such digression on the Jews in his Histories, and he would adorn the Annals with ethnographical flourishes.[107] At the same time, however, his efforts are in general too cursory to warrant the belief that he wanted to write an ethnographical treatise as an end in itself. Just as the Agricola is not simply a biography of Tacitus' father-in-law,[108] so the Germania does not limit itself to a bald and detached description of the German tribes; it seizes every opportunity to make comparisons rather than observations; it is replete with sententiae expressing a decidedly sardonic turn of mind; and it is written in a highly artistic style

Rhine and Danube: from the Sarmatians and Dacians by mutual misgivings or mountains." (Tacitus: Dialogus, Agricola, Germania, p. 265.)

[104] Renata von Scheliha, Die Wassergrenze im Altertum (Breslau: Markus, 1931); Melin (above, note 70), pp. 121-125.

[105] Melin, pp. 113-117.

[106] See Müllenhoff (above, note 9), IV, p. 102; Much, p. 35; Anderson, p. 35. The unusual nature of the expression was remarked by Friedrich (above, note 42), pp. 27-28, while Williams (above, note 5), pp. 224-225 discusses instances in Silver Age poets.

[107] Tacitus, Agr. 10-12; Hist. 5. 2-8; see Ann. 4. 33. 3 (situs gentium as a good topic for digressions). For analysis see Trüdinger, pp. 156-158 and Walser (above, note 28), pp. 82-85.

[108] See above, note 4.

around a carefully controlled structure. There can be little doubt, I think, that Tacitus sought with this treatise to confirm his reputation as a writer of skill and versatility.[109] For the rest, he may well have thought that he was expanding the frontiers of the genre, or writing the ethnographical treatise which no subsequent writer would be able to imitate, let alone surpass.[110] He unquestionably intended to compose an ethnography which would make its mark, and in this aim--unfortunately--he would succeed ultimately beyond his wildest dreams.

As for his choosing the Germanic tribes for topic, it could very well be that he had no real alternative. Quite possibly his work on the Britons had aroused his interest in other northern barbarians; he certainly refers to the Germans in that work, and they figure in his subsequent writings.[111] Possibly, too, his consuming interest in Domitian's activities predisposed him to select a people against whom, so far as he was concerned, the emperor had fought with conspicuously little success.[112] And possibly there was some event in the years between 96 and 98 A.D. which renewed Roman interest in the area.[113] Nevertheless, the Germans and the Dacians appear to have been the only peoples beyond the frontiers to whom ethnographical treatises had not yet been devoted, and when so much more was known about the Germans thanks to the energetic compilations of the Elder Pliny, it would have been thoroughly perverse for an historian with strong literary pretensions to select the Dacians rather than the Germans as the vehicle for his

---

[109] See Gunz (above, note 65), p. 64.

[110] For the differences between Tacitean procedures and those of the Greek ethnographers see Trüdinger, pp. 164-170. By Tacitus' time, however, the various genres--never kept in rigid, watertight compartments--were hopelessly intermingled anyway: see Wilhelm Kroll, Studien zum Verständnis der römischen Literatur (Stuttgart: J.B. Metzler, 1924), pp. 202-224; Leeman (above, note 8), I, pp. 329-330; Williams (above, note 5), pp. 232-233.

[111] Note especially Tacitus, Agr. 11. 2: rutilae Caledoniam habitantium comae, magni artus Germanicam originem adseuerant. His subsequent interest in the Germans is documented by K. Christ, "Germanendarstellung und Zeitverständnis bei Tacitus," Historia 14 (1965), pp. 62-73; see also Sherwin-White (above, note 22), pp. 41-51.

[112] See especially Tacitus, Germ. 37. 2 and 6; Borzsák, pp. 422-424.

[113] Perhaps there is a connection with Nerva's assuming the title "Germanicus"; on that see Peter Kneissl, Die Siegestitulatur der römischen Kaiser (Göttingen: Vandenhoeck and Ruprecht, 1969), pp. 58-70.

manifold interests, historical and ethnographical, literary and stylistic.[114]

Although the Germania, then, must be regarded as history and literature simultaneously, it has seldom been read in this light, least of all by those whom it concerns most intimately. From the moment the manuscript was rediscovered in the fifteenth century, the treatise has been viewed as Holy Writ. At the time of the Renaissance, of course, one could hardly expect otherwise, since historical verity was held to embrace fact and fiction indifferently. "Any written text that purported to be about the past and explicitly eschewed the label of poetry was history."[115] But even the rise of "scientific history" failed to modify the situation significantly. Ranke, or more accurately, the least imaginative amongst his disciples maintained that in a text like the Germania one had only to separate the "facts" from the "opinions," quarrying the former and discarding the latter.[116] It was a naive approach, to say the least, and it failed completely to allow for the way in which the writer's opinion colored, even conditioned the facts he presented, this when there have been few writers more self-willed than Tacitus. Hence, ultimately, the capacity of the Germania to inspire and to haunt the Germans.

On the whole, the results of taking the treatise au pied de la lettre were at first beneficial. Amid the chaos and disunity of the years around 1500, the Germania was a positive inspiration. "In it many German humanists were beginning to see a new ideal for German greatness of culture, prowess in warfare, and moral superiority. Conrad Celtis, the German archhumanist, was the first to create this image.... His successors carried his enthusiastic example to such dynamic heights that the Reformation (although essentially spiritual in its cause) was politically successful in Germany largely because they used the Germania to stir up national patriotic aspirations--providing at once foundation for local movements of civic patriotism and structure for more concerted action in a common national ideology."[117] Tacitus' stress on the military strength which the united tribes had possessed (or would have possessed) inspired the hope that Germany could achieve unity and recover her ancient glory.[118] There was no less enthusiasm for the assertion that the tribes had been indigenous and free from outside influences, since this justified both their right to their country and

[114] See also Syme (above, note 56), I, p. 48.
[115] Frank L. Borchardt, German Antiquity in Renaissance Myth (Baltimore: Johns Hopkins University Press, 1971), p. 175.
[116] See McDonald (above, note 43), p. 480.
[117] Schellhase (above, note 2), p. 30; he discusses the period as a whole at pp. 31-65.
[118] Schellhase, p. 32.

their claim to freedom from alien vices.[119] They had trouble, naturally, with Tacitus' reasons for maintaining this view, namely that only natives would choose to live in so awful a landscape and climate, but that they could dismiss as a misunderstanding or ignore altogether. Similarly, there were few willing to endorse the barbarism which Tacitus had attributed to their ancestors,[120] even though they could no more accept the proposition--advanced promptly by their critics and opponents--that it was subjection to Rome and the Papacy which had brought civilization to their country.[121] And yet it was not the two-edged nature of the Germania which brought this phase to its close in the sixteenth century, but the impossibility of achieving the ideals it had originally inspired; and with that realization polemics yielded place to philology.[122]

The baneful effects of the Germania began to appear much more clearly in the nineteenth century, for there can be little doubt that the treatise encouraged, even if it did not inspire, the Volkish movement which prepared the way, in turn, for Nazi ideology.[123] It was natural enough, after the Treaty of Versailles, that the cult of Arminius should have taken a new lease on life, that scholars should have redoubled their efforts to discover the exact site of his victory over the Romans, and that Ernst von Bandel's monument to the chieftain outside Detmold should have become a center for pilgrims.[124] The Reichswehr might claim that it had been "stabbed in the back," but the war had been lost anyway. Arminius had been a victor, and not for the first time in her history, Germany needed a

---

[119] Borchardt, p. 178; Schellhase, pp. 39, 42, 63.

[120] But see Schellhase, pp. 37 and 53; Borchardt, p. 107.

[121] This view was advanced first by Enea Silvio Piccolomini in the Tractate-Letter published in Leipzig in 1496 (Schellhase, p. 33; Borchardt, pp. 55-56 and 70-71). An accommodation of sorts was subsequently worked out (Borchardt, pp. 95-96).

[122] Schellhase, pp. 50ff., especially pp. 57ff.

[123] In what follows I am indebted particularly to Fritz Stern, The Politics of Cultural Despair: a Study in the Rise of the Germanic Ideology (Berkeley: University of California Press, 1961), and George L. Mosse, The Crisis of German Ideology: Intellectual Origins of the Third Reich (New York: Grosset and Dunlap, 1964).

[124] The Herrmannsdenkmal itself had been erected in 1875, in the first flush of optimism following the unification of Germany, while the bimillennium of the clades Varian in 1909 coincided with the rise of Volkish doctrine and Wilhelmine bellicosity to stimulate discussion in the last years before World War I (Mosse, p. 80, comments on one of the more bizarre results). Nevertheless, literature on the subject grew by leaps and bounds during the Weimar and Nazi periods.

victor to venerate.[125] The influence of the Germania, however, was altogether more pervasive and longer-lived. From the beginning of the nineteenth century through the Weimar era, high school textbooks "praised Volkish ideas, and the destiny of the Volk with its sense of German mission pervaded most of their content. Modernity was universally and irrevocably condemned; the spirit of the Germanic forebears, the primitive but heroic inhabitants of the Teutonic forests were held up as examples to be emulated.... Tacitus' descriptions of the ancient Germans formed the center of Germanic consciousness."[126]

Beyond this, the Germania could be held to endorse a series of specific Volkish tenets. Tacitus' description of Germans as village-dwellers accorded well with the strongly anti-urban attitudes of the movement's followers.[127] More important, his statement that the Germanic tribes were indigenous could be held to provide Germans with the pedigree, the rootedness on which the various exponents of Volkish thought insisted.[128] Then there was Tacitus' declaration that the ancient Germans were a pure race, no small spur to the Rassenreinheit preached by most Volkish and Nazi ideologues.[129] On this basis, indeed, it was even possible to make the clades Variana cause for regret as well as self-congratulation! "Tatsache aber ist, die der rückschauende Beurteiler feststellen darf, daß der Mißerfolg der augusteischen Politik wohl die Zufuhr neuen Blutes aus dem Norden in den Staat der Mittelmeerwelt verhindert hat, daß dadurch jedoch auch die Kräfte des Nordens davor bewahrt blieben, zu früh in den Mischkessel des großen Imperiums hineingerissen zu werden."[130] The most important consideration, however, may rather have been that Tacitus, as a classical author of the first rank, appeared to lend respectability to Volkish precepts. The principal audience for such views, it must be remembered, was the Bürgerstand and, for all the dissatisfaction

[125] For previous invocations of Arminius see Borchardt, pp. 101-102, for the specifically Volkish mentality of the Weimar period Mosse, pp. 137, 226-227, and 254ff.
[126] Mosse, p. 154, building on Ernst Weymar, Das Selbstverständnis der Deutschen (Stuttgart: Klett, 1961), pp. 30-33, 143-144, 148-149, and 163-164.
[127] Tacitus, Germ. 16; see Stern, pp. 130-131; Mosse, pp. 16, 19, 22-23, 26, 108-125.
[128] Stern, p. 130; Mosse, pp. 6-7, 15-18, 20-22, 71, 159.
[129] Weymar, p. 47; Stern, pp. 61-62, 90-91, 201-202; Mosse, pp. 67-107 and 256.
[130] F. Miltner, in Helmut Berve (ed.), Das neue Bild der Antike, II: Rom (Leipzig: Koehler and Amelang, 1942), p. 450. Drexler's paper (above, note 9) also makes a fascinating study when one bears in mind that it was given originally in late 1944 and early 1945.

with Gymnasium and Professoriat during this period, Classical Philology remained an object of awe and wonderment at that level of
society, respectability a prerequisite for existence.[131]

Although the Nazi mentality has been termed an outgrowth of
the "compost heap of bourgeois thought," it cannot be said that the
leaders of the new regime shared the awe in which the Classics were
held;[132] it cannot even be maintained that they possessed a consistent attitude on the subject.[133] But when Himmler succumbed to
the attractions of Volkish theory, as he did early on,[134] it is hardly surprising that the Germania should be one of the books he is
known to have read,[135] or that a classical scholar of the time
should have thanked him publicly for supporting a study of its
manuscript tradition.[136] In a regime which thrust bucolic communi-
ties on an industrialized society, while Nordic barbarians cavorted
amid ferro-concrete neo-Classical architecture, anything was possible, even a Reichskommissar für die Festigung deutschen
Volkstums.[137]

It was no doubt on this basis that Momigliano, remarking that
nobody had yet compiled a list of the one hundred most dangerous

[131]   For the educational system and its problems see Stern, pp.
xxiv-xxv, 74, 78, 172 and 270-271; the drive to respectability is
emphasized by Mosse, p. 309.
[132]   See Volker Losemann, Nationalsozialismus und Antike. Studien zur Entwicklung des Faches Alte Geschichte 1933-1945 (Hamburg: Hoffmann and Campe, 1977), pp.   27-46 and 61-74.   The
anti-intellectual stance generally affected by the Nazi leaders is well
illustrated by Richard Grunberger, The 12-Year Reich. A Social
History of Nazi Germany 1933-1945 (New York: Holt, Rinehart and
Winston, 1971), pp. 44-45.
[133]   Losemann, pp. 17-26. This diversity of opinion, mirroring
what Otto Ohlendorf called "die pluralistische Willkür der obersten
Hierarchen" (Heinz Höhne, Canaris: Patriot im Zwielicht (Munich:
C. Bertelsmann, 1976), p. 212), was of course part of the fragmentation   deliberately   encouraged   by   Hitler   to   assure   his   own
pre-eminence.
[134]   W.T.   Angress   and   B.F.   Smith,   "Diaries   of   Heinrich
Himmler's   Early   Years,"   Journal of Modern History XXXI (1959),
pp. 206-224 at p. 221 n. 86.
[135]   Losemann, p. 23.
[136]   As Losemann, pp. 120-121 and 233 n. 25, points out,
Himmler's interest in this was at best formal; it was not without
reason that one of his own SS generals, Felix Steiner, termed him a
"sleazy romantic": Heinz Höhne, The Order of the Death's Head,
tr. Richard Barry (New York: Coward, McCann, and Geoghegan,
1970), p. 481.
[137]   Höhne, pp. 308-313.

books, the books that cause wars, moved for the inclusion thereon of Homer's Iliad and Tacitus' Germania. This, he said, was "no reflection on Homer and Tacitus. Tacitus was a gentleman and, for all that I know, Homer was a gentleman too. But who will deny that the Iliad and the Germania raise most unholy passions in the human mind?"[138] This is an overstatement, insofar as the Germania was hardly the only source to which lovers of things Nordic could or did appeal.[139] Nor can this one treatise be made to bear all the blame for Volkish, let alone Nazi programs. The conditions of the time and--if you will-the Zeitgeist were perhaps such that events would have followed much the same course even if the Germania had never been rediscovered. But the work was there, it contributed to Germany's problems in the nineteenth and the twentieth centuries, and it did so because it was consistently misread as an historical treatise worthy of the highest respect and the deepest belief. For Tacitus, as I have tried to show, the Germania was above all else a work of art, a blend of history and literature, the historical aspects as often as not taking second place to literary considerations. If only we can begin to read the work in the way he meant it to be read, we may all be the better for it.[140]

[138] Arnaldo Momigliano, Studies in Historiography (London: Weidenfeld and Nicolson; New York: Harper and Row, 1966), p. 113.
[139] It is common to emphasize, perhaps even to over-emphasize, the medieval and feudal aspects of Volkish and Nazi movements: so Mosse, passim; see R. Koehl, "Feudal Aspects of National Socialism," American Political Science Review 54 (1960), pp. 921-933. For the Nordic element see especially Hans-Jürgen Lutz-höft, Der nordische Gedanke in Deutschland 1920-1940 (Stuttgart: E. Klett, 1971).
[140] See F. Graus, "Geschichtsschreibung und National-sozialismus," Vierteljahrshefte für Zeitgeschichte 17 (1969), pp. 87-95, especially pp. 94-95.

POST-REVOLUTIONARY LITERARY HISTORY:

THE CASE OF WILHELM DILTHEY

Peter Uwe Hohendahl

(Translated by Tom Leech)

Whoever mentions the name of Wilhelm Dilthey today, especially in this country, can hardly expect to encounter any great resonance. While there is no lack of scholarly interest in this important historian and philosopher of the nineteenth century, his works seem at first glance to lack the topicality of the writings of Nietzsche or Heidegger despite the fact that they belong in the same context. Dilthey is familiar to Germanists, of course, as the author of the influential collection of essays, Das Erlebnis und die Dichtung, the publication of which, in 1905, had an epochal effect. As a result of his pioneering essays on Lessing, Goethe, Hölderlin, Novalis, written in fact much earlier, Dilthey became the mentor of that trend in German literary studies known as intellectual history ("Geistesgeschichte") or the history of ideas. After 1900, this movement began to combat the Positivist School of Scherer on a large scale. It took over leadership in the twenties and was in turn displaced by the existential approach to interpretation represented by the young Emil Staiger, for example.[1] In the history of literary studies Wilhelm Dilthey is regarded today as a figure of the past from whom, in any case, a revitalizing effect can hardly be expected. The standard reference works in the field of German literature treat Dilthey's works on literary history and poetics as an essentially outdated phase in the history of scholarship.[2]

Dilthey appears in a completely different light, however, when we approach his work in terms of philosophy and method. The

---

[1] Emil Staiger, Die Zeit als Einbildungskraft des Dichters; Untersuchungen zu Gedichten von Brentano, Goethe und Keller (Zurich/Leipzig: Max Niehans Verlag, 1939).

[2] See also Jost Hermand, Synthetisches Interpretieren (Munich: Nymphenburger Verlagsbuchhandlung, 1968), pp. 35-41; Jürgen Hauff et al., eds., Methodendiskussion (Königstein: Athenäum, 1975), II, pp. 10-17.

problem of a hermeneutics of intellectual history, which he first explored fully in its historical and systematic dimension, once again occupies the center of interest. The mention of the names of Hans-Georg Gadamer and Jürgen Habermas suffices to localize this interest. As a result of the famous Positivism debate in sociology, which occupied German scholarship in the sixties (and by no means only the professional sociologists),[3] the old question became topical again of whether the humanities could follow the same methodological principles as the natural and social sciences or whether they could lay claim to a theory and methodology of their own. Speaking for Critical Theory, Habermas formulated a dualistic approach which differentiated rigorously between the natural sciences on the one hand and the humanities and social sciences on the other, without, however, simply reverting to the earlier phase of this debate and the solution offered at that time.[4] To justify this distinction, Habermas called upon philosophical hermeneutics in the form developed by Gadamer in 1960 in Wahrheit und Methode. Gadamer's presentation, which illuminates the historical genesis of its own systematic approach, refers critically to Dilthey and discusses the limitations inherent in Dilthey's historicism in its tensions between Positivism and Philosophical Hermeneutics. Habermas adopted this perspective in his analysis of the epistemological problems involved in the modern concept of an academic discipline in Erkenntnis und Interesse (1968). Like Gadamer, Habermas regarded Dilthey's theory as an example of the contradictions and confusions of historicism in the nineteenth century, which, under the influence of a victorious Positivism, partially abandoned those legitimate interests guiding the cognitive process within the humanities.

Both Gadamer and Habermas considered their task to be the resolution of this situation, although they approached it from different positions. For this reason Dilthey's work is being drawn into the current discussion, and it is appropriate that the interest of the hermeneutic debate is concentrated largely on the studies from the eighties and the nineties, in which Dilthey, after the Einleitung in die Geisteswissenschaften, confronts the question of the self-sufficiency of the humanities and social sciences. The early writings treating German literature and literary history in detail are pushed into the background. Dilthey's hermeneutics, in other words, is being considered as an earlier phase of the present debate. The legitimacy of this procedure cannot be doubted, insofar as every theoretical discussion has to recall its context and background in order to maintain a sense of its own historicity. It

---

[3] Theodor W. Adorno, The Positivist Dispute in German Sociology, tr. Glyn Adey and David Frisby (London: Heinemann, 1976).
[4] Jürgen Habermas, "Gegen einen positivistisch halbierten Rationalismus," in Zur Logik der Sozialwissenschaften: Materialien. (Frankfurt am Main: Suhrkamp, 1970), pp. 41-70.

should not be overlooked, if course, that in this way important aspects of Dilthey's oeuvre are being concealed. These include, if I am correct, the methodology of literary history. In my opinion Wilhelm Dilthey has affected German literary studies more strongly than any historian of the nineteenth century--more strongly, in the final analysis, than Wilhelm Scherer, whose Positivist program was so successful in the late nineteenth century.[5] After 1900, of course, Dilthey's thoughts were developed further, and not only among his students, but also, if less directly, by scholars representing completely different philosophical positions.

I would like to pursue the question of the manner in which Dilthey's conception of literary history was molded by the political and social situation of post-revolutionary Germany and the extent to which his analysis has become accepted as orthodoxy in German literary studies. Walter Benjamin first called attention to this problematic intellectual heritage in the twenties, when he wrote about Germanics: "In this swamp lives the hydra of scholastic aesthetics with its seven heads: creativity, identification (empathy), timelessness, imitation, sympathy, illusion and aesthetic pleasure.[6] The method of identification refers, of course, to Dilthey's hermeneutics, although one must also add immediately that in Dilthey's case more is involved than an impressionism lacking in conceptual content. Benjamin is certainly completely correct in his description of the interpretation of Dilthey in the debates on method within Germanics: the softening of literary criticism to the point that it becomes a form of irrationalism. Lukács emphasized this element later in Zerstörung der Vernunft as the leitmotiv of Dilthey's method, thereby serving also to limit future discussion.[7] On the left the suspicion of irrationalism was enough to ban discussion of Dilthey; in the conservative camp, i.e., in established Germanics, his criticism was discredited from the beginning by the Marxist nature of the attacker.[8] In this way Lukács' verdict cut off the discussion before it succeeded in really approaching the object of its investigation.

We find, therefore, that our way points back to the circumstances in which Dilthey's conception of literary history developed

---

[5] In regard to Scherer see also Hermand, pp. 17-35; Peter Salm, Three Modes of Criticism: The Literary Theories of Scherer, Walzel, and Staiger (Cleveland: Press of Case Western Reserve University, 1968).
[6] Benjamin, "Literaturgeschichte und Literaturwissenschaft," in Angelus Novus (Frankfurt am Main: Suhrkamp, 1966), p. 453.
[7] Lukács, Werke (Neuwied am Rhein: Luchterhand, 1960ff), IX, pp. 363-385.
[8] See also Christofer Zockler, Dilthey und die Hermeneutik (Stuttgart: J.B. Metzler, 1975), pp. 105-107.

in the eighteen-sixties. There are several levels which must be considered--first, the contemporary discussion of method and history which Dilthey encountered and to which he reacted positively or negatively in his works; second, the political ideology of this epoch, i.e., the development of Liberalism in the sixties, especially between 1859 and 1866. Dilthey studied theology and philosophy in the years 1852 through 1856, during the truly reactionary period. As a young doctor of philosophy and "Privatdozent"--his "Habilitationsarbeit" dealt with ethical questions--he experienced the renewal of Liberalism in Prussia under the regent after the abdication of Frederick William IV. In the early sixties he was very sympathetic to political developments and was very close to the important figures of Liberalism in Prussia, although he could never make the decision to exchange the public life of academia for that of politics.[9] He shared the hopes of the liberal party for a greater degree of intellectual and political freedom, but was prepared nevertheless--not unlike the majority of German liberals--to bury these hopes in exchange for national unification under Bismarck's Prussia. Statements in Dilthey's letters leave no room for doubt that in 1866 the Nationalist tradition was more important to him than that of Liberalism, politically as well as culturally.

This attitude is revealed in his works--most obviously, perhaps, in the attempt to develop for the new nation a literary canon of classical authors, a literary and cultural heritage by means of which the nation could establish its legitimacy. This involved not only the inclusion or rejection of specific authors, but also, and with deeper effects, a new total conception of German literary history. More specifically, Dilthey developed the idea that the history of German literature between 1750 and 1830, i.e., the period between Enlightenment and Romanticism, was to be considered as a unified continuum. This apparently merely formal reorganization of history had, in fact, far-reaching consequences. It contained nothing less than an affirmative integration of literature into the Nationalist tradition. German Classicism and Romanticism were seen as preparing the way for the second "Reich." This conception differed significantly from the presentations which the young Dilthey encountered, i.e., the works of Gervinus, Hettner, or Julian Schmidt, for example, who also connected literary history with political history--but in a different way.[10]

[9] See also Bernd Peschken, Versuch einer germanistischen Ideologiekritik (Stuttgart: J.B. Metzler, 1972), pp. 57-72; Zockler, pp. 209-239.
[10] In regard to literary history before 1848 see also Bernd Hüppauf, ed., Literaturgeschichte zwischen Revolution und Reaktion (Wiesbaden: Akademische Verlagsgesellschaft Athenaion, 1972), pp. 3-35; Klaus Weimar, "Zur Geschichte der Literaturwissen-

Dilthey's new conception, therefore, does not originate in a vacuum--either in terms of politics or in terms of literary criticism. It refers to and develops through a confrontation with the liberal historiography of the period preceding the unsuccessful revolution of 1848--figures such as Ranke, Schlosser, and Gervinus. In this confrontation Dilthey stands by no means alone. At about the same time, for example, the young Wilhelm Scherer was developing his Positivist program as a criticism of romantic philology and idealist historiography, while Theodor Wilhelm Danzel had presented a critical program immediately after the revolution. Danzel's program had little effect on subsequent discussion, however, because of the untimely death of its author.

Why did such a confrontation with the older literary histories take place? What separates pre-revolutionary from post-revolutionary literary history? Why did the post-revolutionary situation in Germany, the restriction of political life, have of necessity such a meaning for literature and its history? The correlation of the debate on theory and method with the change in the political climate has, as is to be shown, specific reasons. They can be formulated as the connection between literary and political public life in the period before 1848. The significant literary histories of this period, that of Gervinus especially, serve the cause of Liberalism. The failure of this Liberalism, its inability to hold its own in the long run against the conservative powers as shown in the revolution of 1848, also brought the Liberal cause into disrepute in those sectors, including the sphere of literary history, where there was no direct contact with political decisions.[11] It is the liberals themselves--men such as the Neo-hegelian Robert Prutz or even Theodor Wilhelm Danzel, the Goethe and Lessing scholar--who encourage and carry out the revision of the historical picture. The younger generation, e.g. Dilthey and Scherer, accepts to a great extent this criticism of liberal historiography and turns itself to the task of surmounting the crisis and of formulating a new program.

Let us begin with Danzel's critique of rationalistic literary history. As Danzel shows in his essay "Über die Behandlung der Geschichte der neueren Literatur," it has not yet progressed beyond the level of dilettantism.[12] Its lack of academic character is

schaft. Forschungsbericht," DVLG 50 (1976), pp. 298-363, especially pp. 302-329.

[11] For example Robert E. Prutz, Die deutsche Literatur der Gegenwart. 1848 bis 1858, 2 Vols.

[12] Originally presented as a speech on September 11, 1848, at the University of Leipzig, where Danzel was active professionally as a "Privatdozent." The quotations which follow are from Hans Mayer, ed. Deutsche Literaturkritik im 19. Jahrhundert (Frankfurt am Main: Suhrkamp, 1974), pp. 317-327.

shown in its failure to distinguish methodologically between subject and object, researcher and material in a satisfactory manner. Historians of the period before 1848 immersed themselves in their subject matter and adopted the aesthetic and poetological viewpoints of the literature they treated. In so doing they confused uncritically their own standpoint with the object of their presentation. "It is...the greatest weakness of a work of literary history to take as guiding principles the judgments and viewpoints which serve as points of departure for the Swiss in their critical writings, for Lessing in the Literaturbriefe, for Goethe in this life and for Schiller in his treatise on Naive und sentimentalische Dichtung."[13] In the name of objectivity Danzel demands the complete separation of present and past. "The historian never has the right," so reads his postulate, "to incorporate in his subjective approach the view which he is supposed to be treating at the time with complete objectivity."[14] The problem which concerns Danzel is that of the relationship between historical and aesthetic points of view. Gervinus had already eliminated aesthetic observation from literary history methodologically in order to be able to assume a historical standpoint at all. For the aesthetic perspective is still identical for him with an absolute and ahistorical approach. Such an approach is applicable in the same degree to all works of art and therefore has no interest in historical characteristics. Danzel's criticism is a systematic extension of Gervinus' position. It intends to separate the historian from a specific aesthetic theory and to assign to him a higher position from which aesthetics itself can be viewed as a part of history. The methodological opposition between literary history and aesthetics rests on the inability of Gervinus to recognize clearly the historical nature of aesthetic propositions. For this reason he wishes to exclude them from history as something foreign. Danzel takes the opposite path and adds aesthetics to literary history: even the theories of Lessing, Schiller, and Goethe are historical objects in need of interpretation. The researcher as subject knows himself to be separated from these theories and poetics in the same way that he is separated from past works of art. This means, however, that the historian as subject becomes formalized.

This tendency becomes clearly visible in Danzel's attempt to separate literary history methodologically from the history of philosophy. Idealist history of philosophy had reconstructed the progression of philosophical systems--previously viewed simply as a series--as the history of spirit ("Geist") in such a way that all such systems appeared as logical steps in the development of contemporary philosophy. In this way the history of philosophy becomes the vehicle of the self-consciousness of spirit. Danzel points out rightly that pre-revolutionary literary history took over this

[13] Ibid., p. 318.
[14] Ibid., p. 318.

methodological principle: "The history of modern German literature is treated on the assumption that its course should clarify, indeed should of necessity direct attention to the task of the present."[15] In what follows Danzel describes the rationalistic literary history which takes the interests of the present as its point of departure and goes back to history in order to find answers for the future: "Others, who live completely within the political aspirations of our times, thought that the development in the previous century indicated that literary effort must be followed by efforts directed toward the reorganization of the state, that a period of literature must be followed by a time of action."[16] Although he is not mentioned by name, this passage refers doubtlessly to Gervinus. Danzel reproaches this conception for manipulating the material tendentiously by projecting the interests of the present into the past. The historian is then no different, to use Danzel's comparison, from the preacher who employs the Bible for purposes of edification.

This politically motivated objection becomes meaningful only through its methodological justification, which indeed gives an accurate exposé of progressive bourgeois literary history. The reproach of insufficient empirical proof and of premature construction of syntheses, which anticipates the criticism of the later positivism of the Scherer school, would not be very important as a denunciation. It becomes serious because of its theoretical argument. The attempt to represent historical process as a coherent continuity (by which the literary history of a Gervinus had intended to distinguish itself from the older annalistic works) rests, according to Danzel, on a problematic conception of history. The manner in which the relation between literary history and political history is treated seems to Danzel to be especially dubious. He formulates his objection as follows: "In treating German literature the point of view of the national development has become dominant in recent times. In general there is nothing objectionable in this. If history is to be something more than a mere external chronological ordering of isolated facts, something must be there which develops, a substance, of which individual phenomena are only modifications, and this substance--what should it be but spirit: the manner of thinking of a people, either in general or specifically in terms of poetic production?"[17] The possibility of a historical synthesis depends in the case of Gervinus, as Danzel correctly insists, on two assumptions: the Idealist premise of an autonomously evolving spirit and the specification of this spirit as a national spirit ("Volksgeist"). If one assumes for the historical process an autonomously developing substance, it is possible, even desirable, to

[15] Ibid., p. 319.
[16] Ibid., p. 320.
[17] Ibid., p. 323.

connect literature and politics methodologically, since both are nothing more than modifications of the one spirit.

Danzel's criticism is directed primarily against the nationalistic limitations placed on literary history. He points out that the assumed national developments are fictions which do not do justice to modern history. German literature can only be understood as a part of European literature. This objection is undoubtedly cogent. Danzel's critique of the Idealist premise, however, does not hit the mark completely. As soon as one questions the Idealist conception of history, the connection made by Gervinus between literary and political history no longer holds. Thus Danzel undermines the conception of historical synthesis when he speaks of the different aspects and different tasks of the spirit, all of which have their own independent history. The history of literature, too, would then have to be observed and presented within terms of its own assumptions, specifically that of the connection between aesthetic norms and works. At the end of his essay Danzel suggests an approach in which literary history would be no longer considered a part of political history, but rather as "a kind of history of art." "Its task is the reconstruction of the transformations of poetic production purely in terms of this production itself."[18] There is hardly an allusion to the questions of how this evolution would take place or, above all, of how a historical connection with the realms of philosophy or politics could be made under these conditions. One possibility which Danzel envisions explains the progression of literary production through comparison with contemporary aesthetics and poetics--as the practical accomplishment of tasks formulated by theory or, in reverse, the formulation of new tasks which theory derives from innovative works.

This critique of Gervinus results in the emptying and formalization of the historical subject, whose actual interests are eliminated as illegitimate, and in the separation of literary history from pragmatic history. In other words, by means of methodological criticism, the political charge, as contained in Gervinus' conception of history, is retracted. In the name of a rigorous scientific method literary history withdraws from the public realm and abandons it to popular presentations. The political commitment of pre-revolutionary historiography is denounced by Danzel as dilettantism.

Compared with this penetrating methodological critique, Dilthey's first attempts at confronting existing literary history seem somewhat vague. They do not merit, actually, the name of a critique, since they are intended as an assessment of the accomplishments of Gervinus, Hettner, and Julian Schmidt. The essay

[18] Ibid., p. 326.

126

"Literarische Arbeiten über das klassische Zeitalter" (1866) was intended to prepare the way for Dilthey's own very discursive treatise by presenting a survey of existing scholarship. (At this point in time Dilthey's essay on Novalis had already appeared, and his essay on Lessing would appear shortly thereafter.) The methodological problems which this survey creates become apparent, however, as soon as Dilthey asks himself what task literary history is to accomplish and what form this accomplishment should take.

Dilthey considers literary history as a part of education ("Bildung"). The literary historian's presentation of past literature becomes relevant when the contemporary reader no longer has the leisure to read and react to the works of literature himself. Consequently the objective presentation of information is the guiding principle for Dilthey, since the reader has to be able to rely on the historian. For Dilthey the task of the historian lies in extracting from that which has been handed down the material which has lasting value. "The literary historian should pass judgment about that which deserves today to be preserved from the immeasurable volume of writings and to be presented in detail by a man who values that which has had an effect on men or which is capable of affecting him personally."[19] The main emphasis in Dilthey's case lies clearly on the positive side, specifically on the acquisition of a lasting tradition, and less on the criticism of this tradition. This attitude leads to a critique, although a very cautious one, of the rationalistic literary history of Gervinus and his students, for rationalistic historiography assumes the right to pass judgment on the past. It subjects the past to its moral-political judgment, which takes its scale of values from the goal of the historical process. For this reason rationalistic criticism cannot spare even the Classical authors of German literature, should their works have an effect detrimental to the process of enlightenment. Characteristically, Dilthey considers just this procedure to be lacking in objectivity and thus wrong. He reproaches Gervinus with having transgressed beyond the task of historiography insofar as he makes direct value judgments which go beyond the standpoint of historical effect. "Only when Gervinus abandons the standpoint of historical effect and the great source of this effect in Goethe's autobiography and himself passes judgment on the worth of human beings outside the context of their historical period--only then was he often egregiously mistaken."[20] Dilthey disapproves of an evaluation reflecting present concerns on the grounds that it is morally abstract, and recommends a judgment which is developed from the object itself, as it were, by focusing on the effect of the work in its immediate temporal context. Without emphasizing it explicitly, Dilthey reverses here the perspective of

[19]   Dilthey, Gesammelte Schriften (Leipzig: Teubner, 1914-1958), XI, p. 196.
[20]   Ibid., p. 197.

rationalistic literary history: the point of departure of the historical work is tradition and the canon of significant authors selected
by this tradition, not the concerns of the present.

In these years Dilthey approaches to a degree the positivist
method, e.g., in his desire for rigorous explanation in objective literary history. "We want to survey in uninterrupted sequence, the
concatenation of causes and effects, within which intellectual events
take place in the same manner as do events of political history. In
this case, too, we demand the uncovering of the causal connection
of events."[21] That this demand cannot be separated from the older
Idealist historiography is never mentioned expressly by Dilthey. It
is worth noting, however, that among contemporary literary histories Dilthey preferred after all Julian Schmidt's to that of Hermann
Hettner. In spite of his appreciation for Hettner's extensive knowledge and the force of his presentation, he criticizes no less than
does Wilhelm Scherer the lack of causal derivation. Hettner is merely descriptive, while Schmidt, according to Dilthey, offers a
dramatic presentation which takes account of the causal connections
in a more thorough and appropriate manner. At this point in time
Dilthey finds in Julian Schmidt that which he would like to achieve
himself: an empirically founded intellectual history of the eighteenth century which has freed itself from the theoretical and
methodological principles of Liberal historiography. This verdict
notwithstanding, Dilthey is thoroughly conscious of the fact that
Schmidt's literary history is indebted in its approach to that
pre-revolutionary Liberalism from which he wishes to distance himself. This is made possible by the fact that Schmidt revised his
work a number of times and in the fifth edition, to which Dilthey
refers, a version is presented in which little of the Liberal commitment of the first edition can be detected. Dilthey expresses
specifically his approval of this change of direction, which he views
as an increase in objectivity.

The same cautious aloofness toward rationalistic historiography
is shown in Dilthey's lengthy article on the historian Friedrich
Christoph Schlosser, published in 1865 in the Preussische Jahrbücher. Again Dilthey chooses for his critique the form of a historical evaluation. He traces the evolution of historical thinking in
Germany within the context of the biography and intellectual development of Schlosser and can in this way show the limitations of the
Liberal approach. Dilthey praises Schlosser for opposing Hegel's
teleological philosophy of history and for attempting to construct a
connection in universal history only insofar as it is possible to
reduce "the varied phenomena of history to their causes and these
again to human nature."[22] Nevertheless, the problem of the "evo-

[21] Ibid., p. 198.
[22] Ibid., p. 154.

128

lution of history as a whole"[23] remains unsolved for Schlosser and for his interpreter Dilthey. For Schlosser, the task of history lies in the development of humanity to a more perfect form; he insists, in the same way as did Kant, on the moral-political progress of humanity. It is just this point which, in Dilthey's judgment, indicates his limitations. Schlosser is revealed as a "child of the eighteenth century, whose ideal of the state culminates in 'human rights'."[24] The rationalistic historiography of a Schlosser falters in the face of the manifold nature of spirit. Schlosser "relates literature rigorously to its basic principle, moral culture ("sittliche Kultur"), specifically to moral culture as he understands it, as something in which the direct relationship to active and political life determines everything, and in which, therefore, the world of fantasy retreats completely behind the will and sober reason, as cultivated in this life."[25]

Dilthey's interpretation sees a connection between Schlosser's conception of Progressive history and his Instrumentalist attitude toward literature. The decisive factor is the effect. Dilthey, on the other hand, is concerned with doing justice to all phenomena of intellectual life. In contrast to Schlosser, who is concerned primarily with origin and effect, Dilthey insists on comprehending the phenomenon itself. In this sense Ranke is the model for the younger generation. Dilthey admires obviously the force and the élan of Ranke's presentation, but he points out his lack of constructive and analytical ability. "Ranke seems often to glide over the surface of things: he is unsatisfactory on the point of causal knowledge, but he remains the great teacher, because he does not assume from the very beginning of his presentation those causes which are to be demonstrated, but rather proceeds from great world events to their universal connection."[26] It is not completely clear whether Dilthey considers the lack of sufficient causal analysis to be a disadvantage or an advantage. Dilthey uses the concept of "coherence" ("Zusammenhang"). "The abstract term cause or causality does not quite render what we mean by coherence."[27] Where Dilthey, as in this passage, reaches back to the older historicism, he refers characteristically not to the tradition of Schlosser and Gervinus, but rather to Ranke's descriptive objectivism.

We see that the young Dilthey vacillates between a causal-genetic and a descriptive-genetic conception. Positivism, as represented by his friend Wilhelm Scherer, has a significant attraction for him, since it breaks--at least ostensibly--with the

[23] Ibid., p. 154.
[24] Ibid., p. 157.
[25] Ibid., p. 161.
[26] Ibid., p. 217.
[27] Ibid., p. 218.

speculative philosophy of history and the Idealist concept of progress. The Positivists are no less critical of the rationalistic history of literature than Dilthey. Why does he finally decide against Positivism in favor of an independent humanistic ("geisteswissenschaftliche") method?

The decisive impulse for Dilthey's development of an independent humanistic methodology, presented for the first time in 1875 in the treatise "Über das Studium der Geschichte,"[28] results from his early interest in Schleiermacher and the problem of hermeneutics. In his prize-winning essay of 1860 on Schleiermacher's hermeneutical system the young Dilthey sets himself the task of incorporating the heritage of Romantic literary criticism and interpretive theory into the definition of literary history.[29] In a certain sense Dilthey passes over Hegel and the Hegelian tradition, also still influential in post-revolutionary literary history, and changes the focus of the problem. The emphasis shifts from the question of the possibility of a reconstruction of the historical totality to the question of the possibility of objective text interpretation. Of course these meta-historical points of view are not explored in the prize essay itself, which adheres stringently to the ideal of academic objectivity by dealing exclusively with the presentation of Schleiermacher's hermeneutics in its historical context.

More revealing in terms of the critical self-consciousness of the young Dilthey are the diary entries of the same period, for they reveal more clearly the degree to which Dilthey considers the question of hermeneutics to be related to the question of what it means to understand history. The extensive entry of March 26, 1859, which falls in the period in which the prize essay was being written, is remarkable not least of all for the manner in which Dilthey relates the decisive theoretical-methodological problems of his generation and in so doing attempts an account of the meaning of historical thinking (hardly distinguishing here between history and literary history). Significantly clearer than later, public statements, this entry indicates that Dilthey was quite conscious of the theoretical and methodological limitations inherent in any attempt at historical analysis and understood the inner connection between the methodological approach and the results of the presentation. It was therefore clear to Dilthey that history was the result of a reconstruction ("Nachkonstruktion"). "History, insofar as it deals with the course of intellectual life, is very dependent on the method of its historians. About this method there exists violent

---

[28] Dilthey, "Über das Studium der Geschichte, der Wissenschaften vom Menschen, der Gesellschaft und dem Staat," in Gesammelte Schriften, V, pp. 31-75.
[29] This work is available in print again finally in Volume 14 of the Gesammelte Schriften.

disagreement. Consideration of a work as the expression of an idea produced by the general dialectic; the atomistic analysis of the same into manifold motives and beginnings; the photographic reproduction of works in the smallest possible space; how different the historical pictures produced by such different principles, by means of such different techniques."[30] In a comparative discussion Dilthey examines the different schools of historiography: the philosophy of history of Hegel and his school, the new Positivism, the narrative historicism of a Ranke. He distances himself most explicitly from the Idealist philosophy of history in 1859, possibly as a result of the impression made on him by Haym's book on Hegel. The concept of a direct historical development, unfolding according to the "triad of phases of self-fulfilling dialectic" he considers to be an illusion in nature and history. The irregularity of the world contains no form of reason other than law ("das Gesetz").[31] Nevertheless, Dilthey's critique of absolute reason in history retains the concept of progress as well as that of law, in order to have at least a framework for the comprehension and presentation of historical data. In different formulations Dilthey expresses the same basic principle, i.e., that the human spirit progresses as a result of mechanical laws. The historical process is not advanced by the emanation of the idea, but rather through circumstances. "History has to do with culture as it progresses. The form of spiritual ("geistig") progress is, viewed mechanically, the increasing complexity of ideas and relationships elicited by the reciprocal actions of nations in their historical configuration."[32] In other passages Dilthey speaks of the possibility of explaining the forward movement of history by means of a merely mechanical regularity. This reversal permits him to renounce tentatively the older Idealist premises without sacrificing the concept of progress and the idea of universal history.

There remain, of course, unsolved methodological problems: how can the existence of such laws be demonstrated in the history of spirit and how is progress to be detected in the regularity of history's course? The evolution of history calls for, as Dilthey recognizes, a direction. For this reason Dilthey claims emphatically that the historical process presents itself not as a circle but as a line. This assumption, however, is supported only by the observation that a differentiation of ideas ("Ideen") can be detected by means of historical data. At this point Dilthey brings hermeneutics into play and introduces Schleiermacher into the discussion. After he has discussed the different competing methodological

[30] Clara Misch, ed., Der junge Dilthey. Ein Lebensbild in Briefen und Tagebüchern 1852-1870 (Stuttgart: B.G. Teubner, 1960), p. 92.
[31] Ibid., p. 82.
[32] Ibid., p. 83.

approaches, he writes: "Here is the opinion, the justification of which is one of the main tasks of this investigation, i.e., that the principles of Schleiermacher's hermeneutics offer the first authoritative presentation of the one essential side of the historical method."[33] Although the problem of historiography is raised at first in general terms, it is treated clearly in terms of cultural and intellectual history, for which mechanical positivism is least suited. Before historical laws can be constructed in this area, it is necessary first of all to be certain that we understand the intellectual milieu which presents itself to us in texts. To this extent hermeneutics is the first step for the historian, and one which cannot be ignored. For Dilthey, the methodological understanding of ideas and intellectual systems means always more than the mere reporting of opinions. He is concerned specifically with the "primary original impulses"[34] which give rise to the intellectual systems in question.

Dilthey carries the approach of intellectual history characteristically up to that point at which it finally contradicts the basic assumptions of positivism. He rejects specifically the explanation of intellectual events "from an atomistic mechanism of motives" and demands an understanding "which proceedes from human nature."[35] If, however, the text is taken as the manifestation of human activity and, in the sense of Schleiermacher's hermeneutics, a connection is made between the individuality of the author and the structure of the text, then the question presents itself of how the idea of universal historical coherence, the regularity ("Gesetzmässigkeit") of history, can be maintained in the face of this individualizing approach.

Dilthey recognizes those difficulties inherent in a hermeneutic foundation of the humanities and suggests a combination of hermeneutic and positivistic methods. He demands from the historical method on the one hand that it illuminate a specific work or intellectual system as part of the whole historical process, integrating the specific into the universal law. On the other hand he expects the historical method to enable us to penetrate to the meaning of intellectual statements. For this reason Dilthey remains critical of Schleiermacher, whose philological method is tied too closely to the individual text and its author. He expresses this opinion in his diary in reference to Schleiermacher's interpretation of the New Testament: Schleiermacher's method isolates everything into individualities, understands everything as a closed whole, in its unique composition, in its unique inner form. This method is justified in the realm of art.... The inner law of history, however, demands

---

[33] Ibid., p. 92.
[34] Ibid., p. 93.
[35] Ibid., p. 93.

that continuity be taken with unconditional seriousness."[36] It is remarkable that Dilthey speaks in this passage of inner law and not of mechanical law, thereby at least conceding implicitly that the desired combination of philological hermeneutics and positivism is not without problems of its own. It appears that Idealism was not so easily vanquished as Dilthey had assumed at first under the influence of positivist currents. A diary entry from April, 1861, reveals that Dilthey retains idealist premises in conceptualizing the historical process: "The historical process viewed in general is that the inner characteristics of our moral-intellectual existence as attributes common to many constitute forms of this communality, but that these, like all forms, do not satisfy the generative spirit, which is a progressive infinity, and they rise up against it for different reasons as party and school contradictions."[37] This sentence is undoubtedly nearer to Hegel than Comte; it does not, however, lead back to absolute spirit, but rather to nationalistic history and to comparative anthropology, from which the basic moral-intellectual features are to be derived. This occurs in a form which is already significantly different from the Positivist approach. In 1861 Dilthey distinguishes more clearly than in 1859 between philological-hermeneutic and historic understanding: hermeneutics deals with the individual text as well as its context, while the historical reconstruction is guided in contrast by that point of view which considers the work or philosophical system as a link in "the history of ideas."[38] Dilthey tries to combine both procedures in such a way that they complement each other. The reconstruction of the history of ideas (there is no mention of political history) rests on the preliminary philological work which elucidates the meaning of texts.

We see more clearly now the meaning of Dilthey's censure of rationalistic historiography on grounds of its lack of objectivity. This criticism leads us to hermeneutics as the method through which works can be reconstructed in such a manner that they present themselves a self-evident unity. The meaning extracted from them through interpretation will then, as a second step, be integrated into the history of ideas. In this context the focus shifts for Dilthey in regard to the question of truth. What disturbs Dilthey about liberal historiography is its claim to a direct apprehension of the works and ideas on a moral-political level. These ideas are measured against the goal of history. Dilthey is, however, at the same time more critical in that he sees through the insufficient mediation of the moral approach. At the same time he is less critical in considering the truth of historical knowledge safeguarded through the understanding of texts and the reconstruction of ideas.

[36] Ibid., p. 95.
[37] Ibid., p. 147.
[38] Ibid., p. 151.

Historical tradition, however, is thereby made exempt from critical questioning. Dilthey's turn to political conservatism, which took place according to Bernd Peschken's evidence in 1866,[39] is suggested already on a theoretical level in the Schleiermacher studies and in the earlier statements on hermeneutics. This change is reflected in the diaries in 1865: "The essence ("Wesen") of history is historical movement itself, and if one wants to call this essence purpose, it alone is the purpose of history."[40] In other words, Dilthey shifts the goal of history into history itself--the movement itself is equated with truth, for which works and persons are only signs.

Even the early theoretical treatises refer to history: his essays on Novalis, Lessing, and Goethe, which will appear four decades later and in revised form as the book Das Erlebnis und die Dichtung. Not only Dilthey's selection of authors but also his approach reflect an intense concern with the basic methodological problems of history. Dilthey decides on a biographical approach, without otherwise intending to write biographies. At the same time, however, he conceives these essays as a first attempt at a literary history of the Age of Goethe. This is especially apparent in the methodological deliberations prefacing the Novalis essay, which for the most part were incorporated in Dilthey's inaugural lecture in Basel in 1867. In this lecture--and for this reason it is important to us--Dilthey draws the provisional conclusions suggested by his speculations and applies them to a concrete object, i.e., the history of German literature between 1770 and 1830.

In contrast to older, liberal historiography, Dilthey considers this span of time as a self-contained and unified historical period. "From a sequence of constant historical conditions, there arose in Germany in the last third of the previous century an intellectual movement which ran its closed and uninterrupted course, forming a whole from Lessing up to the death of Schleiermacher and of Hegel."[41] The contents of this conception, very familiar to us today, are combined in the lecture with the basic methodological question of the conditions of historical cognition--but concretely applied to German literature. How is the unity of the period between 1770 and 1830 supported? Dilthey speaks of the impulse "to form a new life ideal" ("Lebensideal").[42] This assumed unity of the period is justified for Dilthey not so much by opinions or works but by the gradual development of a quest for a new world view. Dilthey attributes a specifically German character to this unity. The manner in which he supports this special German position

[39] Peschken, pp. 57-72; also Zockler, pp. 227-239.
[40] Misch, Der junge Dilthey, p. 190.
[41] Dilthey, Gesammelte Schriften, V, p. 13.
[42] Ibid., p. 16.

134

("Sonderstellung") is remarkable. An important argument is taken over from liberal historiography, but its function is changed in such a way as to completely alter its meaning. For Gervinus and Julian Schmidt, Weimar Classicism is characterized by its aloofness toward the political tasks of the German nation or, to exaggerate slightly, by its otherworldliness. Dilthey agrees with this assessment and emphasizes the special position of Germany, contrasting it to the development of England and Spain. In these countries the flowering of literature took place against the background of a flourishing national state. All the great Spanish and English writers formed their material "from the standpoint of a developed national spirit."[43] In Germany, however, this national unity was lacking; there was neither a political nor a cultural center. The German middle class found itself excluded from political participation. Under these conditions, according to Dilthey, cultural life assumes a completely different form: "Thus their total life force ("Lebensdrang"), their total energy in the best years of their ability, is turned inward: personal education ("Bildung"), intellectual distinction become their ideals."[44] Literature, concludes Dilthey, takes the place of political public life.

Gervinus deplored just this tendency in his literary history and called for the politicization of intellectual life. For Dilthey, however, the "German" movement, consisting of three generations, assumes the character of a positive national tradition. Dilthey speaks of a world view in which the German spirit is appeased ("seine Befriedigung finde").[45] Enlightenment, Classicism, and Romanticism appear as three phases of a continuous and uninterrupted development. The selection of representative authors is striking. In his treatment of the Enlightenment Dilthey draws his support almost exclusively from Lessing and ignores writers such as Wieland and Klopstock, since he does not consider their work typical of the spirit of German Enlightenment. It is even more astonishing that the fundamental meaning of Kant for the conceptual penetration of the goals of the Enlightenment is not taken into account. That which gives Lessing precedence over Kant in Dilthey's eyes is his role as a poet, i.e., the advantage of intuitive perception as opposed to the conceptual discourse of the philosopher. Lessing, too, has his place in the latter tradition, i.e., the tradition of Spinoza and Leibniz. "In Lessing Leibniz is delivered of his historical consciousness. From Leibniz' teleological or transcendental position historical phenomena ("Erscheinungen") appear as necessary steps in an evolution, the goal of which is enlightenment and perfection."[46]

[43] Ibid., p. 14.
[44] Ibid., p. 15.
[45] Ibid., p. 13.
[46] Ibid., p. 19.

From this point of view the Enlightenment can only be considered as a preliminary phase of the Age of Goethe, of which the essence, the pantheistic view of nature, is manifested in Goethe himself. The literature of the Enlightenment--and this is what was important in this context--is being depoliticized through selectivity and accentuation. To the same extent the politically motivated criticism of German Classicism made by liberal rationalistic historiography is deflected, for Dilthey attributes necessity, i.e., legitimacy, to the evolution from Storm and Stress to Romanticism. Peschken has pointed out the ideological implications of this conception in discussing Dilthey's Goethe essay of 1871 (conceived in the 1860s). He states that the unity of individual and nature, as emphasized by Dilthey, illuminates "the congruence of monarchist-authoritarian politics with the interests of the Germans" in such a way that political work in parliament becomes of negligible importance.[47] In order to understand this opinion we have to keep the political background in mind. The Prussian victory over Austria in the summer of 1866 sealed the fate of the liberal reform movement in Prussia.[48] As a result of this significant success in foreign affairs Bismarck could ignore the resistance of parliament and insist on his authoritarian political approach as a prerequisite to German unification. In 1866 the majority of German liberals were ready to follow him.[49] Among them was Wilhelm Dilthey.

There is a connection between this political decision and Dilthey's methodological-theoretical deliberations (although he may not have been completely conscious of it). Dilthey's approach based on hermeneutics and the history of ideas, which distances itself critically from the rationalistic literary history of the liberals, anticipates the conservative foundation of the Empire. It is not only the conception of German literary history which is changed here decisively, but also the theory and methodology of this discipline, which is just beginning to win acceptance in German universities. However much Dilthey's point of departure may differ from the positivism of the Scherer school, he arrives at the same results by other paths. Literary history is enlisted in the service of the Second Empire and becomes in the final analysis a science of

---

[47] Peschken, p. 71.

[48] In regard to liberalism in Germany after 1848 see also Theodor Schieder, "Die Krise des bürgerlichen Liberalismus," in Liberalismus, ed. Lothar Gall (Meisenheim: Anton Hain, 1979), pp. 187-207; Rainer Wahl, "Der preußische Verfassungskonflikt und das konstitutionelle System des Kaiserreichs," in Moderne deutsche Verfassungsgeschichte (1815-1918), ed. Ernst Wolf Böckenförde (Cologne: Kiepenhauer and Witsch, 1972), pp. 171-194.

[49] For example Hermann Baumgarten, Der deutsche Liberalismus. Eine Selbstkritik (1866), ed. Adolf M. Birke (Berlin: Ullstein Taschenbuchverlag, 1975).

legitimation. To be sure, this does not happen directly, but rather indirectly, in the form of a critique of liberal literary history exposing the political interests which influenced the perceptions of the liberal literary historians. In the name of objectivity the synthetic constructions of pre-revolutionary historiography are repudiated and replaced by the hermeneutic approach, which affirms tradition.

This intertwining of Romantic hermeneutics with the theory of history, together with the internal support provided the total reconstruction of history by the appropriate understanding of individual works, has already been elucidated in principle by Hans-Georg Gadamer in his chapter on Dilthey. Gadamer, however, draws support primarily from the later writings and fragments. He views Dilthey's efforts as an attempt to formulate an epistemological argument for the epic historicism of a Ranke. "That which was intended to justify his epistemological reflection was basically nothing other than the magnificent epic obliviousness to self of a Ranke."[50] According to Gadamer those problems, left unsolved in early historicism, are taken up by Dilthey and elevated to the level of a problem. In this sense Dilthey is for him a critical successor to objectively inclined historicism--a successor, however, who is not critical enough and therefore finds himself finally ensnared by objectivism as a result of the manner in which he poses his problem.

Gadamer's approach, however, hides the fact that Dilthey does not want simply to understand all aspects of the past, but rather very probably had specific ideas in terms of content about what should be preserved from the past. Gadamer's own traditionalism makes him blind to the manner in which history and literary history are determined through selectivity and accentuation. It escapes him that understanding benefited certain objective social interests, i.e., the ruling class. The acquisition of tradition is more than understanding--it is an act of selective reconstruction, through which social dominance is also confirmed indirectly. This side of Dilthey, which becomes visible immediately through a comparison of his conception with that of pre-revolutionary historiography, is suppressed by Gadamer when he writes: Dilthey "knows himself to stand in a relation of critical self-consciousness to himself and to the tradition in which he has his place. He understands himself in terms of his history. Historical consciousness is a means of self-recognition."[51] Here Gadamer treats historical consciousness as something merely contemplative and overlooks the insoluble connection between the critical consciousness of a tradition no longer accepted as given and the problem of how this tradition should be appropriated. Dilthey decided methodologically as well as in terms

[50] Gadamer, Wahrheit und Methode (Tübingen: J.C.B. Mohr, 1960), p. 218.
[51] Ibid., p. 211.

137

of content against the conception of literary tradition which was offered him by pre-revolutionary historiography, because it lacked scientific objectivity. The concept of objectivity, which in Gadamer's presentation is perceived only on the level of theory and method, is charged with meaning after 1880 on the level of content also--although this was of course never stated explicitly. The power of post-revolutionary rhetoric lies in its letting those interests which dominate the level of content disappear behind the epistemological apparatus.

Gadamer places the emphasis in his critique of Dilthey on the fact that Dilthey took over hermeneutics from Schleiermacher and declared it to constitute the basis of historical recognition. In this way history was reduced to a text. This criticism is justified, but does not suffice to vitiate Dilthey's approach. The early Dilthey is thoroughly aware that hermeneutics cannot solve all the tasks of the historian. The process of historical continuity, the chain of ideas, could not be safeguarded in this way. Where more far-reaching relationships are to be grasped, understanding has to give way to reconstruction.

The later Dilthey retains also the idea of universal historical coherence into which that which is individual can be integrated. He uses the Hegelian concept of objective spirit in order to make the presence of structures recognizable. In the objective spirit history transcends the subjective relation of experience, expression, and understanding, which for Dilthey lies at the base of the hermeneutic process. "Under it (the objective spirit) I understand the manifold forms in which that communality which obtains among individuals has objectified itself in the world of the senses. In this objective spirit the past is for us a lasting and permanent present. Its territory extends from the style of life, the forms of intercourse, to the complex of purposes which society constructed for itself, to morality, justice, the state, religion, art, science and philosophy.... From this world of the objective spirit our self receives from earliest childhood onward its nourishment."[52] Dilthey calls attention to the fact that the historical understanding is certainly affected by the researcher's being a part of this complex. Just this insight, however, makes him, when reflecting on his method, blind to the categorical distinction between the individual and the whole, so that he wants to justify the reconstruction of the whole (totality) on the basis of the experiencing understanding. He argues: "The principles of study of history cannot be formulated in abstract sentences which express equations. They must be based by nature of their object on relationships justified by experi-

[52] Dilthey, Gesammelte Schriften, VII, p. 208.

ence. In experience is the totality of our being ("Wesen"). It is just this totality which we reconstruct in our understanding."[53]

That Dilthey was not satisfied with these deliberations is revealed in those passages where he comes to speak of the formulation of historical concepts. Dilthey is aware that experience ("Erleben") is not sufficient as a basis of knowledge in the face of historical tradition. Tradition consists of remains, of documents from past life, from which the historian, to the best of his ability, reconstructs this past life. The explication of these remains is the art of interpretation, "a hermeneutic art."[54] Here the problem of concept formation arises. In Dilthey's words: "The problem is that of what form it (hermeneutics) assumes, when statements are to be made about subjects which in some sense are aggregates of individuals--cultural systems, nations, or states."[55] Dilthey demands a rational rather than a merely intuitive solution to the problem and in so doing aligns himself with the idealism of a Fichte and a Hegel. He diverges, however, from the method of concept formation in the philosophy of identity, for this philosophy distinguishes according to Dilthey between the logic of cognition and historical reality. Dilthey, in contrast, seeks concepts which proceed from the historical reality itself. He then adds the qualification that just these concepts cannot be reduced to the experience of a single individual. Thus Dilthey sees himself obliged to distinguish between logical and psychological subjects, in other words, to distinguish between experiencing and reconstructive understanding. Dilthey clouds these distinctions again immediately, however, by attempting to justify logical subjects on the basis of individual experiences.[56]

Gadamer's critique of Dilthey leads us finally to the point where a connection can be made between the situation existing during the sixties of the past century and that of the present. It is not a matter of a superficial parallel, but rather of inherited problems. What is the attitude of the historian toward tradition? After Dilthey, historical self-consciousness cannot escape this question. Gadamer poses the problem for himself in a renewed attempt to justify the legitimacy of tradition and authority through a philosophical hermeneutics. In this connection Dilthey is assigned the role of a precursor who has not yet freed himself entirely from orthodox Cartesianism. Gadamer's hermeneutics is conceived as a critique of the critical Enlightenment, as a repudiation of a theory which denounces preconceptions, since such reason has proved to be destructive of that tradition necessary for life. In the concept of the Classical, Gadamer finds an anchor for the historical conscious-

[53] Ibid., p. 278.
[54] Ibid., p. 280.
[55] Ibid., p. 280.
[56] See also ibid., pp. 283 and 311.

ness, for this consciousness encounters here not merely the past as concept, but rather a living force, to which posterity can turn again and again. This is, however, just the situation with which Dilthey has attempted to come to terms critically, i.e., the search for a binding cultural tradition which can serve the future as well as the present as a model. Just as the young Dilthey turns away from liberalism in 1866 in disillusion and places his political hopes in the Prussian state, Gadamer tries again a hundred years later to dismiss the radical Hegelianism of the eighteen-forties as a deviation from tradition.[57]

That a cultural tradition can no longer be taken for granted and that it is not merely the details but the concept of tradition itself which has become problematic in industrial and post-industrial societies--these observations belong to the basic insights of the Critical Theory. For Jürgen Habermas the decline of cultural tradition derives essentially from modern social-historical developments which result from the construction of capitalist social systems. This process is irreversible in principle. To this extent the reconquest of tradition, the insistence that the great cultural achievements of the past are always at our disposal and can be made our own, is an illusion. This illusion becomes an ideology when it makes unsupported claims concerning the relevance of the Classical. The position which Gadamer concedes to tradition is no longer acceptable to Habermas. This difference is expressed in terms of the theory of knowledge ("wissenschaftstheoretisch") in Habermas' delineation of the boundaries which separate not only the natural sciences but also the social sciences from the humanities.[58] The humanities ("Geisteswissenschaften") are withdrawn from the context of the social sciences. A narrower epistemological goal is assigned to them, i.e., the self-conscious renewal of cultural tradition. This decision influences the manner in which he treats Dilthey in two ways: in the first place, Dilthey's hermeneutics is limited from the beginning to the humanities--its inappropriateness for the social sciences has, in Habermas' view, already been established--and in the second place Habermas considers the idea of knowledge as dialogue to be Dilthey's essential problem. In other words, Habermas shifts the aspect of communication into the center of the discussion as the essential concern of Dilthey's hermeneutics. "The hermeneutic sciences are embedded in interreactions conveyed by idiomatic language to the same extent that the

---

[57] See also Zockler, pp. 131-139, especially p. 138.
[58] Presented systematically for the first time in the Frankfurt inaugural lecture of 1965, reprinted in: Habermas, Technik und Wissenschaft als "Ideologie" (Frankfurt am Main: Suhrkamp, 1968), pp. 146-168. (English version in Knowledge and Human Interest, tr. Jeremy J. Shapiro (Boston: Beacon Press, 1971), pp. 301-317.)

empirical-analytical sciences are embedded in the circle of functions of instrumental action."[59] The task of hermeneutics is thus, according to Habermas, the safeguarding of the intersubjectivity of communication in speaking and acting (practice).

In this respect Habermas' attitude toward Dilthey is positive. Dilthey's attempt to protect the humanities against the positivism of the natural sciences he considers legitimate and in need of further development. This takes place in Habermas' work through a consciousness of those interests affecting knowledge on the practical level. Following Gadamer, Habermas takes issue with Dilthey only at that point at which he suspects a misunderstanding of methodology on Dilthey's part. Dilthey's efforts to justify the objectivity of the humanities he regards as a misguided attempt which resulted in the final analysis from Dilthey's making concessions again to the positivism of his times. Dilthey constructs an opposition between the scientific-theoretical and the practical tasks of the researcher, between generally valid objectivity and subjective predisposition.[60] This opposition he considers as a insoluble problem inherent in his approach. Habermas questions just this limitation, however, and calls attention to the distinct interests which affect knowledge in the natural and human sciences. Referring to Dilthey he says: "Just as did Peirce, Dilthey remains in the end under the sway of positivism to the extent that he abandons the self-consciousness which characterizes the humanities just at that point at which practical interest in knowing is perceived as the possible foundation of hermeneutic knowing, rather than its corruption, after which he falls back into objectivism."[61]

Habermas' objection, not unlike Gadamer's, is made on the methodological and metatheoretical level. What Dilthey understands by tradition in terms of content, how he interprets the history of German literature, for example, becomes invisible. It should be remembered that Dilthey in the 1860s does not assume that the presentation of larger historical connections can be justified only by hermeneutics. The explication of the individual work is subject to hermeneutic rules, while the historical processes through which the works are related to one another are to be reconstructed as chains of ideas. Habermas is justified in criticizing Dilthey's model of identification ("Einfühlung"), by means of which the role of dialogue in the integration of past works into the personal world view of the reader is to be emphasized. Meanwhile he overlooks the other task of the historian, i.e., the production of a connection among individual works and authors. Habermas' hermeneutics as

[59] Habermas, Erkenntnis und Interesse (Frankfurt am Main: Suhrkamp, 1973), p. 221.

[60] Dilthey, Gesammelte Schriften, VII, p. 165.

[61] Habermas, Erkenntnis und Interesse, p. 225.

dialogue isolates the works as discrete objects with which the reader must come to terms.

This aspect of Habermas' hermeneutics reflects the concern of the late Dilthey, who in the treatise on the origin of hermeneutics speaks in 1900 of the coherence of the whole human past and raises explicitly the understanding of the single instance as the basis of any systematic knowledge aspiring to general validity.[62] In other passages Dilthey returns, as we have shown, to the strategy of the sixties. He uses the concept of coherence of effects ("Wirkungszusammenhang") in order to clarify the problem of historical connection. It is this problem which the historian encounters in moving from the explication of the single work to the illumination of a process or an epoch. The later Dilthey no longer thinks of this coherence of effects as causality, but rather as the formation of a total force ("Totalkraft")[63] which elects and determines all discrete events within a specific epoch.

Habermas implies that Dilthey has made the hermeneutic basis so general that he wants to derive historiography as well as systematic structural sciences from it. He objects consequently that Dilthey has overtaxed hermeneutics and does not do justice to the requirements of the systematic humanities. Habermas argues: "For the systematic humanities the methodological foundation of the historical humanities (i.e., hermeneutics) is obviously too narrow."[64] It does not seem to me to be entirely clear, however, that the later Dilthey wants to entrust the study of history or for that matter that of the systematic cultural sciences (philosophy, jurisprudence, political theory) exclusively to hermeneutics. Alongside the well known passages to which Habermas refers there are other remarks which suggest a pluralistic procedure.

Those concerns which persist for Dilthey into the eighties are clearly expressed in his eulogy for Julian Schmidt (1887). In reviewing Schmidt's development Dilthey detects a significant change of approach after the year 1866. He connects this change with political events, i.e., the victory of Prussia over Austria and the increasing attractiveness of a political solution excluding Austria from the "Reich." The possibility of national unification gave literary history a new perspective. In Dilthey's words: "The standpoint of our conception of our modern literature changed again completely when in 1866 the nation, the unity of which had lain till then in its intellectual life, became a political whole. Now the creative meaning of our great literature for our national state also became clearer. There was now more sympathy for that which men

---

[62] Dilthey, Gesammelte Schriften, VII, pp. 317ff.
[63] Ibid., p. 165.
[64] Habermas, Erkenntnis und Interesse, p. 232.

such as Kant, Schiller, and especially Herder had done in this respect."[65] The mature Dilthey finds Schmidt's literary history superior to that of Gervinus because it makes "the coherence of our national formation" recognizable, while he considered Gervinus to have offered only literary vignettes.[66] This surprising judgment, which is all too inclined to take the late works of Schmidt at face value, contains a good bit of projection on Dilthey's part. In 1887 Dilthey still identifies with the shift to national liberalism of 1866, which cut the ground from beneath rationalistic literary history. He desires the accommodation of German literary history to national unification under the sign of conservative Prussian hegemony. In the final analysis the consciousness of method ("Methoden-reflexion") serves this conception of the formation of a German nation.

Dilthey clarifies this context again in his reference to Wilhelm Scherer. In his eulogy for this contemporary he is able to project himself to an even greater degree into the other's situation and give at the same time a sketch of his own goals.

Even Scherer's biography--the fact that the native Austrian cast his lot with Prussia and Berlin and lamented the loss of the German tradition in the Austrian state--becomes meaningful here.[67] Although it is clear to Dilthey that his methodology differs from that of Scherer, he finds connections and parallels nevertheless--especially in respect to their conception of a national tradition. The philological training which Scherer received from the older Germanists joins with contemporary positivism to form the methodological foundation of modern literary history: on the one hand the method of the natural sciences characterized by causal derivation and comparison, on the other the contribution of philological criticism. Dilthey describes this synthesis in the following terms: "The rigorous linguistic and metric observation and the different levels of criticism founded upon it, as developed by German philology and applied to the monuments of our antiquity. All this he applied to works of modern literature.... The aesthetic categories of the Idealist school are exhausted; our current treatises on aesthetics and on the history of art reveal one basic tendency: the desire to understand the contemplation of works of art and to grasp their aesthetic value by means of the synthetic techniques employed within a single art form."[68] The parallel to Dilthey expresses also quite clearly that which justifies the method. It serves to safeguard the meaning of German literary history which Dilthey found developed in Scherer's presentation. While Dilthey remarks on the

[65] Dilthey, Gesammelte Schriften, XI, p. 235.
[66] Ibid., p. 236.
[67] See also ibid., p. 241.
[68] Ibid., p. 250.

methodological differences between Scherer and himself, his reaction toward Scherer's analysis of the content of German literature is basically positive, for this analysis emphasizes the evolution of the German national spirit. In the emphatic formulation of the eulogy: "Scherer appeared predestined to represent scientifically the immortal function of poetry in the life of the nation in the midst of the material and political interests of our times, in contemporary Berlin,"[69] a mission with which Wilhelm Dilthey could well identify!

[69] Ibid., p. 253.

SIMULTANEOUS FUTURES AND THE BERLIN AVANT-GARDE

John H. Zammito

The catastrophic event of the Great War of 1914-1918 presented literary intellectuals in Germany with a decisive challenge. This essay explores the effort of the Berlin avant-garde to develop a coherent vision of the world which could provide not only a sense of identity and solidarity among themselves after the debacle of the war, but also serve to mobilize and guide the larger society around them.[1] Finding a basis upon which to build and to discriminate, which could allow for both artistic and social hope, proved a desperate enterprise. The Great War had devastated every conventional foundation. During the years 1914-1923, one word more than any other came to be applied by German participants and by later interpreters: the word Zusammenbruch. The Great War had induced a systemic collapse of massive proportions in Germany.[2]

---

[1] In this essay I present some of the results of a longer study, Simultaneous Futures: Americanism and Bolshevism in the Berlin Avant-Garde, 1917-1932. I wish to express my gratitude to the Social Science Research Council, the German Academic Exchange Service and the Mabelle McLeod Lewis Memorial Foundation for their generous assistance in the pursuit of this study.

[2] Obviously, in the compass of this brief essay it is impossible to do justice to the complexity of the war's impact on Germany. The abbreviated summary which follows is founded upon my forthcoming larger study and the major secondary interpretations upon which it leans. See in particular: Jürgen Kocka, Klassengesellschaft im Kriege: deutsche Sozialgeschichte 1914-1918 (Göttingen: Vandenhoeck and Ruprecht, 1973); Gerald Feldman, Army, Industry and Labor in Germany 1914-1918 (Princeton: Princeton University Press, 1966); Eberhard Kolb, Arbeiterräte in der deutschen Innenpolitik, 1918-1919 (Düsseldorf: Droste, 1962); Peter von Örtzen, Betriebsräte in der Novemberrevolution (Düsseldorf: Droste, 1963); Ulrich Kluge, Soldatenräte und Revolution (Göttingen: Vandenhoeck and Ruprecht, 1975); Gerald Feldman, Eberhard Kolb and Reinhard Rürup, "Die Massenbewegungen der Arbeiterschaft in Deutschland am Ende des Ersten Weltkrieges (1917-1920)," Politische Vierteljahrsschrift 13, No. 1 (1972); and Eberhard Kolb,

The Germans had not only lost the war; they believed they had also lost their traditional forms of government, their economic stability, their socio-economic status structures, their cultural and moral security. The war experience corroded the moral fibre and sapped the physical energy of the nation. Censorship deceived Germans at home (and even in some measure on the front) regarding the dire straits of the situation, so that the plea for armistice in October 1918, which culminated in revolution, came as such a shock that it utterly discredited the established government. That was the occasion for the term Zusammenbruch--the collapse of governmental legitimacy from October to November, 1918. Yet the Zusammenbruch was not simply a loss of faith in former leaders; it proved far more to be a dissolution of societal institutions. German society lost orientation in the course of events.

Initially, this disorientation was forestalled for some, in that new hopes fanned by the Russian Revolution and by Wilson's Fourteen Points gave some measure of significance to the Zusammenbruch.[3] It could be construed as a revolution. That conception proved fruitless, however, as the revolution misfired. It is striking how those who spoke in terms of "revolution" in November 1918 came to speak in terms of Zusammenbruch shortly thereafter.[4]

ed., Vom Kaiserreich zur Weimarer Republik (Cologne: Kiepenhauer and Witsch, 1972).

[3] The major histories of the German revolutionary council movement of 1917-1920 cited above are available only in German and deserve English translation. For those without German, there have recently emerged a series of penetrating English-language studies, foremost among them David Morgan's The Socialist Left and the German Revolution (Ithaca: Cornell University Press, 1975) and the first parts of Charles Maier's broader Recasting Bourgeois Europe (Englewood Cliffs, N.J.: Prentice-Hall, 1975). For a stimulating presentation of current historiographical positions, see Charles Bertrand, ed., Revolutionary Situations in Europe, 1917-1922: Germany, Italy, Austria-Hungary (Montreal: Interuniversity Center for European Studies, 1977).

[4] A case in point is Philipp Scheidemann, the man who declared Germany a republic amid revolutionary fanfare in November 1918, but whose memoirs recapitulated the events under the rubric of Zusammenbruch. The pioneer historian of the revolution and the Republic, Arthur Rosenberg, presented a penetrating account of this shift in language. The events in Germany in 1918-1919 were an embarrassment for real revolutionaries, since they did not go far enough, and a disgrace for conservative republicans, since they muddled the constitutional transition from the war government to the new Republic. There was no one to preserve the memory or the meaning of the German Revolution. See Rosenberg's A History of the German Republic, tr. Ian F.D. Morrow and L. Marie Sieveking

Utopian aspirations projected onto the subsequent peace from the depths of wartime deprivation had been dashed. Disillusionment intensified when the terms of the Versailles Treaty were announced in May 1919. The economic complications of that settlement caused Germans to undergo an even more debilitating inflation through 1923.[5] Fortunes were lost, futures foreclosed, customs of a lifetime forsaken. Zusammenbruch meant pervasive disorientation in German society. That disorientation was mirrored by the literary intellectuals, who felt the additional desperate burden that it was precisely their responsibility to find an orientation, to make sense of the chaos, not only for themselves but for society.

With very few exceptions, avant-garde artists and intellectuals in Germany prior to the First World War had developed little political consciousness.[6] At most, they played at "literary politics." Yet the clarion call to political responsibility had been given in 1910 in Heinrich Mann's key essay "Spirit and Deed."[7] For Heinrich Mann, the relation of the artist to democracy was the great issue of the day. The times demanded that intellectuals "become agitators, align themselves with the people against authority" and "support the people's struggle with all their eloquence." But the initial enthusiasm with which the young generation of Expressionists flocked into the ranks in August 1914 belies any serious grasp of Mann's message. Only the war, which harrowed the spirit of Expressionism and robbed it of many of its greatest voices, awakened the avant-garde to political matters. Only then did "engaged" anti-war Expressionism arise. It centered around key literary

(London: Methuen, 1936), and Reinhard Rürup, "Problems of the German Revolution of 1918-1919," Journal of Contemporary History 3, No. 4 (1961).

[5] The social impact of the inflation was captured in what remains the classic account by Franz Eulenburg, "Die sozialen Wirkungen der Währungsverhältnisse," Jahrbücher für Nationalökonomie und Statistik 67, No. 3 (1924), pp. 748-794. For recent historical interpretations of this complex event, see Gerald Feldman, Iron and Steel in the German Inflation (Princeton: Princeton University Press, 1977) and the proceedings of the conference on the German inflation held in Berlin, Summer, 1976: Historische Prozesse der deutschen Inflation, ed. Gerald Feldman and Otto Busch (Berlin: Colloquium Verlag, 1978).

[6] See, for example, the two works which trace the activation of political commitment in the German Expressionist avant-garde: Eva Kolinsky's Engagierter Expressionismus (Stuttgart: J.B. Metzler, 1970); and Friedrich Albrecht, Deutsche Schriftsteller in der Entscheidung (Berlin: Aufbau Verlag, 1970).

[7] First published in the journal Das Forum in 1910, and reprinted in W. Rothe, ed., Der Aktivismus 1915-1920 (Munich: Deutscher Taschenbuchverlag, 1969), pp. 23ff.

journals: Franz Pfemfert's Die Aktion, René Schickele's Die Weissen Blätter, Wilhelm Herzog's Das Forum, Kurt Hiller's
Ziel-Jahrbücher, and Wieland Herzfelde's Neue Jugend.

Expressionism swiftly refracted into a spectrum of responses
under the trauma of the war. At least three main directions of
response seem discernible. First, horror, pathos and an explicitly
religious fervor for redemption pervaded much of Expressionist literature in the war years. The poetry of Alfred Ehrenstein and
Franz Werfel, or Leonhard Frank's novel, Der Mensch ist gut,
exemplify this direction.[8] The increasingly ecstatic and aesthetically limp poetry of late Expressionism, the poetry of "O Mensch"
and exclamation points, belongs in this line.[9] A second line reacted
more violently to the violence, more destructively to the
destruction. The realization that "culture" had done nothing to
prevent the carnage of war, the betrayal of popular rights and the
violation of basic human dignity, but had in fact served to instigate
or legitimize these things, provoked rage, bitterness and hatred
and gave rise to Berlin Dada.[10] Third, there emerged a disillusioned sobriety bordering on cynicism which took the measure both
of the soaring hopes for redemption of the one and the total misan-
thropic nihilism of the other line of avant-garde reaction and sought
to find a posture of lucidity which avoided their excesses.

[8] For a particularly clear statement of this religious orientation
by one of its major proponents, see Franz Werfel, "Die christliche
Sendung: Offener Brief an Kurt Hiller," Tätiger Geist. Zieljahrbuch II (Munich: G. Müller, 1918).
[9] The classic anthology of Expressionist poetry, Menschheitsdämmerung, edited by Werfel's close friend Kurt Pinthus, is
thronged with such poetry. Originally published in early 1920
(Berlin: Rowohlt), it has been reprinted (Hamburg: Rowohlt,
1960).
[10] There are several accounts of Berlin Dada, of which two articles by J.C. Middleton are of particular note: "Dada versus
Expressionism or the Red King's Dream," German Life and Letters
15, No. 1 (1961), and "'Bolshevism in Art': Dada and Politics,"
Texas Studies in Literature and Language 4, No. 3 (1962). The
classic locus for the spirit of nihilism in Berlin Dada is the work of
George Grosz--both visual and verbal. See Das Gesicht der herrschenden Klasse (Berlin: Malik, 1921) for the visual side, and "Die
Kunst ist in Gefahr," in D. Schmidt, ed., Manifeste, Manifeste
(Dresden: Verlag der Kunst, 1965) for a verbal statement. Rich-
ard Huelsenbeck's En avant Dada, reprinted in R. Motherwell, ed.,
The Dada Painters and Poets: An Anthology (New York: Witten-
born, Schultz, 1951), and Walter Mehring's Berlin Dada (Zurich:
Verlag der Arche, 1959) round out the picture of the Berlin circle.

Intellectual sanity required that the war and its costs have some meaning, that all the horror not have been in vain. For many, the Russian Revolution gave the sense of world-historical meaning to the carnage. As the novelist Alfred Döblin put it, the revolution meant that the war, despite its malignancy, did have a rational outcome: it brought the old order to dissolution; it opened the epoch of revolution and the reorganization of human affairs along lines of social justice.[11] The Russian Revolution accentuated all three strains of Berlin avant-garde response to the war experience. For the ecstatic-religious strain, the Russian Revolution crystallized the chiliastic impulses and raised them to feverish heights.[12] In the ranks of Berlin Dada, the response was equally to amplify the position already taken. When Richard Huelsenbeck proclaimed "Dada is German Bolshevism," he was asserting that Bolshevism, like Dada, embraced nihilism, that both aimed to dispel all lingering remnants of the "swindle" of European civilization. Since this conflation reinforced the old-European dread of Bolshevism as a new barbarism, Dada gave plausibility to the conservative notion of "cultural bolshevism."

It remains clear that such "Bolshevism" had little to do either with events in Russia or with Leninist theories. Still, for the entire avant-garde it made the question of the political redemption of the war central and aggravated. The introduction of the idea of "Bolshevism"--either as "dictatorship of the proletariat" or as cultural nihilism--shattered the apparent solidarity of anti-war Expressionism and in the wake of the Zusammenbruch produced a polarization into hostile camps. Prior to the war, Marxism had not been a significant force in avant-garde circles. They had been far more taken with anarchism.[13] But the war and the Russian Revolution changed all that. The editor of the great Expressionist journal Die Aktion, Franz Pfemfert, perhaps the most important leader of anti-war Expressionism, turned to Marxism, to Bolshevism, and ultimately to left-extremist Proletkult, over the

---

[11] Alfred Döblin, "Es ist Zeit," in Die Neue Rundschau, reprinted in Schriften zur Politik und Gesellschaft, vol. 15 of Ausgewählte Werke, ed. Walter Muschg (Freiburg: Walter Verlag, 1960ff).

[12] A work which is infused with this spirit is Ernst Bloch's classic Geist der Utopie (Munich and Leipzig: Duncker and Humblot, 1918; rpt. Frankfurt am Main: Suhrkamp, 1971).

[13] See, for instance, H.E. Jacob's memoir of pre-war Berlin Expressionism and the journal Die Aktion: "Communism? Not a bit of it. But anarchism, pacifism, anti-authoritarianism, and anti-militarism. How the young poets were attracted by this!" reprinted in P. Raabe, ed., The Era of Expressionism, tr. J.M. Ritchie (London: Calder and Boyers, 1974), p. 18.

course of the war and the Zusammenbruch.[14] He demanded the "dictatorship of the proletariat," sole rule by workers-and-soldiers-councils, and the exclusion not only of the bourgeoisie but of the collaborationist Social Democrats from the governing alliance of a new socialist republic in Germany.[15]

If Pfemfert and the Dadaists embraced "Bolshevism," others in the avant-garde repudiated it just as swiftly. Most prominent in this repudiation was the editor of another great anti-war Expressionist journal, René Schickele of Die Weissen Blätter.[16] For Schickele, the Bolsheviks represented the "cossacks of socialism," imbued with the same militarism and violence as the warmongers. Red praetorians, he feared, would merely displace white. "I am a socialist," he wrote. "But if I were persuaded that socialism could be realized only by Bolshevik methods, I--and not I alone--would renounce its realization."[17] This dread of Bolshevism was shared by writers for Die Weltbühne like Siegfried Jacobsohn, Willy Wolfradt and Kurt Tucholsky.[18]

Most anti-Bolsheviks opted for "idealism." For the religious-utopian Expressionist, "Humanity" had become so manifestly sacrosanct in the wake of the war that human brotherhood displaced politics and it sufficed to cry "O Mensch!" Others in this "idealist" camp argued that any political compromise would only sully the moral integrity of opposition, and ruin the hope for a just world. Finally, on this "idealist" side were intellectual megalomani-

[14] On Pfemfert see: P. Raabe, ed., Ich schneide die Zeit aus: Expressionismus in Franz Pfemferts 'Aktion' (Munich: Deutscher Taschenbuchverlag, 1964) as well as his "Einführung und Kommentar" for the reprint of the journal Die Aktion. See also Lothar Peter, Literarische Intelligenz und Klassenkampf: 'Die Aktion' 1911-1932 (Cologne: Pahl-Rugenstein, 1972).
[15] For these particular positions, see Pfemfert's manifestos: "Freunde, Kameraden der Aktion!" Die Aktion 8, No. 41/42 (1918); "Aufruf der Antinationalen Sozialistischen Partei Gruppe Deutschland," and "Soldaten! Kameraden der A.S.P.! Freunde der Aktion!" Die Aktion 8, No. 45/46 (1918); "Nationalversammlung ist Konterrevolution!" Die Aktion 8, No. 49/50 (1918).
[16] On Schickele, see Albrecht, Deutsche Schriftsteller in der Entscheidung, pp. 88ff.
[17] René Schickele, "Revolution, Bolschewismus und Ideal," Die Weissen Blätter 5, No. 6 (1918), p. 125.
[18] See Weltbühne 14, No. 47 (1918) for comments from Jacobsohn and Wolfradt. On them and on Tucholsky, see István Deák, Weimar Germany's Left-Wing Intellectuals: A Political History of the Weltbühne and Its Circle (Berkeley: University of California Press, 1968).

acs like Kurt Hiller and his Rat der geistigen Arbeiter.[19] All the excesses of Berlin Dada on the line of Bolshevism are paralleled in the excesses of idealism in Hiller's enterprises. In the zany days of early 1919 it was sometimes hard to tell which of these two factions produced the more fantastic manifestos.

To plunge to either extreme proved sterile. Pfemfert's left-radicalism whirled him off through a series of splinter groups into obscurity and impotence.[20] Berlin Dada disintegrated in short order.[21] Schickele and Hiller, with their idealistic humanism and intellectual elitism, lost touch with the realities just as swiftly.[22] By 1920 the avant-garde was clearly verging on collapse. All the major Expressionist journals had ceased publication or lost their élan. Critics proclaimed the death of Expressionism.[23] The impasse of the extremes forces our attention back upon the third line, that of disillusioned sobriety, as the last hope for viability in the avant-garde.

A few Berlin intellectuals found themselves between the competing polarities of intellectual megalomania and Proletkult anti-intellectualism. In the wake of the botched revolution of

[19] On Kurt Hiller and his Rat der geistigen Arbeiter, see the program of the Rat, reprinted in Albrecht, Deutsche Schriftsteller in der Entscheidung, pp. 497ff.; Kurt Hiller, "Geist werde Herr!" reprinted in P. Pörtner, ed., Literaturrevolution 1910-1925 (Darmstadt: Luchterhand, 1960); the four volumes of Hiller's Zieljahrbücher, 1916-1920 (I and II: Munich: G. Müller, 1916, 1918; III and IV: Leipzig: K. Wolff, 1919, 1920); and Hiller's autobiography, Leben gegen die Zeit (Hamburg: Rowohlt, 1969ff).
[20] See Peter, Literarische Intelligenz und Klassenkampf. The decline of Die Aktion is reflected in the increasingly sectarian monologue of the volumes after 1920. Pfemfert had lost completely the leadership of the Berlin avant-garde.
[21] The last event of Berlin Dada was the great Dada Messe of 1920, and by then the circle was already disintegrating. Huelsenbeck and Hausmann went their separate ways. Franz Jung, another stalwart, hijacked a German freighter and went to Soviet Russia. The Grosz circle abandoned the artistic effrontery of Dada for a humorless prosecution of Proletkult.
[22] Hiller's Rat der geistigen Arbeiter collapsed in early 1919 as even within the avant-garde his megalomania provoked distaste. See Siegfried Jacobsohn's comment upon withdrawing his journal, Die Weltbühne, from affiliation with Hiller's Rat: "Antworten," Die Weltbühne 14, No. 50 (1918). As for Schickele, his Die Weissen Blätter ceased publication in 1920.
[23] See the critical pronouncements reprinted in P. Raabe, ed., Expressionismus: Der Kampf um eine literarische Bewegung (Munich: Deutscher Taschenbuchverlag, 1965).

1918-1919, political integrity required unequivocal rejection of the regime, while intellectual integrity required independence of judgment, the refusal to suspend criticism for the sake of tactical or organizational considerations. Under the circumstances the middle was a desperate position. The third leading editor of wartime Expressionism, Wilhelm Herzog of Das Forum, took this position, and he spelled out its dilemma: "Because one struggles (not simply on ideal, but also on real-political grounds) for purity in political life, against shameful compromises with the bearers of the old regime--what is one called because of this? A Bolshevik."[24] By the right they were labelled "Bolsheviks" for their political commitment, but by the party-line Communists and the left-extremist Proletkult, they were condemned as either elitists or opportunists for their independence. For themselves these intellectuals could establish only a minimal identity: they saw themselves compelled to a general negativism.

Negativism meant commitment to radical change; it meant intellectual criticism and autonomy. It meant insistence upon the necessity of destroying the old regime, and suspicion and hostility towards the traditions of bourgeois Europe. It was politically radical and aesthetically avant-garde. But what it lacked was the confidence of imminent political victory. It could not accept the cadre-like Bolshevik Party with its putschist and authoritarian propensities, nor could it retain faith in the spontaneous revolutionary potential of the masses in the face of the betrayal of socialist leadership and the brutal employment of counter-revolutionary force. In addition to reassignation there remained only remonstrance: constant, abrasive criticism designed to stir up, convert and mobilize the progressive forces in German society. Kurt Tucholsky's essay, "Wir Negativen," March 1919, was the paradigmatic expression of this stance of negativism. In it, Tucholsky rejected the criticisms voiced in several quarters that the Weltbühne circle did nothing but criticize and found nothing positive about the German situation. For Tucholsky, that was simply because there was indeed nothing to affirm. "We know only one thing: that we must sweep away with an iron broom all that is rotten in Germany."[25]

Perhaps the most brilliant representation of this negativism came in Alfred Döblin's powerful essay of May 1920, "The German Masquerade," where he wrote:

[24] Wilhelm Herzog, "Besinnt Euch!" editorial in Republik, reprinted in Das Forum 3, No. 3 (1918), p. 186.
[25] Kurt Tucholsky, "Wir Negativen," Die Weltbühne 15, No. 12 (1919), reprinted in his Gesammelte Werke, ed. Mary Gerold-Tucholsky and Fritz J. Raddatz (Hamburg: Rowohlt, 1960ff), Vol. I., p. 376.

And then there was a republic....One didn't know
what to make of it....Five minutes before the thing
was set up, the country was monarchist. Monarchist to the bone....It is one of the most important
tasks of the Republic not to rub the monarchists
wrong, especially if they are military. For,...the
Republic was brought into the Holy Roman Empire
by a wise man from abroad. He didn't say what to
do with it; it was a Republic without directions for
use. The military could smash it up, and then
what would one have left?[26]

A Republic whose greatest responsibility was to be inoffensive to
monarchists and militarists: German democracy seemed merely dictatorship in masquerade. Everywhere the war had produced bitterness and dissension. The front-line soldiers felt disgust with the
homeland to which they returned. The working class fragmented
into so many little sects. Germany was not ready for a republic in
1918. In the aftermath of the Kapp-Putsch of March 1920, Döblin
dispensed with optimism and settled in for a guerilla war of words.
"Weakness, thy name is democracy," he wrote.[27]

Yet it remains that he was committed to democracy. For Döblin
democracy was not a matter of institutions or constitutions. He
denied the existence of "universal constitutions for all
peoples..."[28] A democratic government was one which promoted
the independent decision-making of the masses. By the masses, he
meant all those who had been excluded from political affairs, all
those who had been mere subordinates (Untertanen) in German
authoritarianism. His great concern was for the growth and
self-discovery of these masses. As he put it:

> The industrialization of the earth has had as its
> consequence a fantastic concentration of masses,
> orgies of organization. The concentrating masses,
> despite organizational centralization, become ever
> more forcefully the masters of their situation
> through their very massiveness and their partic-
> ular conductivity. Anonymity is on the rise.[29]

---

[26] Alfred Döblin, "Der deutsche Maskenball" (1920), reprinted in
Der deutsche Maskenball von Linke Poot. Wissen und Verändern!,
vol. 14 in Ausgewählte Werke, p. 100.
[27] Alfred Döblin, "Neue Jugend" (1922), reprinted in Schriften
zur Politik und Gesellschaft, p. 215-215.
[28] Döblin, Der deutsche Maskenball von Linke Poot, p. 275.
[29] Döblin, "Überfliessend von Ekel" (1920), in Der deutsche
Maskenball von Linke Poot, p. 277.

Döblin's model for mass democracy was derived from Walt Whitman's portrayal of American populism. On several occasions he referred to Whitman and marvelled over his characterization of American masses whose self-assured egalitarianism stood in no awe of rulers.[30]

If Döblin, Tucholsky and Herzog turned out to be negativists, it was not for lack of intellectual or political values. The historical situation made these values inaccessible. By 1920 these leftist intellectuals recognized that they faced a hopeless situation. The forces of the left were fragmented and irreconcilable and the masses disheartened and drained. When Germany emerged from the Zusammenbruch once more on a course of conservative and even militarist nationalism, they adopted a posture of resolute defiance. Negativism must therefore be stringently differentiated from nihilism, for it embraced the values of democracy and socialism. And it must be equally distinguished from withdrawal, for it was active and critical, as the biting political commentaries of Tucholsky, Herzog and Döblin attest. The problem of these negativists was to find some basis for continuing, some alternative vision upon which they could found their artistic and their political activities and carry on in the wake of the war and the botched revolution. What was so important about these Berlin negativists was their staunch effort to rescue something from the ruins of civilization in the wake of war, and above all to keep faith with modernity. They sought to orient themselves in the new mass social order confronting them after the war without a trace of the ornamental "idealism" of Wilhelmian culture.

The attempt to rescue intellectual and artistic integrity and to secure a sustaining vision of the future after the First World War proved problematic and paradoxical from the outset. Even if sobriety displaced outrage, the sense of ruin and disillusionment was all-pervasive. All these artists shared with Ernest Hemingway the plight of a "lost generation" and an ineradicable suspicion of grand rhetoric. "Abstract words such as glory, honor, courage or hallow were obscene," Hemingway wrote.[31] Terse sobriety and matter-of-factness--Sachlichkeit--became the overriding imperative not only of literary style but of intellectual identity. Throughout Europe the First World War had shattered the conventions of traditional European culture. Romain Rolland wrote its epitaph with deep pathos in 1916: "Farewell, Europe, queen of thought, guide of humanity! You have lost your way, you tramp through a grave-

    [30]   Döblin, "Republik" (1920), in Schriften zur Politik, p. 119-120; "Die Drahtzieher" (1919), in Der deutsche Maskenball von Linke Poot, p. 46.
    [31]   Ernest Hemingway, A Farewell to Arms (New York: Scribner, 1929), p. 185.

yard. That is where you belong. Lie down! And let others rule the world."[32] Paul Valéry had this same sense, writing of an "extraordinary shudder" which "ran through the marrow of Europe" in the Great War, as it became aware of its mortality. "Thousands of young writers and artists have died; the illusion of a European culture has been lost, and knowledge has been proved impotent to save anything whatever."[33] Ezra Pound put it more crudely, terming Europe "an old bitch gone in the teeth,/...a botched civilization."[34] This was the experience of the Berlin negativists as well. Herzog commented in 1914 that "spirit and art must declare themselves bankrupt in the face of such a war...."[35] Later in that year he forsook his old idea of Europe, since it had "given itself over to self-mutilation in civil war."[36] The old European order had lost its lustre forever.

The new order in the world could not come from the old centers and old ideas of Europe, but only from beyond, from the transatlantic United States and the new, revolutionary Russia. Wilson and Lenin set the parameters of the new age.[37] Germany's left-wing intellectuals had to find their place in a world in which the only progressive conceptions of modern society seemed to be lodged in Americanism and Bolshevism. American and Bolshevik Russia, after 1917, came together, stood together in many ways against the old world of Europe. While Europe still seemed embroiled in the old machinations of power, Wilson and Lenin advocated a peace of understanding. While Europe still dreaded the "rise of the masses," Wilson and Lenin proclaimed with unprecedented vigor notions of popular sovereignty and self-determination. While European civilization appeared dubious

[32] Romain Rolland, Demain: Pages et Documents, 11/12 (1916) cited in Arno Mayer, Political Origins of the New Diplomacy (New York: H. Fertig, 1969), p. 29.
[33] Paul Valéry, "The Crisis of the Mind," in Paul Valéry: An Anthology, ed. J. Lawler (Princeton: Princeton University Press, 1956), pp. 94ff.
[34] Ezra Pound, Hugh Selwyn Mauberley in Ezra Pound: Selected Poems, ed. T.S. Eliot (London: Faber and Gwyer, 1928), p. 176.
[35] Wilhelm Herzog, "Der Triumph des Krieges," Das Forum 1, No. 5/6 (1914), p. 262.
[36] Wilhelm Herzog, "Der Unfug der Moral," Das Forum 1, No. 9 (1914), p. 460.
[37] On Wilson and Lenin and their impact on Europe in 1917, see above all, Mayer, Political Origins of the New Diplomacy. See also: Norman Gordon Levin, Woodrow Wilson and World Politics (New York: Oxford University Pres, 1968); and E. Hölzle, "Die amerikanische und die bolschewistische Weltrevolution," in Weltwende 1917. Monarchie, Weltrevolution, Demokratie, ed. Hellmuth Rössler (Göttingen: Musterschmidt-Verlag, 1965).

about the value of technology, industry and the metropolis, these two new civilizations, America and Bolshevik Russia, raised technology to the pinnacle of their values. While Europe conceived of itself as the guardian of high humanist culture inherited from the past, both America and Bolshevik Russia embraced mass culture and the future.

In this context, America and Bolshevik Russia merged to form an alternative to old Europe in the minds of the Berlin avant-garde. That coalescence I have termed simultaneous futures. For the Berlin avant-garde, in the words of Wilhelm Herzog, "the question is not Wilson or Lenin, but Wilson and Lenin."[38] Erich Mendelsohn gave perhaps the most lucid account of this German perception in his book Russia, Europe, America.[39] Whereas before the war "Europe was used to being at the center of things," and America and Russia languished on the peripheries, the war changed everything. The peripheries overwhelmed the center. "America...is master of the world," and "the new Russia actively reaches out toward America." What drew the two orders together was the primacy of technology and its abolition of the past. "The new Russia recognizes the values of the New World," Mendelsohn wrote. "Technology is anti-God."

In the words of Maria Ley-Piscator, wife of the avant-garde theater director, the Berlin avant-garde built itself up around a "startling contradiction."

> It invented "America." Everything that was useful, effective, expedient, operative, performing properly and instrumental for productivity was called American. Even time had an American tempo and was valued as such. None of them had seen America.... They admired what seemed real to them: the objective existence of the land of plenty, its material genius, with its prosperity, its slogans, and the great god--the machine.[40]

[38] Wilhelm Herzog, "Der geistige Typus des Revolutionärs," Das Forum 3, No. 3 (1918), p. 183.
[39] Erich Mendelsohn, Rußland, Europa, Amerika. Ein architektonischer Querschnitt (Berlin, R. Mosse, 1929); rpt. as Russia--Europe--America in Images: Reprint of Four Volumes of Architecture published in Germany in the Twenties, ed. C. and T. Benton (Great Britain: Open University Press, 1975), especially pp. 11-15.
[40] Maria Ley-Piscator, The Piscator Experiment: The Political Theater (New York: J.H. Heineman, 1967), p. 26.

America captured the imagination of the Berlin avant-garde while "at the same time, the period was idealistically entangled with the new Russia."

What the two great peripheral powers shared was their commitment to modernity, to contemporaneity, to mass society, technology and the future. In this they stood together against a traditionalist Europe which had lost direction and authority. As Hermann von Wederkop, the maverick editor of Der Querschnitt, put it: "Russians and Americans are opposite poles in many things, to be sure, but they are both clearly conscious of the principle of contemporary life."[41] Willy Wolfradt, art critic for Die Weltbühne, put it this way: "We stand at the conflux of two winds....The one blows out of the east, the other out of the west. They level many old European forms, such as studio art, art as a calling. For Americanism, it is no viable calling; for the Russians, no appropriate art."[42] The intervention of this new and energizing vision of the future which swept into Germany and especially into Berlin from the far peripheries of America and Soviet Russia allowed the avant-garde to transcend the dilemma of negativism and resume a futuristic posture embracing both political hope and intellectual creativity. Simultaneous futures, curiously interwoven, dispelled paralysis with fantasies and illusions and wooed the avant-garde away from despair. So it was that the left-wing intellectuals of Weimar raised up against a corrupt German socialism and a reactionary old regime a bizarre image which fused the revolutionary aspirations of socialism with the practical rationality of Americanism. Americanism was a fantasy and Bolshevism was an illusion, but fantasy and illusion were all that sustained artistic and political vision in Weimar Germany, all that shielded the left-wing intellectuals of the Berlin avant-garde from despair.

Simultaneous futures allowed the Berlin avant-garde to reassert a commitment to the modern world, to Sachlichkeit. In early 20th-century Germany that term had become a shorthand designation for modern values. It represented urbanism, technology and "mass society," but also a particular life-style and cultural orientation which embraced "mere utilitarian values" and affirmed the democratization and universal dissemination of culture. The avant-garde went so far as to argue for the greater aesthetic and intellectual integrity of the new forms of Zivilisationswerte over those of traditional "high" culture.[43]

---

[41] Hermann von Wederkop, "Querschnitt durch 1923," Der Querschnitt III, p. xii.

[42] Willy Wolfradt, "George Grosz," Jahrbuch der jungen Kunst (Leipzig: Klinkhardt and Biermann, 1921), p. 97.

[43] For this position see especially Adolf Loos, "Kulturentartung," and "Die Überflüssigen" in Sämtliche Schriften

Between 1918 and 1924, Alfred Döblin welded together for the Berlin avant-garde the ideas and values embraced in the syndrome of simultaneous futures: it was for the city, for technology, for mass society and for mass culture. Döblin carried into the twenties all the elements of Sachlichkeit that the pre-war years had to offer: the Sachlichkeit of the city of Berlin itself, the programmatic Sachlichkeit of Adolf Loos and the new spirit of functionalism in architecture, and the Sachlichkeit of engagé Naturalism, with its struggle for perspective on the social questions of the epoch. He brought with him a Futurist fascination with urban-technological order, and a Whitmanesque reverence for populism. All this allowed him to weld together capitalism and socialism, America and Soviet Russia, under the single rubric of a "new naturalism," the spirit of an age dedicated to the masses and technology. For the young generation of artists who emerged in the twenties, at their forefront George Grosz, Bertolt Brecht and Erwin Piscator, he provided the only plausible way to see the world, a "new matter-of-factness."

Döblin based all his writing in philosophy, art and culture on one principle: "to recognize what is, that is the first commandment."[44] As he put it in another, more pointedly political context, "it is the great misfortune of the country in whose language I write, that its sense of reality did not develop at the same pace as its general intellectual development."[45] Döblin's arguments urged a return to facts, to practical life, to the concrete realities of the contemporary world. This insistent Sachlichkeit across the board, from politics to metaphysics to art, made him the most rigorous theorist of Neue Sachlichkeit. The major task of contemporary intellectual culture, Döblin argued, was to "get free from clap-trap," to "create clarity and purity."[46] There was far too much traditionalism, "ancestor worship," in European society, and it was time to dispense with it. The commitment to clarity, to "perceiving the thing objectively and without mythology," entailed an acute awareness of historicity, a concern to be up-to-date, in line with the spirit of the age.[47]

In perhaps the single most important elaboration of his viewpoint, "The Spirit of the Naturalistic Epoch," 1924, Döblin drew a

(Vienna: Herold, 1962ff) and Hermann Muthesius, "Die moderne Umbildung unserer ästhetischen Anschauungen," in Kultur und Kunst (Jena: E. Diederich, 1904).

[44] Döblin, "Krieg und Frieden" (1920), in Schriften zur Politik, p. 169.

[45] Döblin, "Die Drahtzieher," in Schriften zur Politik, p. 42.

[46] Döblin, "Jenseits von Gott," in A. Wolfenstein, ed., Die Erhebung I (rpt. Nendeln, Liechtenstein: Kraus, n.d.), p. 395.

[47] Döblin, "Male, Mühle, Male," Die Neue Rundschau 31, No. 7 (1920), p. 881.

basic distinction between old European "high humanism" and the "naturalistic epoch" of modernity.[48] It seemed clear to Döblin that the transcendentalist, high-humanist worldview had become obsolete. "We stand at the beginning of the naturalistic epoch," he proclaimed. Its harbinger was technology. The "naturalistic spirit" dissolved the old transcendental categories, yet since it had not yet completed its task, the "present is still a confusion," Döblin wrote. Ruins and raw materials, old and new energies existed side by side. This was why so many saw the modern epoch as one of barbarism, uncertainty and pessimism. "The barbarism of this period has a double source: the incongruity of intellectuality and practice, and then the lack of intellectuality of the young technical drive itself." The great object and symbol of this new technological drive was the metropolis.

> Why is the new naturalistic spirit--at the moment--so closely bound up with the cities, more closely than the spirit of earlier epochs? Because it creates a form adequate to itself in the cities. The technical impulse ultimately requires great collectivities, masses, for its realization. The cities, particularly the metropolises, are technical work centers. Consequently, they reflect at once what is characteristic for this epoch: the monotony, the uniformity, the specific rationalization of this age.[49]

It was only natural that cities would become the targets of romanticist opprobrium. But such charges of "materialism," "banality," etc., ultimately reflected the anachronism of the critic rather than the flaw of the new naturalism, Döblin insisted. He attacked Oswald Spengler specifically for this posture. The distinction of Kultur from Zivilisation could be seen as the rear-guard action of an antiquated worldview. "What pulses powerfully in the cities, in the industries, cannot be stilled by contempt," Döblin admonished.[50] "Despite materialism, despite the powerful grasp of mechanization, there remains something living in these European countries including America."[51]

If the naturalistic epoch expressed itself first in technology rather than in the domain of culture, the key to this lay in the lack

---

[48] Döblin, "Der Geist des naturalistischen Zeitalters" (1924), reprinted in Aufsätze zur Literatur (vol. 8 in Ausgewählte Werke), p. 64.

[49] Ibid., p. 72.

[50] Döblin, "Revue" (1920), in Der deutsche Maskenball von Linke Poot, p. 80.

[51] Ibid.

of contemporaneity of culture. Most intellectuals construed their task to be that of preservation, not extension of culture. As a result, "they do not live in the same age as their practical contemporaries..." and therefore "are not in a position to give practical men directions of any kind."[52] The lack of contemporaneity signified that different worldviews drawn from disparate historical moments existed simultaneously, with for the most part anachronistic results. "The majority of artists and of art-lovers is still stuck manifestly around 1800 or 1600 even now." For Döblin the intellectual establishment of Germany was "unrepresentative of the spirit and the art that this epoch requires."[53] He contrasted German intellectuals to the Italian Futurists to make his point. He saw Futurism as "the drive of literature into the really living realm," the city and technology. The Germans, though they lived in a far more industrial society, could not perceive it. "The entire problem of iron and steel did not penetrate into the consciousness of these pseudo-intellectuals."[54] German art remained caught up in agrarian romanticism, and, even more alarming, German thought remained caught up in aggressive nationalism.

Under the authoritarian regime, German intellectuals had succumbed to "Deutschland, Deutschland über alles." Historians trumpeted German destiny. German "Classicism" decorated power-mongers with the trappings of civility. For Döblin the Classicism of Goethe and Schiller had become hopelessly contaminated by the teachers who attached themselves to its stately verbiage like parasitic moss. This perception developed into a general social theory: "Slowly there emerged a link between the classical ensemble, including school and teaching staff, and the obtuse bourgeoisie." The Classicists "helped to build castes, in that they bedecked the propertied classes in a fabulous ideology."[55]

It was against this perversion, the so-called "Kulturstaat," that Döblin believed the avant-garde had emerged in Germany as an act of creative rebellion. "They tried to push through meanings which were not used up, keen insights, unhemmed productivity."[56] They waged war against a civilization of clichés. They declared independence from Goethe and the entire classical tradition. But all

---

[52]   Döblin, "Der Geist des naturalistischen Zeitalters," in Der deutsche Maskenball von Linke Poot, p. 78.
[53]   Döblin, "Von einem Kaufmann und einem Yoghi" (1921), reprinted in Die Zeitlupe: Kleine Prosa, ed. W. Muschg (Olten: Walter-Verlag, 1962), p. 29.
[54]   Ibid.
[55]   Döblin, "Mireille, oder zwischen Politik und Religion," in Döblin, ed., Minotaurus (Wiesbaden: F. Steiner, 1953), p. 51.
[56]   Döblin, "Die Vertreibung der Gespenster," in Schriften zur Politik, p. 126.

this availed the avant-garde nothing: "We made an intellectual revolution.... But they made the war." The outbreak of the Great
War and the complicity of the intellectual establishment in its genesis and conduct helped Döblin to grasp the fatal dilemma of
post-war avant-gardism:

> Now one can see whence came the despair of the
> artists who worked in the last few decades driven
> by hatred of the bourgeois. This despair which
> carries forward to this very day and drives one
> toward nihilism. One understands the artists of
> the one side, who consider art to be pointless and
> who place engagement and the struggle over
> engagement at the forefront, and those of the other
> side for whom art becomes almost an external
> game.[57]

Art proved insufficient for dealing with the problems of the modern
world. Döblin wrote of "a desperate time for artists with a strong
penchant for fantasy and artifice."[58] They lived through a "night
between two days." Meanwhile, a very stern "conscience of the
age" set the scope of the possible. That conscience concerned
itself with making roadways fit for automobiles, not with the deli-
cate sensibilities of an aesthete.

Artists no longer had the right to ask for interest in their
intimacies. Döblin made it clear that he wanted a radical transformation of artistic orientation: "I am for a ceremonious burial of the
remaining artists of this genre and the installment of diligent,
bright-eyed journalists as their successors."[59] The literary intellectual had other responsibilities in the naturalistic epoch. "Critics
are needed, matter-of-fact minds, men who observe, who are interested in the laws and coloration of life." Germany, Döblin
commented acidly, had "enough profound dough-balls already."

Secularized modern civilization, with its liquidation of tran-
scendence, called for some painful adjustments in human
self-esteem. One had to realize "that we have lost our central place
in the universe," that individual human life no longer enjoyed the
absolute sanction of an immortal soul.[60] Yet the modern world ush-
ered in a new "feeling of freedom and independence." Everything

---

[57] Döblin, "Republik," in Schriften zur Politik, p. 126.
[58] Döblin, "Der deutsche Maskenball," in Schriften zur Politik,
p. 96.
[59] Döblin, "Kannibalisches" (1919), reprinted in Der deutsche
Maskenball von Linke Poot, p. 23.
[60] Döblin, "Der Geist des naturalistischen Zeitalters," in Schriften zur Politik, p. 66.

had to be started afresh, and there prevailed a sense of energetic action. "The loss of the transcendental faith absolutely does not lead to despair. It comes to this: The starry heavens above me and the railroad tracks beneath me," Döblin asserted. Kant's "moral law within me" had been replaced by the technical-practical activism and freedom of secular civilization. "Practical reason" could no longer abide smuggling God in the back door.

Two great orders of things obsessed Döblin in the new secular perspective: the plenitude and autonomy of the natural order and the dynamism and transformation of the urban-technological order. For Döblin the great word for the new age was anonymity. This anonymity expressed itself both in the oneness felt with organic matter and the totality of nature on the one hand, and in the solidarity and collectivity of human existence, the realm of the masses, on the other. "Anonymous, the magical term, the leading term. The individual person plays no role."[61] Döblin insisted upon the recognition of the objectivity of the world as manifested in the recalcitrance of things to the human will, in the autonomy with which even his own technical civilization determined his fate.[62] In Döblin's words:

> Once the intellect hit upon electricity and steam, it had set its course for a few centuries and predetermined its fate.... Our task for a few centuries is the industrialization of the world by means of electricity, steam and other steel mechanisms, without a care for the consequences. Nothing will deter us. We will see, after time, what we have made.[63]

He suggested that in the modern epoch the process of urban-technological development had begun to extend the realm of human social organization beyond the unit of the nation. "The prior, loose existence of people side by side is ever more overcome by railroads, industry and technology. These are themselves expressions of the social drive."[64] Döblin termed this a "supranational disposition," and he believed it increasingly displaced the mere "tender feelings" expressed in ideas of universal morality or brotherhood in literature and religion with technological forces of

---

[61] Döblin, "Die Natur und ihre Seelen," Der neue Merkur 6 (1922/1923), p. 9.
[62] Döblin, "Landauer," (1919), reprinted in Schriften zur Politik, p. 100.
[63] Döblin, "An die Geistlichkeit" (1919), in Der deutsche Maskenball von Linke Poot, p. 47.
[64] Döblin, "Krieg und Frieden," in Der deutsche Maskenball von Linke Poot, pp. 161-162.

"reality and consequence" which could enforce a supranational order. Initially, to be sure, technology, by bringing the human community into closer proximity, occasioned national clashes, but the long-term propensity of these forces was away from war, subordinating national unities to vaster patterns of technical and economic organization. The forces of urban-technological development would lead--even through the abyss of war--to vaster forms of planetary organization, world economic planning.

This idea of economic planning and technological organization resulting in a peaceful world brings us to the heart of the idea of simultaneous futures. Döblin spelled out this central premise:

> The intellectual suction of the technical-industrial order is so strong that differences within society like capitalism and socialism are petty compared with it. Both of these worlds want to industrialize; this is their common dogma; contemporary socialism is the legitimate child of industry and will not betray its parents; in all else capitalism is a leftover from the period of small industries.[65]

The possibility of reconciling capitalism and socialism as modern visions contrasted to old European civilization was the essence of "simultaneous futures" as a syndrome. The technological impulse proceeded to marshall the forces of both capitalism and socialism against obsolescent humanism and individualism, as well as anachronistic agrarianism and nationalism.

Subliminally, the constructions of technology were altering the world, and with that, the horizons of intellectual life. "Railroads, dynamos, these seemingly merely external things have enormous intellectual consequences."[66] In the modern world, Döblin believed, "natural science and industry have the say in the intellectual realm."[67] The literary intellectual had to come to terms with this epoch, for there could be no evasion of it, and it cried out for his labors. Radical secularism meant abandonment of absolute values. Those intellectuals who resisted were still caught up in the myths of the old order. "What has become of the questions and the problems of a philosophical, religious, aesthetic nature which they raised? The answer: contemporary man has solved them all in the

[65] Döblin, "An die Geistlichkeit," in Der deutsche Maskenball von Linke Poot, p. 48.
[66] Döblin, "Der Geist des naturalistischen Zeitalters," in Der deutsche Maskenball von Linke Poot, p. 70.
[67] Döblin, "Male, Mühle, Male," in Der deutsche Maskenball von Linke Poot, p. 881.

easiest way: he let them lie."[68] The old wisdom, the "cultivation of the twelfth through the eighteenth centuries," had no place directing the new world. Humanistic culture might persist, but it had no claim to rule the new order. The Cathedral at Cologne was a great monument to the old spirit, but the dynamo was a monument of equal power for the new spirit. (Shades of Henry Adams!) Emil Fischer's synthesis of sugar could match any humanistic achievement. "Technology and natural science conquer the world in their own way, the way of bright and powerful men. In their drive there is nothing of the old pieties. These men really say calico instead of God. But calico is no more a joke to them than God had been for earlier generations."[69]

This did not mean there was no place left for literary intellectuals. "There are voices which say that it is hopeless for intellectuals, that they can do nothing of consequence in the state, that the great forces of industry, technology and commerce have become almighty, that against them the highest ideas are inadequate."[70] Döblin disagreed fundamentally. Industry and technology merely laid the foundation; it was necessary for human beings to elaborate their social drive into a coherent cultural order. And it was here that the writer fit in: his was the responsibility to articulate a humane vision of society. The task of the artist-intellectual of the "new naturalism" was to bring the masses into a participatory role in culture and society.[71] "One knows that the enormous masses of the so-called lower orders will and must take an ever greater part" in cultural life. But to reach them it would be necessary to "become simpler...more comprehensible and more lively." There were two key projects in this transformation of the writing profession in Germany in accordance with the "new naturalism." First, it would be necessary to "defeat the monopoly on education" among the elite strata of German society through educational reform. But second, German artists had to "turn toward the broad masses of society," even if this should mean to "lower the general level of literature."[72] The artists had to recognize that their responsibility was no longer to sustain the high literary level of the elite but to "become conscious of their new social task and provide intellectual support" for the masses.

[68] Döblin, "Der Geist des naturalistischen Zeitalters," in Der deutsche Maskenball von Linke Poot, p. 68.
[69] Ibid., p. 68-69.
[70] Döblin, "Staat und Schriftsteller" (1921), reprinted in Aufsätze zur Literatur, p. 54.
[71] Ibid., p. 57.
[72] Döblin, "Vom alten zum neuen Naturalismus" (1930), reprinted in Aufsätze zur Literatur, p. 145.

Döblin's program for the writer was an even more radical reformulation of Heinrich Mann's program of 1910. Not only was Döblin prepared to dispense with the elitist mystique of art, but he proceeded to challenge all the esotericist and absolutist values behind which artists took refuge from modernity. If Expressionism had hankered after a new world, billowing off into clouds of vapid humanism, Döblin's Neue Sachlichkeit opted for this world. The thematic concerns of the movement he led revolved around the city: the city as jungle, the city as collective, the city as symbol and principle of the technological order. Technology and the domination of nature, the collective and the subordination of the individual, social change and the liquidation of transcendence--all these received prime emphasis. The technological epoch was seen as a radically new civilization rising out of the ashes of the old, primitive and naive in its newness, raw and powerful in its organizing principle and its propensity towards accelerated change. Neue Sachlichkeit was the artistic effort to find a cultural stance affirming urbanism, technology, mass democracy and mass culture by fusing the modernist images of Americanism and Bolshevism into simultaneous futures.

THOMAS MANN AND HIS JOURNALS

Hans Mayer

As the seventies drew to a close, two lengthy and remarkable publications appeared in quick succession on the literary scene. Indeed, in view of their contents, arrangement and style, they should have created something of a sensation. One was soon left with the impression, however, that the critics and reviewers were not really aware of the importance of these works. I am, of course, talking of the journals of Cosima Wagner, Richard Wagner's widow, and of the three volumes of Thomas Mann's journals, which permit the reader to peep over the distinguished author's shoulder, as it were, at eight years of his life, 1918 to 1921 and 1933 to 1936, day by day, moment by moment. [1]

Richard Wagner's significance in our more recent cultural history is just as obvious as Thomas Mann's importance for the literary and ideological history of the twentieth century. I certainly don't have to make special mention here of the fact that a quite definite interrelationship exists between the literary output of Thomas Mann and the artistic accomplishments of Richard Wagner. Although only 24, Thomas Mann, who had just completed that epic work Buddenbrooks, his early novel about the decline of a German middle-class family, was positively proud of the fact that for the first time in literary history he had succeeded in applying Richard Wagner's technique of using the leitmotif, in particular as used in the Ring of the Nibelung.

Cosima Wagner's first entry in her journals, which were to record in all their minutiae the daily events of her life together with Richard Wagner, was made on the 1st of January, 1869. The final entry was made on February 12, 1883, in the Palazzo Vendramin in Venice. The following day Richard Wagner died of a heart attack. Here the journal comes to an abrupt end. From this moment on, the

---

[1] Cosima Wagner-Liszt, Die Tagebücher, ed. Martin Gregor-Dellin and Dietrich Mack (Munich: Piper, 1982), 2 vols. (1869-77; 1878-83). Thomas Mann, Tagebücher, ed. Peter de Mendelssohn (Frankfurt: S. Fischer, 1981-82), 3 vols. (1918-1921; 1933-1934; 1935-1938).

widow made up her mind that there was nothing worthwhile recording any more.

Originally, her journals were intended as a kind of review for
the children of this--initially adulterous--relationship between
Cosima von Bülow, daughter of Franz Liszt, and Richard Wagner,
24 years her senior. To put it even more succinctly, the journals
were really intended for the benefit of their only son, Siegfried
Wagner. The fact that Siegfried Wagner probably never even set
eyes on the journals is just one more in a long line of intrigues and
Wagner family fights, which so often bring to mind scenes from
Greek tragedy. Siegfried's older sister, Eva, who was married to
that English ideologue Houston Stewart Chamberlain, remained
childless, preferring to look after their aged mother in Villa Wahn-
fried. It was Eva who came into possession of the journals. She
sealed them up from prying eyes and laid down in her testament
that the journals should be opened and assigned over to the town of
Bayreuth forty years after her death. This is what happened.
Because they had been compelled to rely on Richard Wagner's own
statements and numerous insincerities, not even all the previously
published secondary sources taken as a whole have been able to
throw such clear light on Richard Wagner's life and views as do
these journals.

"No, he was not a likable person," Thomas Mann said of Richard Wagner in 1951.[2] He was perfectly correct. The numerous
outbursts of anger and inconsequential jumps from one idea to
another, so faithfully recorded each and every evening by Cosima
in her journals, are disturbing to say the least. Often enough,
they are utterly absurd, particularly the repeated anti-Semitic
explosions of hate and the abuse Wagner heaped on composers and
writers he loathed. It was of no great consequence to him to offer
his opinion on Robert Schumann, who had haughtily snubbed him as
a young man, as someone quite incapable of composing even a conventional melody. Johannes Brahms' second symphony led Wagner
to remark that it was a sign of the general decadence of the times
that such a shoddy piece be taken seriously at all.

On the other hand, reading these journals leaves us with a
sense of strangeness: Wagner seems to be completely spontaneous,
thoroughly naive, and curiously innocent in a rather odd way. By
the same token, lofty and profound ideas are expressed and
musico-dramatic difficulties are discussed in all their complexities.
The Cosima Wagner journals, therefore, are a fascinating document,
indispensable to our understanding of German cultural history.

---

[2] Thomas Mann, Gesammelte Werke (Frankfurt: S. Fischer,
1960), X, p. 796.

"No, he was not a likable person..." Thomas Mann's remark about Richard Wagner can be taken equally well as a motto for an analysis of his own journals. These, too, are documents which either utterly fascinate the reader, or anger him, even repel him. They disclose detail after detail of daily life. The meticulousness of Thomas Mann's entries are more than a match even for a Cosima Wagner. Cosima was a loving wife who deliberately played a servile role. She recorded in exact detail whether Richard had slept well or not and what dreams he had had, these being narrated to her the next morning in his own rather free fashion. She avoided raising any kind of objection and never permitted herself even to consider contradicting him. Anything even remotely concerning Richard Wagner was exceptional.

Thomas Mann himself recorded in great detail his experiences, thoughts and even dreams. Entries concerning the latter occur less frequently than they do in Cosima's journals. On the other hand, when they did occur Thomas Mann wrote them down exactly as he remembered them. For instance, the unexpected appearance of his father, who then assumed the features of his hated elder brother, Heinrich Mann, during the course of the dream. Aided by nothing more than the material contained in these journals, a pschoanalyst could write an extensive treatise. Cosima merely informs us as to whether Richard Wagner slept well or not, even though we are now able to reach the not unimportant conclusion that Richard Wagner suffered from severe heart disease in the latter years of his life, something that has been inadequately taken into account in all past Wagner literature. As is now obvious, his doctors did not take his complaints and pains seriously enough, even though he described them with great accuracy.

Thomas Mann was capable of precise self-observation, and he took pleasure in contemplating everything with something like an "evil eye" and then putting it down on paper. The amounts and kinds of sleeping draughts and medicaments he took are accurately recorded, as are the complaints about his health, his strong emotions and his sexual impulses, which he described in his journals both ironically and with amusement as "excesses."

One could even deduce a kind of monstrous narcissism from all this, but this rather obvious reproach does not really hit the nail on the head. Certainly, Thomas Mann was continuously occupied with himself because he knew perfectly well that the events of his life and the experiences he had had were to form the framework for his art and work. The Greek Narcissus was in love with his own reflection. But Thomas Mann was not in love with himself. Hamlet's "Thou comest in such a questionable shape" is quoted time and again by Thomas Mann in his later essays, always referring to himself. Indeed, Thomas Mann really did think of himself as a person "of a questionable shape." Almost ruthless toward himself and his family, although he was the father of six children, he observed in his journal that people like himself should not have children at all. Later he remarked that "bringing children into this world of ours creates more suffering quite apart from one's own, objective suffering, something one does not actually feel oneself but which one observes being felt, which in turn gives one a feeling of guilt."[3]

Thomas Mann sealed the journals before he died, having laid down in his testament that they were not to be opened again until twenty years after his death, in other words August 1975, and that they could then be published. Many readers and critics of the journals are filled with indignation, repeatedly asserting that these most private writings should not have been published at all. Even if Thomas Mann himself was hardly a heroic writer, this is just a case of hanging up yet another heroic picture, which was not to be defamed nor fouled; not even by Thomas Mann himself.

There is abundant cause for indignation contained in the journals already published: whether in the journal spanning the four years from 1918 to 1921, written by a man in his forties, or in the journals covering those first years of emigration, in which Thomas Mann describes, among other things, his sixtieth birthday on June 6, 1935, in Switzerland. The grotesque anti-Semitic invective he used is hardly less potent than the well-known anti-Semitic utterances of Richard Wagner.

Notwithstanding this, Thomas Mann was married to a Jewess whom he greatly respected and even worshipped. He counted numerous Jews among his friends; even his noted publisher Samuel Fischer was a Jew. We can now see quite clearly that his anti-Semitic invective was really directed both against the Pringsheims, his unloved parents-in-law, and against the Jewish Expressionist friends of his brother Heinrich Mann. Certainly, these are very private motives, but the end result is genuine anti-Semitism. For example, following the visit of a Jewish guest Thomas Mann invariably commented on the fact that he or she was a Jew. Equally numerous are the political follies he committed over matters like the First World War, the German Reich, the revolution, the French and the English and the Americans, the Bavarian Soviet Republic in Munich, and the counter-revolution of the German generals. There is more than enough material here for an attentive reader to feel disgusted and to resolve that this is all he ever wants to know about Thomas Mann.

But this is doing Thomas Mann a grave injustice and is also a complete underestimation of these journals. Cosima Wagner was not born in Germany; her natural language was French. To be sure,

[3] Mann, Tagebücher (1918-1921), pp. 76-77.

170

she writes accurately enough, but without any particular refinement or elegance. The journals of Thomas Mann are those of a great author, even if his style is sometimes sloppy when written in a hurry, and, once in a while, he even makes the most astonishing spelling mistakes. Anyone truly interested in Thomas Mann the writer and his work, and thus some of the masterpieces of twentieth century German literature, has to analyze these journals both seriously and critically. Thomas Mann kept a diary his entire life, obviously starting as early as his schooldays in Lübeck and continuing into his eightieth year. The actual arrangement of the diaries has been known to us since the publication of his journals covering the years 1933 to 1936. All daily events were clinically and precisely noted down. First of all he recorded his state of health, whether he had slept well or not, whether he had to take medicines or not, then his daily walk, the situation at home, the family's visitors, who were always individually characterized and more often than not in a most unfriendly way, then the progress or lack of progress on the work currently on his desk.

As is well known, Thomas Mann burned all the journals covering the years before his emigration in the garden of his home in Pacific Palisades, California. This seemed to preclude any sort of conclusive answer to the question as to whether the earlier journals differed not merely in content, which is obvious, but also in structure from the later journals of the famous author and Nobel prize-winner. On his fifty-eighth birthday on June 6, 1933, he was without a homeland and was later to become stateless.

It appears, however, that an approximate answer can now be put forward. Twenty years after his death in Zurich, August, 1975, the sealed packets containing the journals were opened, something the author had expressly put in writing. Not only did the packet contain the journals beginning with 1933 but also an astonishing bundle of manuscript pages that had somehow escaped the incineration in California. These were the journal entries spanning the four years from 1918 to 1921. Just how this material came to be salvaged is something Peter de Mendelssohn, who carefully edited and commented the journals, has a completely plausible explanation for.

At the time of the destruction of all other journals up to 1933, which had been brought from Munich to Switzerland under dramatic circumstances and had been fervently awaited by Thomas Mann, the author was hard at work on his novel about the German composer Adrian Leverkühn, in other words Doctor Faustus. As is well known, the action of this distinguished later novel takes place on three separate time planes: at the beginning of the twentieth century, during the twenties, and finally during the Second World War, when Adrian Leverkühn died of softening of the brain and his friend and biographer, Zeitblom, set to work to describe and write about this Faust-like German composer.

Of necessity, the 1918, 1919, 1920 and 1921 journals deal with the final stages of the First World War, the defeat, the November revolution, the dictated peace of Versailles, the founding of the German republic, the failure of the rightwing coup by a man named Kapp, which was quickly brought to nothing by means of a general strike, the erratic devaluation of currency, the workers' insurrections, and a great many other happenings as well. All this forms the writer's working material for Doctor Faustus at a time when the Weimar Republic was ousted; one could say it was a posthumous victory for Kapp and Ludendorff because it led to the outbreak of a second world war--this time kindled by Germany. For the time being, therefore, Thomas Mann emphatically amnestied these four years. The journals were needed as an aide-mémoire for Doctor Faustus. Was it only intended as a temporary reprieve for the journals, which were then to have been incinerated as soon as the epic work was completed, possibly escaping this fate because Thomas Mann became severely ill? We don't know. Whatever the reason may have been, the reader can now acquaint himself with this important part of Thomas Mann's highly personal writings, which were obviously intended for no one but himself. The answer to our initial question is thus fairly straightforward: there is no real difference in structure between the evening or nocturnal entries of the 45-year-old Thomas Mann and those of the 60-year-old diarist in 1935.

The circumstances surrounding his life as described in the entries of 1920, and those of 1935, are astonishingly similar. This appears at first to be somewhat self-contradictory because Thomas Mann was living in his attractive Munich home at the end of the war. A daughter, Elizabeth the "toddler," had joined the four older children. Katia Mann was pregnant again, something the couple learned only after a somewhat elaborate false diagnosis. A sixth child was thus on the way. This time Thomas Mann awaited it with more than just a little ill-humor. Since the birth of his youngest son Michael, something like paternal irritation can be encountered in the journal entries concerning this new dependent. The difficult, unhappy and brief life of Michael Mann is obviously overshadowed from the very beginning by such paternal emotions.

Naturally enough, all this differs considerably from the situation during Thomas Mann's emigration in the thirties. He had, however, been able to salvage a large part of his wealth. The Mann's style of living with their six children and servants was therefore secure in Zurich; it was secure enough, at any rate, to ensure the progress of that epic work, the Joseph novels.

There are strange parallels in the ways Thomas Mann understood the world in 1920 and later in 1935; above all, in the ways he
understood himself. In these seemingly so differing circumstances,
the journals speak consistently of his self-doubt and indeed of a
great deal of objective humiliation. After the First World War had
ended, the German nationalist and author of Reflections of a
Non-Political Man was humiliated by the literary and political world.
His association with a Germanomaniac composer such as Hans Pfitzner could not make him forget that the then young and potent
literary and artistic movement of Expressionism wanted to have
nothing at all to do with the author of Royal Highness and Death in
Venice. Their Mann is the older brother Heinrich, Thomas Mann's
antagonist and adversary, whom Thomas hated to a degree which
even the journals only begin to hint at. One is left with the
impression that all of Thomas Mann's important works were from the
outset directed against Heinrich, his concept of literature and politics, his style and tradition. While on a visit to Vienna to attend a
performance of his somewhat unsuccessful play Fiorenza, he
remarked, not without reason, that he had actually begun writing
against his brother Heinrich as early as the first decade of the century. This was a direct reference to Fiorenza, which is a
counter-story to the vitalistic and Nietzsche-like earlier Renaissance stories of Heinrich Mann.

There is the humiliation of an ideologically defeated warrior
around 1920 and the humiliation of the emigrant Thomas Mann by
the Third Reich, by passport offices and conference chairmen, by
the Nazi and the emigrant press. The latter failed to understand
why Thomas Mann still did not make the essential and urgent break
with the Third Reich. This was because of consideration for the
safety of his publisher, Gottfried Bermann.

Adrian Leverkühn's clinical type of character was
ever-present within the diarist himself. At the same time,
however, that thoughtful biographer of the Doctor Faustus novel,
the Gymnasialprofessor Serenus Zeitblom, was also present. In a
later journal Thomas Mann, writing about the origins of Doctor
Faustus, confirmed that the two protagonists of his novel, Leverkühn and Zeitblom, were not all that sharply drawn because each of
them had a lot to hide: the secret of their identity. To what
degree this holds true, not just for this great later novel but also
for the attitude of Leverkühn and Zeitblom to their lord and master,
Thomas Mann, is shown by the previous journals hitherto unpub-
lished.

The diarist was attempting to be sincere, and in his own way
he was. Far more radical and pitiless than André Gide or Brecht,
to say nothing of Rousseau, Thomas Mann the writer was nobody's
fool. As I mentioned earlier, he was not in love with himself.
Rather he loved meticulousness. An entry in the journal of 1919

tells us everything about his marriage: "Evening stroll with Katia, who loves me very much and to whom I am eternally grateful."[4]

On his engagement to Katia Pringsheim Thomas Mann already knew perfectly well why he was unable to promise himself more than "exacting happiness." It is now an indisputed fact that his deeper erotic inclinations were always directed towards the male sex. Even without the journals this can be clearly traced throughout his literary output. Here too, Thomas Mann is meticulous and honest. He noted down erotic difficulties in his marriage and traced his sexual inclination quite correctly, deep into his literary output.

On September 17, 1919, he noted in his journal: "There is no doubt whatsoever in my own mind that Reflections of a Non-Political Man are a manifestation of my sexual invertedness."[5] That is a strange way of putting it, and at first somewhat baffling. Are we to suppose that Thomas Mann's deeply rooted preference for young men should have manifested itself not only and quite unmistakably in works such as Tonio Kröger or Death in Venice, but also improbably in that vast 1918 essay, Reflections of a Non-Political Man?

It is true enough, however, and it demonstrates the clear, one could almost say "evil-eye" view Thomas Mann had of his environment and of himself. Reflections of a Non-Political Man is inspired by two sources. The negative source is his feeling of hate and his will to self-assertion regarding everything personified by his elder brother Heinrich. Heinrich Mann had acidly assailed his younger brother in his celebrated essay on Emile Zola, published during the war. In his journals we discover that Thomas Mann had been ill for weeks after reading the essay. When he had sufficiently recovered, he wrote the essay about foreign policy and the assumed German "non-politics." Even while working on it, he secretly regarded the essay with a feeling of deep unease.

Only the positive element of self-assertion is directly ascribable to the differences existing between himself and Heinrich. These were not merely ideological, but almost physiological in their intensity. Thomas and Katia Mann viewed the girls and women in Heinrich Mann's life and work with considerable misgivings. In Heinrich Mann's Professor Unrat ("The Blue Angel") the narrator's sympathies obviously lie with the depraved "artiste Fröhlich." During his lifetime Thomas Mann was fascinated by what one can best describe as pleasing scamps: the presumptuous but handsome, even beautiful Joseph, son of Jacob, and the confidence man Felix Krull. Heinrich Mann as essayist essentially concerned himself with works and figures from French literature. Thomas Mann reacted in

---

[4]   Ibid., p. 295.
[5]   Ibid., p. 303.

174

Reflections of a Non-Political Man to Heinrich Mann's support of
Emile Zola as the tribune in the Dreyfuss affair with the antitype of
Eichendorff's Taugenichts (Good-for-nothing) and Pfitzner's Pales-
trina; in other words, with German Romanticism and the so-called
Late-Romanticism.

These two opposites could be pursued still further: Heinrich
Mann's faith in existing Western European parliamentarism as
opposed to Thomas Mann's commitment to "machtgeschützte Inner-
lichkeit"[6] and to a conjectured non-political Germanism. On the one
hand, there is the political tribune Heinrich Mann, on the other the
younger brother in his commitment to distinguished isolation à la
Friedrich Nietzsche. From Thomas Mann's hate-filled viewpoint
Heinrich was seen as a speaker for the Western bourgeoisie. By
contrast, Thomas Mann presented himself as a German Bürger of a
romantic and pure nature.

Seen in the light of this great interrelationship, which went
well beyond the mere contraposition of the writers and their characters, Thomas Mann's self-characterization becomes comprehensible.
This helps us understand why Reflections of a Non-Political Man can
be seen as the expression of his erotic inversion. Thomas Mann
interpreted his brother's world as that of a political petticoat government in that "township Paris," as Dostoevsky called it, a phrase
Thomas Mann almost gleefully made use of in Reflections of a
Non-Political Man. Part of this world was apparently parliamentarism, shallow and ephemeral literature, political salons, and
naturalistic novels in Zola's immediate entourage.

Careful perusal of this vast essay shows us that the German
non-political world is indeed to be understood as the author's declaration of love for a certain type of blue-eyed, blonde German male,
who appears repeatedly in Thomas Mann's works: from Hanno's
schoolfriend Kai Graf Mölln in Buddenbrooks to the musician Rudi
Schwerdtfeger in Doctor Faustus. These are the type of romantic
German youths described by Eichendorff as well as the likable ras-
cals of Thomas Mann's later years. The journal entries in the
summer of 1919 provide us with additional substantiation for Thomas
Mann's self-knowledge with respect to existing links between sexual
inversion and epic creativity. The journal entries about two young
Holstein youths during a vacation stopover in Glücksburg could
have been taken straight from one of Thomas Mann's earlier or later
stories.

Thomas Mann was never really fond of Reflections of a
Non-Political Man, whose wistful and almost involuntary comic origins can be traced in the 1918 and 1919 journals; but he never

[6] Mann, Gesammelte Werke, XI, p. 419.

actually rejected them. In his eightieth year, however, he was perfectly willing to abandon <u>Reflections</u> instantly if his later political
writings and speeches could be included in the twelve-volume edition of his work being prepared in East Berlin in honor of his
birthday. While on the subject, the grand old man was most
emphatic that "Schriften zur Politik" ("Political Writings"), should
not appear in the title or subtitle, rather "Schriften zum Zeitge-
schehen" ("Writings on Contemporary Events"). Once again this
was an indirect commitment to "non-politics."

Just how little Thomas Mann really understood or even wanted
to understand about the revolution and counter-revolution, the
Bavarian Soviet Republic and courts martial while still in Munich is
shown by some entries in his journals. At a time when Germany's
defeat could be clearly foreseen, was the author really clear in his
own mind when he wrote on October 18, 1918, that he was in fact
censuring himself: "The heroic fight, which brought forth unparal-
leled feats of bravery, has been lost because of hideous military
and political errors and because of the completely ill-adapted intellectual quality of the German for such battles...." Shortly
afterwards he wrote in angry terms: "This people has proved itself
completely unfit to hold power. I would be content if the Reich
were to be dissolved and if non-political powerless collaboration of
the republics with a Prussia and a Germany-Austria (or these individually) were to issue forth."[7]

In a pinch Thomas Mann was even prepared to accept the
Bavarian Soviet Republic were it not for the fact that so many Jews
had a hand in it, as well as men of letters who supported his brother Heinrich to a man. Confronted by the Western "Zivilisationsli-
terat," Thomas Mann constructed a new utopia for himself, as if it
were an old Prussian-Bolshevik structure: "I would be quite prepared to run into the streets and cry 'Down with our deceitful
Western democracy! Long live Germany and Russia! Long live
Communism!'"[8] This was written on March 24, 1919. Only weeks
later, when people were being summarily executed on the orders of
military courts, the diarist, who had intended to run out into the
streets in their support, wrote on April 13, 1919: "I welcome the
temporary downfall of the Bavarian Soviet Republic...and I loathe
the reckless schemers who compromise the intellect just as much as
I do those persons who have mismanaged everything this time. I
would have nothing against shooting them as one does rodents,
even though care will be taken not to."[9] But care was not taken.

[7] Mann, <u>Tagebücher</u> (1918-1921), p. 73.
[8] Ibid., p. 178.
[9] Ibid., p. 196.

As Joachim Fest correctly put it in his analysis of the journals, Thomas Mann lumped together "Liberalism, Conservatism, Socialism and occasionally even Communism in wild transient 'political marriages' almost at random." The conclusion he infers from this is also correct: "Never for a moment did he intend to have anything to do with politics; he invariably moved with a kind of awkward sensitiveness at the edge of the crowd; his boisterous flag-waving does not conceal the hard facts."[10] This is perfectly true and applies equally well to the later Thomas Mann, the political orator, the radio commentator and political publicist, particularly when, examined in the light of history, he even uttered the right things and defended democratic positions.

Seen in retrospect, it strikes us that Thomas Mann's associations with the important writers of his time, an era he characterizes in a noteworthy speech held on the occasion of his 75th birthday in 1950 as "my time," was marked by his lack of contact with the most important writers of his day. His correspondence with Hermann Hesse is certainly interesting seen as a historical political document, but there is no question of their correspondence being of any literary worth. His relationship to Hofmannsthal was one of embarrassed politeness. Hofmannsthal's comedy Der Schwierige generated more expressions of boredom than of respect in the journals. A comedy "that naturally enough occasionally reaches a high level, but not something I would be proud of."[11] For varied and occasionally extremely unjust reasons, the most interesting writers of his time, in our judgment anyway, more or less determinedly rejected Thomas Mann the writer: Döblin and Brecht, Gottfried Benn and Hans Henny Jahnn, critics such as Karl Kraus or Walter Benjamin. Most of them, especially the young Gottfried Benn, felt themselves more strongly drawn to Heinrich Mann than to his younger brother. The indignation felt by the diarist towards the young and potent literature of the time was thus well founded. Throughout most of his life he entertained more frequent and cordial relations with the minor literary figures of the day. Often enough he wrote benevolent publicity blurbs for them, so much so that these were publicly being sneered at as the twenties drew to a close. Thomas Mann was well aware of this and deliberately continued to write them.

The withering commentaries in his journals, however, show us just how scornful he really was of those he so openly praised. Continually comparing himself with the greatest writers, he was always trying to write up to Goethe's standard. In his own eyes none of his contemporaries were on a par with himself. Least of all Heinrich

[10] Joachim Fest, "Das Dilemma eines Unpolitischen," Frankfurter Allgemeine, 13 October 1979, Literature Section.
[11] Mann, Tagebücher (1918-1921), p. 507.

Mann. Nonetheless, the journals covering 1933 to 1936 show that he increasingly recognized the importance of Marcel Proust and particularly Franz Kafka, although his courteous published remarks about Kafka are far more non-committal in content than are the journal entries concerning the author of Die Verwandlung (The Metamorphosis).

Early on, Thomas Mann evidently did not know very much about Kafka, despite the fact that Carl Sternheim had the cash award which came with the Kleist Prize transferred to the writer Dr. Kafka in Prague during the world war--with an emphatic reference to Kafka's high stature. But Thomas Mann does record a visit by that skillful reciter Ludwig Hardt on August 1, 1921. It was Hardt's habit often to include Kafka texts in his evening readings. As a matter of interest, he also recited early Thomas Mann stories. The journal records: "Tea with L. Hardt, who read me some prose by a writer in Prague, Kafka. Strange enough. Otherwise rather boring."[12] But this opinion was revised as early as September 22: "I was most interested in Franz Kafka's writings, recommended by Hardt, the reciter."[13] Another entry is just as intriguing: "Annette Kolb to dinner, I find her somewhat displeasing....She extolled a French novelist, named Proust or something like that. Accompanied her to the tram."[14] Proust or something like that!

Richard Wagner's extremely copious autobiographical writings were of two kinds, on the one hand the stylized and manipulated, and on the other the almost impulsive entries concerning daily life by Cosima. Probably Wagner never imagined that Cosima's journals might one day be published and thus put before the eyes of a curious public well beyond the reach of any attempts at stylization or manipulation. We now know that Wagner repeatedly checked Cosima's journal entries to verify that everything had been correctly recorded.

Thomas Mann was also driven by a restless penchant to autobiography to use his own words. He too makes a distinction between the barely concealed private records and the stylized and well-prepared works intended for publishing and the public. The latter too can be split up in two ways: Firstly, by using the journal entries as material for his own writings, culminating in the utilization of the journals for the creation of Doctor Faustus; and secondly, through the selection and readying of certain journal entries for publication. The most important examples are the political reflections covering the initial period of the Third Reich, which Thomas Mann selected for publication after the war, giving them the

[12] Ibid., p. 542.
[13] Ibid., p. 547.
[14] Ibid., p. 456.

title "Suffering under Germany," and the essay about the genesis of Doctor Faustus, which was characterized in its subtitle as the "Story of a Novel."

Nonetheless, there can be absolutely no doubt about the fact that Thomas Mann did not look upon his own journals as publishable material. This was the reason behind his almost despairing dread that the journals left behind in Munich might conceivably fall into the hands of the Hitlerites. This also explains his decision to free himself from all future worries about the journals by incinerating them in the garden of his California home. The basic reasons behind all this have to do with his harsh character and the almost alarmingly clinical perspective of the diarist towards himself.

When the journals were opened, considerable astonishment was expressed that Thomas Mann had considered the journals that had escaped the auto-da-fé as being "of no literary worth," as he described them on the paper he used as packing material. For the modern reader the journals are doubly valuable, both as the output of a great writer, and as sincere, often even deeply disquieting biographical documents.

Nevertheless, Thomas Mann's denial of their literary value was probably meant seriously enough. In direct connection with Goethe and German classicism, he was possessed with the idea of literary perfection. It was a matter of continual importance to him to transform the uncertainness of his own existence into a work of art in the Goethean sense through the instrumentality of "special forms." True to Friedrich Schiller's aesthetics, which accompanied Thomas Mann throughout his entire life, the subject matter was to be "consumed" as it were by the form, that is: arrangement and style. This always occurred whenever he was able to transform material from his life in an artistic sense; such as his experiences of the Bavarian Soviet Republic in Munich in The Magic Mountain, and also the love of the elderly Thomas Mann for a young man from Düsseldorf named Klaus Heuser, which was initially included in his plan for a short novel about Goethe's late love for Ulrike von Levetzow, a plan he later abandoned, and then worked into his story Die Betrogene, in which Klaus Heuser appears as the American student Ken Keaten. Thomas Mann deliberately retained Klaus Heuser's Düsseldorf environment, transforming himself into the aging Madame Rosalie von Tümmler.

In all these and many other cases, the journal material, indeed Thomas Mann's entire life, is "turned to account" as a literary framework, thus turning it into something of great value. As the waiter Mager in Thomas Mann's novel Lotte in Weimar would say, it becomes very much an "event worth writing down." Whenever this was not the case, however, as with the larger part of the material contained in the journals covering his long and troubled life, the

179

diarist looks upon his nocturnal notes as being of "no literary worth."

Since publication of the journals, a lively controversy has raged in German intellectual circles as to whether all the numerous admissions of unkindness, of obvious political blindness, of moments of greatest intimacy should be published or not. Even among the surviving children of Katia and Thomas Mann there is a difference of opinion. There is no secret about that. Even the well informed editor and commentator of the journals himself, Peter de Mendels-sohn, had begun his work on the journals full of unease.

In spite of all this, it is my opinion that it is well worth becoming acquainted with these unique documents. Transcending Thomas Mann's enjoyable stylization in his autobiographical writings, they show us an extremely hard life in which the quest for "happiness" had to take second place to the quest for "dignity." Happiness and dignity were postulated by Friedrich Schiller as contradictions. He knew perfectly well why he kept them so strictly apart. Thomas Mann permitted Aschenbach to die in Venice, but Aschenbach nevertheless continued to exist within his creator until Thomas Mann's eightieth birthday—and a few weeks beyond. His journals are not significant for the history of literature alone; that indeed would be too little and would not justify their publication. A great writer does not live to write for any future secondary sources. Thomas Mann's journals are great primary literary sources. In spite of all their faults and their lack of dignity, but above all because of their embittered battle for a literary life's work, the journals are unique literary and cultural-historical documents.

A ONE-SIDED HISTORY: BRECHT'S HITLER PLAYS

David Bathrick

If historians have been forced of late to consider the poetic structure of historical imagination,[1] the dramaturgical legacy of Bertolt Brecht has long since suggested that the opposite is also the case. Basic to his system of dialectical theater is the understanding that poetic representation is historical representation; that the narrative arrangement of fictive events assumes historical emplotment; finally, that the struggle of epic theater to counter the entrappings of traditional drama is at the same time a decoding of the bourgeois history implicit in its form. At every register of his dramatic theory, from formal structure to audience response to his theory of estrangement, Brecht reorganized the dramaturgical game around a battle of historiographies. Just as Aristotelian drama was retroactively historicized by Brecht into 19th-century bourgeois drama, into a writing of bourgeois history, so Brecht's avant-garde theater was a Marxist reading of that history to put it firmly on its feet. Hence the Brechtian paradigm Dramatic vs. Epic is not a frozen juxtaposition. Rather, it is the sublation of the one by the other--the grounding of a history based on universals, kings and battles back into the substratum of dialectical matter which is its greater truth and overcoming.

Nowhere was Brecht's struggle for historiography waged in greater earnest than in the fight against fascism. In opposition to those who viewed in Hitler's rise the emergence of barbarism as a kind of historical "Betriebsunfall" (accident), Brecht stressed from the very outset its absolute congruence with the bourgeois order:

> Capitalism exists in fascist countries only as
> fascism and fascism can only be fought as capital-
> ism, as the most naked, most oppressive and most
> deceitful form of capitalism.[2]

---

[1] See Hayden White, Metahistory (Baltimore: Johns Hopkins University Press, 1973).
[2] Bertolt Brecht, Gesammelte Werke (Frankfurt am Main: Suhrkamp, 1976), XVIII, pp. 226-7.

This reduction of fascism to a sub-component of capitalism, in conformity as it was with the then-prevailing Comintern position, had a number of implications for Brecht's dramaturgy and his political work in the 1930s. As a theory of history, dialectical materialism offered a paradigm with which to counter the obfuscating mythologies of both Nazi and some anti-Nazi historiographies. Against those "idealists" and "neo-romantics" who saw in German fascism a virulent perversion of the German spirit--"the horrors were the result of a war-like and thoroughly disgusting spirit, which had somehow gained the upper hand"[3]--Brecht's insistence upon the primacy of economics and class struggle provided him with an anchor both for his psychological well-being and for the emplotments of his dramas. At the center of the theory lay the one immutable truth which would be the cornerstone for his entire anti-fascist activity: If fascism results from the calculated maneuverings of the bourgeoisie in crisis, then it can and will be overcome only by that force in whose material interest it is to do so--the working class. Thus at the level of philosophy and at the level of practice, Brecht remained an optimistic child of the Enlightenment, with his own debt to German idealism: linked to the progressing forces of material production, the proletariat as exploited and hence revolutionary subject of bourgeois history--as the embodiment of historical reason itself--will necessarily transcend the system.

While it is true that the forces and relations of production provided for Brecht the Archimedean point from which to comprehend and challenge fascism--in a very real sense the epic voice of Brechtian theater--it is also the case that during this period his analysis undergoes a marked shift of focus from the political economy to a politics of culture. In his dramatic writing, this shift is most observable when comparing his anti-Hitler plays: The Roundheads and the Peakheads (1934) and The Resistible Rise of Arturo Ui (1941). In point of fact, Brecht's increasing and one must also say "unmarxist" fixation on the personage of Hitler[4] and the psychodynamics and theatricality of the Nazi spectacle showed a reliance on cultural categories which threatened to subvert the historical paradigms derived from orthodox Marxism.[5] It is within the

---

[3] Brecht, Gesammelte Werke, XX, p. 185.
[4] Brecht also wrote numerous poems about Hitler, whom he referred to as the "Whitewasher" (Anstreicher).
[5] Brecht's move away from economics is commented upon by Manfred Wekwerth, Brecht's successor at the Berliner Ensemble, in his notes to the 1959 production of Arturo Ui: "Fascism does not evolve immanently from economic development, but rather from the exceptional situation of violating laws (Dogsborough's dock aid scandal). It will be necessary to think about how to show the immanent emergence of fascism." Notate. Über die Arbeit des

dynamics of Brecht's struggle to broaden and "umfunktionieren" the orthodox position that we shall trace his development in exile.

Our primary concern, then, is to interrogate the relationship between literature and history within the work of a playwright who consciously thematized and grappled with that relationship at the level of formal representation. Brecht's writing of a new drama was at once the reading and writing of a new history through the rereading and rewriting of the old. That we have chosen fascism as the point of intersection is founded upon the hypothesis--to be demonstrated--that the solutions and failures which emerged from this most desperate confrontation of a literary imagination with historical truth were profoundly to affect and shape all of his theories and work from that time on. Put more polemically, the categories which have come to be understood as quintessentially and I might add ahistorically Brechtian are themselves in many regards an expression of and response to these dark times.

Certainly Brecht himself gives occasional, if somewhat veiled, allusion to the relationship between the realities of fascism and his own political and aesthetic representations of the time. In a number of poems written between 1933 and 1945 he openly apologizes for their failure to address certain aspects of human experience; for having to concern themselves with "the business of politics" and "the dry unworthy vocabulary of dialectical economy." The final verse of his famous poem "An die Nachgeborenen" beseeches those who come after to be gentle when assessing the weaknesses of the ones who wrote under fascism and to understand the historical reasons why:

> For we went, changing our country more often than
> our shoes,
> In the class war, despairing
> When there was only injustice and no resistance.
> For we knew only too well:
> Even the hatred of squalor
> Makes the brow grow stern.
> Even anger against injustice
> Makes the voice grow harsh. Alas, we
> Who wished to lay the foundations of kindness
> Could not ourselves be kind.
>
> But you, when at least it comes to pass
> That man can help his fellow man,

Berliner Ensembles 1956 bis 1966 (Frankfurt am Main: Suhrkamp, 1967), p. 42.

Do not judge us
Too harshly.[6]

From one angle, Brecht is calling for the same "critical-historical" reading of his work which he himself practiced in his own writing of theory and plays. The struggle against fascism, he seems to be saying, has taken its toll: it has distorted the features and hoarsened the voice. Yet there is another reading of Brecht's poetic persona from exile which says that he is not really "apologizing" at all, but rather provocatively, if also ironically, sketching the framework for a new aesthetic. This attitude is even more pronounced in an earlier poem:

Exclusively because of the increasing disorder
in our cities of class struggle
a few of us have decided in these years
Not to speak about harbour cities, Snow on the
roofs, women
The smell of ripe apples in the cellar, joys of the
Flesh
All those things
which make humans round and human
But rather to speak only about disorder
that is to be one sided, dull, bound up in the
business
Of politics and the dry unworthy vocabulary
Of dialectical economy[7]

The rationale for such dualism is revealing: too close an intertwining of economics and eroticism, or in the words of our class-conscious persona, "tempted flesh and class justice," may induce enjoyment, indeed even approval of a "bloody" world which could produce such contradictions in such close proximity. Better then one remain "einseitig."

What is significant at this point in Brecht's thinking is the radical impulse to characterize such things as feeling, nature, Freundlichkeit, sexuality, even beauty itself--qualities quite often associated with subjectivity or the non-utilitarian--as suspect, and to favor instead the very instrumental, indeed "rational" values of economics and class struggle. As he even more aggressively put it in an essay about fascism: "I realize of course that such words as private ownership of the means of production are not beautiful, not very romantic, not at all poetic. But none of us are using these words because of their beauty. The fact is, they are simply necessary. By that I mean: to say what they say is necessary. And if

[6] Brecht, Gesammelte Werke, IX, p. 722.
[7] Ibid., p. 519.

184

one is confronted with the choice of using such unbeautiful and dry and doctrinaire words and of speaking about such lowly things as earning one's board or earning enough or, on the other hand, of letting fascism triumph, then one ought to make the choice to use them..."[8]

We have learned, of course, to take skeptically the postures and articulations of any authorial voice--be it a fictional or discursive-analytical one. Bertolt Brecht's consciously "unpoetic," unrhythmical appeal for non-poetry--in the carefully honed, grandeured language of non-poetry--is a brilliant ruse, a highly "poetic" device with which to overcome in formal eloquence the very antinomies one claims are there in content. Reinhold Grimm, in an essay focussing on the poem "Exclusively because of the increasing disorder" has shown convincingly how Brecht anticipates and then proceeds to answer affirmatively Adorno's now epochal question concerning whether it is possible to write poetry after Auschwitz. The "reply," Grimm tells us, emerges in practice, not in theory: the classical power and grace of Brecht's simple prosaic verse is itself the poetic "Aufhebung" of the classical aesthetic.[9]

While Brecht's success in forging poetic beauty out of despair permits him to right the foundering ship of aestheticism, such interpretive Hegelian sleight of hand cannot cover up the deeper contradictions revolving around society and self which remain submerged and yet articulated within the Brechtian "solution." So let us begin by taking at face value the assertions of Brecht's beleaguered persona, viewed for a moment within the crisis of the times and as yet one more example of a modern writer's attempt to cope with the dissolution of subjectivity; indeed as an admission of its own very real infirmities in the face not only of fascism, but before the global process of reification and commodification of social life in the latter period of the Weimar Republic.

It is true that Brecht's manifesto of toughness and stoicism unequivocally repudiates the romantic individual subject and the Kantian system of beauty and disinterest which has been associated with and sustains it. Yet in scorning the ineffectualness of affirmative culture, Brecht's subject is equally disdainful of the subjectivization of individual experience, of the overly psychologizing, sometimes solipsistic forms of expression he came to associate with

---

[8]   Brecht, Gesammelte Werke, XX, p. 188.
[9]   Reinhold Grimm, Brecht und Nietzsche oder Geständnisse eines Dichters. Fünf Essays und ein Bruchstück (Frankfurt am Main: Suhrkamp, 1975), pp. 11-54.

some facets of the modernist gesture.[10] Indeed, what is notable about Brecht in both poetry and drama of this period is his metonymic submission of individual sensibility to the symbolic paradigms of collective experience. The Brechtian "I," deprived now by history of its beauty-loving, subject-centered "authentic" experience, reconstitutes itself as the embodiment of an objective historical reality principle. This de-centering of the ego, begun so radically in Mann ist Mann and culminated in the interchangeable parts of the Lehrstück--emerges in the early exile years as the postulated epic "we" of machine-age culture and its superego, proletarian history. Yes, Brecht achieves a grandeur of style--the rebirth of aesthetics in the "unbeautiful" "dry" "doctrinaire" language of Marx's political economy--but at a price. The relegation of feeling, nature, subjectivity to the realm of historical impracticality in favor of reason reveals the psychological-political foundation of indeed a one-sided poetic episteme which was later to help but also to hinder him in his very struggle against fascism. This essay will trace Brecht's efforts to overcome that limitation.

Certainly the economistic thrust in Brecht's writing is evident in his first anti-fascist play, The Roundheads and the Peakheads. Based loosely on Shakespeare's Measure for Measure and written between 1932 and 1934, the three-version genesis of the play was ideologically very much in accord with the then-evolving official position of the communist party as defined at the 13th Plenum of the executive committee of the Communist International, which stated: "Fascism is the open, terroristic dictatorship of the most reactionary, the most chauvinist, the most imperialist elements of finance capitalism."[11] In The Roundheads and the Peakheads--Empire and Empire flock together, we are given in the dialectical tension of title and subtitle the political message of the work. "Reich und Reich gesellt sich gern" is obviously a play on the saying "Gleich und Gleich gesellt sich gern," in English, Birds of a Feather flock together. The birds of a feather or in this case the basis upon which people really share interests is determined by class relations, not by whether one has a rounded or a peaked head--or by analogy, whether one is Jewish. In the words of the prologue:

> ...I see a difference
> But the difference, which I see
> It is greater than that between heads
> > only
> And it determines good times and bad

[10] For an excellent discussion of modernism and fascism, see Fredric Jameson's Fables of Aggression. Wyndham Lewis, the Modernist as Fascist (Berkeley: University of California Press, 1979).

[11] Quoted from Arthur P. Mendel, ed., Essential Works of Marxism (New York: Bantam Books, 1961), p. 412.

> And I shall name it for you now:
> It is the difference between poor and
> rich.[12]

The parable that Brecht develops to demonstrate this teaching is a complicated one. The mythical land of Yahoo is in an economic crisis of overproduction and threatened by an uprising of the poor tenant farmers under the leadership of the Sickel movement. The Viceroy of Yahoo is pursuaded to meet the crisis by handing over the power to Angelo Iberin, a demagogue of the petit bourgeoisie who promises that he will deal with the situation. He does so by inventing a theory which proclaims the racial superiority of the Roundheads over the Peakheads, the Tschuchen over the Tschichen. Thus we have the myth of both the play and fascism: the race question merely confuses the more important economic contradiction.

How does this work in practice? The landowner de Guzmann has seduced the daughter of a tenant, the peasant Callas. Under the control of the new regime, he is brought to trial on two counts: first, because he is a peakhead and has ruined the honor of a roundhead; secondly, as a landowner he is accused of exploiting unfairly the poor tenant farmer. After a long and uncertain trial and through the eventual intervention of Iberin himself, de Guzmann is sentenced to death to restore to Callas his <u>honor</u>, not his <u>property</u>. Thus he is convicted only on the first count, his membership in a race, and not because of exploitation. When Callas demands restitution of property by stealing de Guzmann's horses, the court upholds property relations, again with intervention from Iberin. Then and only then does Callas realize that his real interests are not represented, but it is too late. The Sickel movement has been crushed and ultimately de Guzmann himself is released. The final scene shows the retreat of the Iberin-Hitler figure to the political wings and the re-establishment of overt bourgeois rule with the return of the Viceroy. We also see the retreat of de Guzmann as specifically as Jew when he sits down at the table with his capitalist roundhead brothers. The message, then, is a clear one: birds of a monetary feather flock together. Were it not for the phantom of racism, birds of a disenfranchised, exploited feather would also.

What is significant about the play from the standpoint of history is its emphasis upon the fact that capitalism and racism are intertwined and self-supporting. Brecht demonstrates well the interlocking and totalistic nature of fascist ideology: anti-semitism's juxtaposition of the purity of Volk to Jewish capitalism, Jewish modernization, Jewish decadence was clearly a way in

---

[12] Brecht, <u>Gesammelte Werke</u>, III, p. 910.

which social and economic problems were displaced and ultimately mystified into the realm of biological difference. Brecht shows this, and at a time prior to the Nuremburg laws and later open war against the Jews.

Also important is Brecht's focus on the political and ideological role of the middle class as a basis for both the leadership and backing of the Nazi movement. Anticipating much of the later scholarship and in direct disagreement with the more economistic theories of the Comintern, Brecht demonstrates through the Iberin figure the central function of ideological manipulation in the building of a mass movement and the "solving" of economic crisis.

Yet, as gratifying as such insights are, it is also clear from hindsight that the historical emplotment of the play profoundly distorts a number of the political realities of the time. Let us start with the figure of Hitler. While it is true that Brecht's overall fixation with this "individual" clearly ran counter to his own view of individuals being metonymical expressions of larger social forces, in this first play it is the class paradigm that ultimately writes the text. Once he has executed his juggling act, Iberin is absorbed back into the labor-capital dialectic, thus illustrating the "real" laws that are operable in the historical process. That such a subsumption seriously underestimated the aura, if not to say erotics of Hitler's power is as obvious from a viewing of Riefenstahl's Triumph of the Will as it is from Brecht's own changing views on the subject.

Even more questionable is the playwright's treatment of the racial question in the play, for again we find the historical emplotment of class struggle pinning to its procrustean bed the dynamics of an infinitely more complicated process. The point is not simply that the harmless return of the capitalist-peakhead de Guzmann to his bourgeois fold subsequent to crisis failed to anticipate the very "historically irrational" slaughter of six million Jews. The point is rather that Brecht's epic voice as the epistemology of productivist-proletarian reason would have to subsume any irrational phenomenon into the larger text of a world without Freud, a history without its discontents. What such reductions ignore and fail to grasp is the level at which the racial and the Hitler question must also be understood in terms of libidinal needs and unconscious fears which lie beyond such rationalist explanatory models.

Brecht's problem with racism is particularly clear when viewing the figure of Callas in the play. As a member of the materially oppressed, the peasant Callas is given to us as an absolutely rational being with one set of needs--namely economic ones. The issues of sexual assault and racial defilement are coded ultimately as non-issues, pseudo-issues--outside the need-structure of real history. Until Iberin-Hitler suggests to Callas that perhaps there is a loss of honor involved in his daughter being seduced by de Guzmann, it has never occurred to Callas that Nanna might have been abused. Indeed, up to the first trial scene, Callas has only thought of the material advantages of Nanna's liaison with de Guzmann and of her work in a brothel:

> Iberin: The Landlord misused his economic position of power, in order to drive your daughter to ruin?
> The Tenant Callas: Ruin? She had nothing but advantages! She never had to work. But we! You try ploughing without horses![13]

Thus in the face of such consistently materialist-conscious class interest, the ideology of racial defilement can only result in temporary false consciousness. Furthermore, by introducing the round-head-peakhead myth as a ruse, as the discovery if not invention of the Hitler figure, Brecht trivializes the very real social-psychological history of anti-semitism by relegating it to the realm of a secondary contradiction. Unlike Ernst Bloch, who glimpsed in the perversions of such propaganda an appeal to the very real sub-histories in which smolder the needs and dreams ("Wünsche und Urtriebe") of social substance, the Brechtian model posits it all as a trick to be swept aside by reason and insight; something which has momentarily clouded the mind of our historical subject to lure him away from the real task. Characteristically, one of the central songs in the play is entitled "The Song of the Whitewash," the singing of which becomes an allegorical statement as Iberin's men whitewash over the cracks peeling in the houses of the city.

One need only think of the very successful anti-semitic film Jud Süss (1940) to see how much more effectively Veit Harlan and his crew grasped the interlocking relationship between the race question and sexuality. Süss Oppenheimer has taken complete financial control of the Duchy of Baden-Württemberg, but it is only when he rapes the beautiful blond daughter of the estates, driving her to suicide, that the populace is pushed to revolt and execution. Thus in one emblematic but living figure--Süss Oppenheimer--sexual degeneracy, defiling of the Volk, capitalist greed and cosmopolitan decadence are spun together into a monolithic anti-German conspiracy, rooted in long-standing traditions.

With the personifying of historical forces in the figure of Süss, we necessarily return to our central concern, namely the relationship between historical and poetical representation. In this regard it is important to emphasize how the structural principles of epic, avant-garde theater were consonant for Brecht with the writing of another history. Where the fascist culture industry used

[13] Ibid., p. 954.

189

ing of another history. Where the fascist culture industry used sexuality to play on deep-seated historical anxieties, Brecht's enlightenment response displaced the libidinal politics to their sup-posed deeper roots. In point of fact the entire play is constructed and organized formally around the process by which epiphenomena of appearance are pierced through to perceive the real subsurface of reality.

For instance, plot in Roundheads is not guided by the fate of any one individual, but is consistently linked dynamically and interpretively to events occurring in the economic sphere. This is particularly highlighted in the two trial scenes, which are key "turning points" in the action for Callas. The use of newspaper flashes telling of the distant class struggle is watched closely by Iberin as he formulates his race theory (when things look bad) and finally refuses retribution at the moment that the Sickel movement is defeated. The inverted use of tychoscopy here as epic device pro-vides a dramatic metaphor for the dualism and monocausality in Brecht's thinking: the messages beamed from a more primary sphere register truth from the substratum of materialist history, making the stage into an ideological reflex of some other reality rather than a force field of social contradiction. Similarly, the ges-tic techniques, episodic montage, inclusion of song and consistent use of Verfremdung--in fact, every facet and interchange of the parable form--point inexorably to a universalized historical truth which would break the myths of fascist history by denying them authenticity. Peering through all this is the epic voice of progres-sive history reminding us of his allegorical message:

> I will write for you a parable ("Gleichnis")
> in which I prove to everyone
> That this difference is the only significant one. [14]

In understanding Brecht's treatment of the Jewish question as related to his emerging representation of history, it should also be noted that at no point in the ensuing years was he able or it seems willing to come to terms with this phenomenon. His poem "The Jew, a Misfortune for our People" treats the issue once again merely as an ideological mystification of the fact that real misfortunes come from the Ruhr captains of industry and property owners, a stance that he is to repeat ad infinitum in other writings of the period. While he was ready to admit at one point that "as a socialist, I have no conception of the race question," his insistence upon relegating the Jewish question to the "political application of the race

<hr>

[14]   Ibid., p. 910.

question"[15] indicates the extent to which he remained confined to the original paradigm. Certainly Brecht was not alone, either on the left of elsewhere, in his refusal to face fully the enormity of the horror that was happening to the Jews. What is important, however, is the extent to which his blindspot on this question in part derives and is sustained by the "one-sided" political foundations of epic theater itself. The prevailing opposition between a reified illusion founded on the manipulative potential of feeling, and a "real" world made evident by rational, authentic materialist visions of truth helped create its own set of myths and simplifications: the myth of the historical process being grounded in some primary ontological way on the all-encompassing category of the political economy; the simplification of a political avant-garde theater founded on an unmediated notion of rational demystification. The abstractions of Brecht's undialectical Marxism and dualistic use of Verfremdung go hand in hand.

Brecht's next play dealing with Hitler was completed in 1941 and signals in its very title the change in focus. Whereas the title Roundheads and Peakheads places the dramatic configuration in the realm of true and false collectives, de-escalating, as it were, the powers of personal and sexual aura, Brecht's Resistible Rise of Arturo Ui relocates the emphasis back onto the shoulders of the "great" historical individual and back into the arena of classical theater. The rises and falls of people emanate from the language of bourgeois historiography just as the language of bourgeois historiography is itself organized around the poetics of tragedy. By making this rise resistible, Brecht seeks to subvert the paradigm from within, rather than confronting it with a counter-aesthetic. The entire play is dedicated to unmasking the facade of bourgeois-fascist rule by demystifying the poetic-historical legends which have imbued it with staying power. The shift is important. The principle of his dramaturgical strategy is no longer merely to reduce outer appearance to capitalist truth, for Brecht has come to take seriously and wage direct struggle with the aura of the spectacle itself.

Certainly such a change of attitude is manifest in Brecht's theoretical writings from this period, particularly in the Arbeitsjournale and those sections of the Messingkauf dialogues[16] which deal directly with what he calls "the theatricality of Fascism." Like

---

[15] In a letter to Per Knutzon, April/May 1934 quoted in Werner Hecht, Hans-Joachim Bunge, Käthe Rülicke-Weiler, Bertolt Brecht. Sein Leben und Werk (Berlin: Volk und Wissen, 1969), p. 128.
[16] For two thorough discussions of Brecht's theory of fascism see Wolfgang Emmerich, "Massenfachismus und die Rolle des Ästhetischen. Faschismustheorie bei Ernst Bloch, Walter Benjamin, Bertolt Brecht," in Antifaschistische Literatur, ed. Lutz Winckler, Vol.

Walter Benjamin, friend and colleague during this period, Brecht comes increasingly to understand the importance of the cultural realm as constitutive of contemporary politics and particularly the Fascist culture industry. Where the communist politicizes art, Benjamin argues in "Art in the Age of Mechanical Reproduction," by bringing it into the service of the people in their struggles to better their lot, fascism aestheticizes politics by creating the illusion of truth and the beautiful, the appearance of involvement and authenticity. For instance, the beauty of the labor movement started by Robert Ley in 1934 was a false aestheticizing of an ugly reality. What we have are not shorter work hours or better pay, but the beautification of the work place as the appearance of the upgrading of labor. Similarly, the mass ceremonies and parades represent a self-revelation and celebration of the "Volk" precisely at a time when they were being deprived of their real rights at the ballot box and the work place. One of Albert Speer's great inventions was the Cathedral of Light, where 130 anti-aircraft spotlights were placed around an open field shining upward into the sky to create an aura in which modern war technology is aestheticized into a religious glorification of the body politic.

In the writings of Brecht, quite logically, it was the theater which became a living metaphor for fascist domination. For him the Nazi public sphere was one great Gesamtkunstwerk--an Aristotelian drama in which Hitler himself was scriptwriter, director and main actor. Repeatedly he refers to the "Theatralik des Fascismus" and to Hitler's ability to direct ("Regie führen") instead of rule ("regieren"). His two favorite examples for the staging of politics in the Third Reich were the burning of the Reichstag in February of 1933 and "the Night of the Long Knives" in June of 1934. Both were political-theatrical events, both symbolic representations conceived as theatrical gestures for the purpose of political manipulation. Certainly one of the narratives of the killing of the SA leadership has all the markings of a well made play--with the Führer cast as hero. It was said that Hitler himself pounded down the door of Ernst Röhm to catch him in bed with a young boy and send him to his execution. Not surprisingly, the Röhm murder becomes a central scene in Ui, as does the trial scene of the Reichstag burning.

Brecht's conception of Hitlerian politics as theater of empathy ("Einfühlungstheater") par excellence, the realization of bourgeois high culture into the enactments of the political sphere, very much determined the counter to this "theater" that he was to develop in

I: Konspekt I (Kronberg/Ts: Scriptor-Verlag, 1977); F.N. Mennemeier, Modernes Deutsches Drama. Kritiken und Charakteristiken, Vol. II: 1933 bis zur Gegenwart (Munich: W. Fink, 1979), pp. 42ff.

Ui. If high culture in the garb of classical theater was the historical coding of politics in the Third Reich, then the principles of
modernism and estrangement would be its disruption and
overcoming. The avant-garde as the negation of high culture was
to become eo ipso anti-fascist. Its assault upon the institution of
autonomous art would now include the larger institutional framework
with which high culture is associated.

To realize this, Brecht created another parable, with important differences from Roundheads and Peakheads. Most important
was the building of emplotment around political rather than economic
narratives. The focus upon major events and key figures in the
crucial years 1932-1934 lends emphasis to the primacy of politics as
something other than secondary reflection. Conversely, Ui also
shows a receding of the economic categories of Brecht's earlier
work. The proletariat is all but invisible as the resistance; if anything, the implicit critical subject of resistance for this play is the
intellectual audience who will be open to its subtleties. The economics of power are trivialized into the petty dealings of small-time
racketeers. Clearly, the whole paradigm of figural representation
is one in which economic, political and cultural phenomena are
intertwined rather than causally reduced to a single denominator.

In realizing this shift, Brecht avails himself of a double Verfremdung. The allegory of Third Reich history is set into contex-
tual relationship with both the rise of a petty bourgeois gangster in
the underworld of Chicago and the narratives and codes of classical
drama: Schiller, Goethe, Shakespeare. Arturo Ui is not just the
shady character Al Capone, but also Richard III, Faust, even Hamlet. The language of political discourse is not just unmasked as the
butcher's jargon of small-time petty crooks, but is spoken in the
classical rhythms of blank verse and Shakespearean declamation.
The most immediate effect of this triangular referent system is to
break the allegorical codes in a number of directions and open up
the possibilities of exploring political legitimation as a total system.

Certainly Arturo Ui is most successful at the level of cultural
Ideologiekritik. Here again Brecht operates in a number of different registers. Like the Mauler scenes in his earlier play Saint Joan
of the Stockyards, there is clear satire of so-called autonomous culture whose values of beauty become unmasked as what Herbert Marcuse has called affirmative culture. The capitalist-meatpacker
Mauler's Schillerian odes to cows are as revealing of the emptiness
of high culture in service of butchering as is Ui's "high style" in
the service of political domination. Once again, we find in the
Brechtian reading a form of historicizing--not the repudiation of the
classics per se, but a rejection of their function as a mode of
manipulation.

If Brecht's Ui succeeds more generally as a parable about cultural legitimation, it is still somehow inadequate in its grasp of Hitler--and for some of the same reasons as the earlier endeavor. While it is certainly important to emphasize the petit-bourgeois base of Nazism as well as the Führer's self-creation as a grand actor in a political drama, Brecht's ultimate peek behind what he perceives as the "facade" reveals him still in part unaware as to what constitutes real power. To be sure, his political writings and Arbeitsjournale demonstrate significant changes in attitudes toward the Führer since the early 1930s. Unlike Feuchtwanger and other exile intellectuals, who would write off Hitler as aberrant, Brecht would now concede his status as a "great" man: "Only by comprehending the fact that Hitler is a real national phenomenon, a sly, vital, unconventional and thoroughly original politician," Brecht says, "can we understand how corruption, inadequacy and brutality really come into play."[17] It is clear that for Brecht, Hitler is no longer a mere puppet in the hands of the ruling elite, but has achieved a certain independence. Moreover, the concept of the petit-bourgeois also permits Brecht to consider the pathological side of the fascist phenomenon as itself the social expression of a class between: "...the pathological is something completely class based. Hitler's neurasthenia is the neurasthenia of the postal secretary. Everything goal-directed is necessarily pure ideology, bad myth, unreal."[18]

The final line in the preceding quotation is important. Although Brecht has come to acknowledge the charisma and individual accomplishment of Hitler, he still views the aura created as "pure ideology" and "bad myth." The greatness, as he tells us in his notes to Ui, lies in the enormity of Hitler's deeds rather than any inherent quality of self. "The ruling classes in the modern state make use of very average people for their tasks...they are not great political criminals but rather the committers of great political crimes."[19] Brecht's emphasis upon mediocrity here does not really contradict his acknowledgement of Hitler's greatness, for the emphasis in his whole outlook in Ui and elsewhere is upon the appearance rather than the substance of power. And it is Brecht's focus here upon mediocrity of personality that gives us insight into his view of history as well as of the potential audience of the play.

For an intellectual looking in from exile upon the tantrums of Third Reich politics, the events of the hour may have indeed seemed like petit-bourgeois mediocrity run amok. And we can certainly sympathize with Brecht's intention to unmask the imposter, to "destroy the usual dangerous respect for the great murderers."

[17] Brecht, Arbeitsjournale, ed. Werner Hecht (Frankfurt am Main: Suhrkamp, 1973) I, p. 380.
[18] Ibid., p. 381.
[19] Brecht, Gesammelte Werke, XVII, p. 1177.

But the real question, it seems to me, concerns the authentic substance of history and its relation to myth. Regardless of how seriously Brecht takes the manipulations of the cultural apparatus or how beautifully he dissects the interlocking nature of its power, his view of history remains one in which all modes of thought, memory, experience or the unconscious which do not correspond to the most advanced levels of material culture are relegated to the realm of false consciousness. In terms of the Ui play, petit-bourgeois thinking is ridiculous ("lächerlich"), not simply because it is spoken by mediocrity, but because when viewed from the vantage point of "real" material needs, it is historically obsolete. Myth for Brecht, then, is alienated thinking, false synthesis; the fascist appeals to community, Volk and nature are socially irrelevant in the light of the deeper truth of a progressing productivist history.

Given this view, it is not surprising that it was the Marxist Ernst Bloch and not Bertolt Brecht who, with the help of his theory of the synchronous and the non-synchronous, was able to historicize fascist mythology rather than simply dismiss it.[20] Bloch's view of history stressed its unequal development and argued that in modern, highly industrial societies there remain remnants and pockets ("alogische Räume") which resist or are immune to the cultural life at the centers of production. It is in such pockets of resistance that we find the social experiences, the dreams, the repressed drives and fantasies which, while "irrational" when viewed from that center, retain an explosive power, or even a utopian thrust to the future. The peasantry, youth, the petit-bourgeoisie--all represent the social ground for such thinking. More important, its political potential is highly ambivalent. Clearly the fascists have exploited it. But progressives should too, he says.

Bloch's notion of history gives us critical insight into Brecht with which to conclude our remarks. The extent to which the historiography at the heart of the productivist avant-garde fails to acknowledge the historical substance of fascist mythologies, is the extent to which its very critique of fascist "empathy" results in but another kind of abstraction. It is absolutely unimportant whether Hitler was "average" or not. What matters was his ability to produce an aura of authenticity by organizing real existing social needs, not simply synthetically produced or aberrant, pathological ones. Brecht's theater of demythification does not begin to deal with the public fantasies and social needs which helped create a Hitler in the first place. The needs for pageantry, for ecstasy, for the sensual spectacle of figural and cultic representation are not

---

[20] Ernst Bloch, Erbschaft dieser Zeit (Frankfurt am Main: Suhrkamp, 1962). See also the discussion of Bloch's theories by Anson Rabinbach, "Ernst Bloch's Heritage of Our Times and Fascism," New German Critique 11 (Spring, 1977), 5-21.

adequately mediated in a theater of simple estrangement. For as long as Brecht's estrangement technique remained limited to an episteme of a traditionally rationalist historiography, it will and must forfeit areas of experience to the other side.

In his poem "Exclusively because of the Increasing Disorder" Brecht admits not being able to talk about the smell of apples in the cellar and the sensitivities of the flesh...i.e., all that makes human beings "round and really human." We were forced to do this, he says, because of the times. My argument is, yes, that is true, but we should also keep in mind that if Brecht had worked the "pleasures of the flesh" into his theory of fascism, he might more fully have come to terms with why it was so successful and how to combat it.

BIBLIOGRAPHY

Ableitinger, Doris and Helmut Gugel, eds. Festschrift Karl Vretska. Heidelberg: Carl Winter, 1970.

Abraham, H.C. and E.L. Freud, eds. A Psycho-Analytic Dialogue: The Letters of Sigmund Freud and Karl Abraham, 1907-1926. New York: Basic Books, 1965.

Adorno, Theodor W. and Max Horkheimer. Dialektik der Aufklärung. Philosophische Fragmente. Frankfurt: Fischer, 1969.

Adorno, Theodor W. The Positivist Dispute in German Sociology. Tr. Glyn Adey and David Frisby. London: Heinemann, 1976.

Ahrens, Dieter, ed. Festschrift Max Wegner. Münster: Aschendorff, 1962.

Aktion. Rpt. See Union List of Serials.

Albrecht, Friedrich. Deutsche Schriftsteller in der Entscheidung. Wege zur Arbeiterklasse 1918-1933. Berlin: Aufbau Verlag, 1970.

Althusser, Louis. Eléments d'autocritique. Paris: Gallimard, 1974.

Anderson, John G.C., ed. Corneli Taciti de origine et situ Germanorum. Oxford: Clarendon Press, 1938.

Angress, W.T. and B.F. Smith. "Diaries of Heinrich Himmler's Early Years." Journal of Modern History 31 (1959), pp. 206-224.

Anselm of Canterbury. Truth, Freedom, and Evil: Three Philosophical Dialogues. Ed. and tr. by Jasper Hopkins and Herbert Richardson. New York: Harper and Row, 1967.

Apel, Karl Otto. "The Apriori of Communication and the Foundation of the Humanities." Man and World 5 (1972), pp. 3-37.

Aquinas, St. Thomas. Summa Theologiae. Turin: Marietti, 1952-53.

Aristotle. Poetics. Tr. Preston H. Epps. Chapel Hill: University of North Carolina Press, 1942.

Augustine, Aurelius, St. Contra Academicos, Bk II. In Vol. I of Opera Omnia. Ed. J.-P. Migne. Paris: Garnier, 1841-1902.

Augustine, Aurelius, St. De Vera Religione. In Vol. III of Opera Omnia.

Augustine, Aurelius, St. Soliloquia, Bk. II. In Vol. I of Opera Omnia.

Axelrod, Charles David. Studies in Intellectual Breakthrough. Freud, Simmel, Buber. Amherst: University of Massachusetts Press, 1979.

Baldwin, Barry. "Rulers and Ruled at Rome: A.D. 14-192." Ancient Society 3 (1972), pp. 149-164.

197

Barfield, Owen. Saving the Appearances: A Study in Idolatry. London: Faber and Faber, 1957.

Barthes, Roland. "Le discours de l'histoire." Information sur les sciences sociales 6 (1967).

Barwick, K. "Die Gliederung der Narratio in der rhetorischen Theorie und ihre Bedeutung für die Geschichte des antiken Romans." Hermes 63 (1928), pp. 261-287.

Baumgarten, Hermann. Der deutsche Liberalismus. Eine Selbstkritik. (1866). Berlin: Ullstein Taschenbuchverlag, 1975.

Becker, Carl L. Detachment and the Writing of History: Essays and Letters of Carl L. Becker. Ed. Phil L. Snyder. Ithaca: Cornell University Press, 1958.

Becker, Carl L. Everyman His Own Historian: Essays in History and Politics. New York: F.S. Crofts, 1935. Rpt. El Paso: Texas Western College Press for Academic Reprints, 1960.

Béguin, Albert. L'âme romantique et le rêve. Essai sur le romantisme allemand et la poesie française. Paris: J. Corti, 1956.

Ben-David, Joseph and Randall Collins. "Social Factors in the Origin of a New Science: The Case of Psychology." American Sociological Review 31, No. 4 (1966), pp. 451-465.

Benjamin, Walter. Angelus Novus. Frankfurt am Main: Suhrkamp, 1966.

Berkhofer, Robert F., Jr. Behavioral Approach to Historical Analysis. New York: Free Press, 1969.

Bernard, Claude. Introduction to the Study of Experimental Medicine. Tr. Henry Copley Greene. New York: Schuman, 1949.

Bertrand, Charles, ed. Revolutionary Situations in Europe, 1917-1922: Germany, Italy, Austria-Hungary. Montreal: Interuniversity Center for European Studies, 1977.

Berve, Helmut, ed. Das neue Bild der Antike, Vol. II, Rom. Leipzig: Koehler and Amelang, 1942.

Bickerman, E.J. "Origines Gentium." Classical Philology 47 (1952), pp. 65-81.

Bielefeld, G. "Der kompositorische Aufbau der Germania des Tacitus." In Festschrift Max Wegner. Ed. Dieter Ahrens. Münster: Aschendorff, 1962. Pp. 44-54.

Bloch, Ernst. Erbschaft dieser Zeit. Frankfurt am Main: Suhrkamp, 1962.

Bloch, Ernst. Geist der Utopie. Munich and Leipzig: Duncker and Humblot, 1918. Rpt. Frankfurt am Main: Suhrkamp, 1971.

Bloch, Marc. The Historian's Craft. Tr. Peter Putnam. New York: Knopf, 1962.

Böckenförde, Ernst W., ed. Moderne deutsche Verfassungsgeschichte (1815-1918). Cologne: Kiepenhauer and Witsch, 1972.

Boehringer, Hannes and Karlfried Gruender, eds. Aesthetik und Soziologie um die Jahrhundertwende: Georg Simmel. Frankfurt am Main: Klostermann, 1976.

Boissier, Gaston. Tacitus and Other Roman Studies. Tr. W.G. Hutchison. London: A. Constable, 1906.

Borchardt, Frank L. German Antiquity in Renaissance Myth. Baltimore: Johns Hopkins University Press, 1971.
Borzsák, Stefan. "P. Cornelius Tacitus." In Pauly-Wissowas Realencyclopädie der classischen Altertumswissenschaft. Stuttgart: J.B. Metzler, 1894ff. Supb. XI, cols. 373-512.
Brecht, Bertolt. Arbeitsjournal 1938-1955. 3 vols. Ed. Werner Hecht. Frankfurt am Main: Suhrkamp, 1973.
Brecht, Bertolt. Gesammelte Werke. Werkausgabe. 20 vols. Frankfurt am Main: Suhrkamp, 1976.
Bringmann, Wolfgang G. and William D.G. Balance. "Wilhelm Wundt 1832-1920: A Brief Bibliographical Sketch." Journal of the History of the Behavioral Sciences 11 (1975), pp. 287-297.
Bry, Ilse and Alfred H. Rifkin. "Freud and the History of Ideas: Primary Sources, 1886-1910." In Science and Psychoanalysis. Vol. 5 (Psychoanalytic Education). Ed. Jules H. Masserman. New York/London: Grune and Stratton, 1962. Pp. 6-36.
Büchner, Karl, tr. and ed. P. Cornelius Tacitus: die historischen Versuche: Agricola, Germania, Dialogus. Stuttgart: A. Kröner, 1955.
Burke, Kenneth. A Grammar of Motives. Berkeley: University of California Press, 1969.
Burke, Kenneth. A Rhetoric of Motives. Berkeley: University of California Press, 1969.

Cabell, James Branch. Figures of Earth. A Comedy of Appearances. New York: McBride, 1921.
Canary, Robert H. and Henry Kozicki. The Writing of History: Literary Form and Historical Understanding. Madison: University of Wisconsin Press, 1978.
Carr, Edward H. What is History? London: MacMillan; New York: St. Martin's Press, 1961.
Chaplin, James P. and T.S. Krawiec. Systems and Theories of Psychology. 3rd Edition. New York: Holt, Rinehart and Winston, 1974.
Christ, K. "Germanendarstellung und Zeitverständnis bei Tacitus." Historia 14 (1965), pp. 62-73.
Clive, Geoffrey, ed. The Philosophy of Nietzsche. New York: New American Library, 1965.
Comte, Auguste. Correspondance générale et confessions. Vol. I (1814-1840). Ed. Paulo E. de Berredo Carneiro and Pierre Arnaud. Paris/The Hague: Mouton, 1973.
Coser, Lewis A., ed. Georg Simmel. Englewood Cliffs, N.J.: Prentice-Hall, 1965.
Couissin, P. "Tacite et César." Revue de philologie 58 (1932), pp. 97-117.
Cousin, J. "Rhétorique et psychologie chez Tacite." Revue des études latines 29 (1951), pp. 228-247.

Danzel, Wilhelm. "Über die Behandlung der Geschichte der neuren Literatur." In Deutsche Literaturkritik im 19. Jahrhundert. Ed. Hans Mayer. Frankfurt am Main: Suhrkamp, 1974. Pp. 317-327.

Darnoi, Dennis N. Kenedy. The Unconscious and Eduard von Hartmann. A Historico-Critical Approach. The Hague: Martinus Nijhoff, 1967.

Davies, William Robertson. The Manticore. New York: Viking, 1972.

Deák, István. Weimar Germany's Left-Wing Intellectuals: A Political History of the Weltbühne and its Circle. Berkeley: University of California Press, 1968.

Decker, Hannah S. Freud in Germany. Revolution and Reaction in Science, 1893-1907. New York: International Universities Press, 1977.

Decker, Hannah S. "The Interpretation of Dreams: Early Reception by the Educated German Public." Journal of the History of the Behavioral Sciences 11 (1975), pp. 129-141.

Derrida, Jacques. Of Grammatology. Tr. Gayatri C. Spivak. Baltimore: Johns Hopkins University Press, 1977.

Derrida, Jacques. "Structure, Sign, and Play in the Discourse of the Human Sciences." In The Languages of Criticism and the Sciences of Man. The Structuralist Controversy. Ed. Richard Macksey and Eugenio Donato. Baltimore: Johns Hopkins University Press, 1970.

Dihle, A. "The Conception of India in Hellenistic and Roman Literature." Proceedings of the Cambridge Philological Society 10 (1964), pp. 15-23.

Dilthey, Wilhelm. Gesammelte Schriften. 14 vols. Leipzig: Teubner, 1914-58.

Döblin, Alfred. Aufsätze zur Literatur. Vol. 8 in Ausgewählte Werke. Ed. Walter Muschg. Freiburg: Walter Verlag, 1960ff.

Döblin, Alfred. Der deutsche Maskenball von Linke Poot. Wissen und Verändern. Vol. 14 in Ausgewählte Werke. Freiburg: Walter Verlag, 1960ff.

Döblin, Alfred. "Es ist Zeit." In Schriften zur Politik und Gesellschaft. Vol. 15 in Ausgewählte Werke.

Döblin, Alfred. "Male, Mühle, Male." Die neue Rundschau 31, No. 7 (1920), p. 874-881.

Döblin, Alfred, ed. Minotaurus. Dichtung unter den Hufen von Staat und Industrie. Wiesbaden: F. Steiner, 1953.

Döblin, Alfred. "Die Natur und ihre Seelen." Der neue Merkur 6 (1922/23), p. 5-14.

Döblin, Alfred. Die Zeitlupe: Kleine Prosa. Ed. Walter Muschg. Olten: Walter Verlag, 1962.

Dorey, Tom Alan, ed. Latin Historians. London: Routledge and Kegan Paul, 1966.

Dorey, Tom Alan, ed. Tacitus. London: Routledge and Kegan Paul, 1969.

Drexler, H. "Die Germania des Tacitus." Gymnasium 59 (1952), pp. 52-70.

Durkheim, Emile. Rev. of Philosophie des Geldes by G. Simmel. L'Année Sociologique 5 (1900-01), pp. 140-145.
Dyson, Freeman. Disturbing the Universe. New York: Harper and Row, 1979.

Earl, Donald C. The Moral and Political Tradition of Rome. Ithaca: Cornell University Press, 1967.
Ebbinghaus, Hermann. "Psychologie." In Die Kultur der Gegenwart. Ihre Entwicklung und ihre Ziele. Teil 6. Ed. Paul Hinneberg. Berlin, Leipzig: Teubner, 1907. Pp. 173-244.
Ehrentheil, Otto F. "The almost forgotten Feuchtersleben: Poet, Essayist, Popular Philosopher and Psychiatrist." Journal of the History of the Behavioral Sciences 11 (1975), pp. 82-86.
Eng, Erling. "Karl Philipp Moritz' Magazin für Erfahrungsseelenkunde 1783-1793." Journal of the History of the Behavioral Sciences 9 (1973), pp. 300-305.
Engel, Josef. "Die deutschen Universitäten und die Geschichtswissenschaft." In Hundert Jahre Historische Zeitschrift 1859-1959. Beiträge zur Geschichte der Historiographie in den deutschsprachigen Ländern. Ed. Theodor Schieder. Munich: Oldenbourg, 1959. Pp. 223-378.
Eulenberg, Franz. "Die sozialen Wirkungen der Währungsverhältnisse." Jahrbücher für Nationalökonomie und Statistik 67, Nr. 3 (1924), pp. 748-794.

Faye, Jean Pierre. Langages totalitaires. Paris: Hermann, 1977.
Feigl, Herbert and Michael Scriven, ed. The Foundations of Science and the Concepts of Psychology and Psychoanalysis. Minneapolis: University of Minnesota Press, 1956.
Feldman, Gerald D. Army, Industry and Labor in Germany 1914-1918. Princeton: Princeton University Press, 1966.
Feldman, Gerald D. and Otto Busch, eds. Historische Prozesse der deutschen Inflation, 1914 bis 1924: ein Tagungsbericht. Berlin: Colloquium Verlag, 1978.
Feldman, Gerald D. Iron and Steel in the German Inflation. Princeton: Princeton University Press, 1977.
Feldman, Gerald D., Eberhard Kolb, and Reinhard Rürup. "Die Massenbewegungen der Arbeiterschaft in Deutschland am Ende des Ersten Weltkrieges (1917-1920)." Politische Vierteljahrsschrift 13, No. 1 (1972).
Fest, Joachim. "Das Dilemma eines Unpolitischen." Frankfurter Allgemeine Zeitung, 13 October 1979.
Feuchtersleben, Ernst von. Lehrbuch der ärztlichen Seelenkunde. Vienna: Gerold, 1845. (English: The Principles of Medical Psychology. London: Sydenham Society, 1847.)
Fischer, David H. Historians' Fallacies. New York: Harper and Row, 1970.
Foucault, Michel. Histoire de la folie à l'age classique. Paris: Plon, 1961.
Foucault, Michel. Les mots et les choses. Paris: Gallimard, 1966.

Freud, Sigmund. An Autobiographical Study. In Standard Edition XX. London: The Hogarth Press, 1975. Pp. 7-61.

Freud, Sigmund. Creative Writers and Day-Dreaming. In Standard Edition IX. London: The Hogarth Press, 1975. Pp. 143-153.

Freud, Sigmund. Delusions and Dreams in Jensen's "Gradiva." In Standard Edition IX. London: The Hogarth Press, 1975. Pp. 7-95.

Freud, Sigmund. The Goethe Prize. In Standard Edition XXI. London: The Hogarth Press, 1975. Pp. 207-214.

Freud, Sigmund. The Interpretation of Dreams. In Standard Edition IV and V. London: The Hogarth Press, 1975.

Freud, Sigmund. Introductory Lectures on Psychoanalysis (Parts I and II). In Standard Edition XV and XVI. London: The Hogarth Press, 1975.

Freud, Sigmund. New Introductory Lectures on Psychoanalysis. In Standard Edition XXII. London: The Hogarth Press, 1975. Pp. 5-182.

Freud, Sigmund. On the History of the Psycho-Analytic Movement. In Standard Edition XIV. London: The Hogarth Press, 1975. Pp. 7-66.

Freud, Sigmund. On the Teaching of Psycho-Analysis in Universities. In Standard Edition XVII. London: The Hogarth Press, 1975. Pp. 171-173.

Freud, Sigmund. The Question of Lay Analysis. In Standard Edition XX. London: The Hogarth Press, 1975. Pp. 183-258.

Freud, Sigmund. Studies on Hysteria (with Josef Breuer). In Standard Edition II. London: The Hogarth Press, 1975, Pp. 1-311.

Friedrich, W.-H. "Stilistische Symptome der Geschichtsauffassung des Tacitus." In Festschrift Karl Vretska. Ed. Doris Ableitinger and Helmut Gugel. Heidelberg: Carl Winter, 1970. Pp. 23-39.

Frye, Northrop. Anatomy of Criticism. New York: Atheneum, 1967.

Frye, Northrop. Fables of Identity: Studies in Poetic Mythology. New York: Harcourt, Brace and World, 1963.

Gadamer, Hans-Georg. Wahrheit und Methode. Grundzüge einer philosophischen Hermeneutik. Tübingen: J.C.B. Mohr, 1960.

Gall, Lothar, ed. Liberalismus. 2nd ed. Meisenheim: Anton Hain, 1979.

Gassen, Kurt and Michael Landmann, eds. Buch des Dankes an Georg Simmel. Briefe, Erinnerungen, Bibliographie. Berlin: Duncker and Humblot, 1958.

Gay, Peter. Style in History. New York: Basic Books, 1974.

Giancotti, Francesco. Strutture delle Monografie di Sallustio e di Tacito. Messina and Florence: G. D'Anna, 1971.

Giesebrecht, Wilhelm. "Zur Charakteristik der heutigen Geschichtsschreibung in Deutschland." Historische Zeitschrift 1 (1859), pp. 1-17.

Gilbert, Felix. "Reflections on the History of the Profession of History." In History, Choice and Commitment. Ed. Arno J. Mayer. Cambridge, Mass.: Harvard University Press, 1977. Pp. 441-453.

Glucksmann, André. Les maîtres penseurs. Paris: B. Grasset, 1977.

Goldstein, Leon J. Historical Knowing. Austin: University of Texas Press, 1976.

Gooch, George P. History and Historians in the Nineteenth Century. 2nd ed. London, New York: Longmans, Green, 1952.

Gossman, Lionel. "History and Literature: Reproduction or Signification." In The Writing of History: Literary Form and Historical Understanding. Ed. Robert H. Canary and Henry Kozicki. Milwaukee: University of Wisconsin Press, 1978.

Graus, F. "Geschichtsschreibung und Nationalsozialismus." Vierteljahrshefte für Zeitgeschichte 17 (1969), pp. 87-95.

Griesinger, Wilhelm. Die Pathologie und Therapie der psychischen Krankheiten. Stuttgart: Krabbe, 1845. (English: Mental Pathology and Therapeutics. A facsimile of the English edition of 1867. New York: Hafner, 1965.)

Grimm, Reinhold. Brecht und Nietzsche oder Geständisse eines Dichters. Fünf Essays und ein Bruchstück. Frankfurt am Main: Suhrkamp, 1975.

Grosz, George. Das Gesicht der herrschenden Klasse. Berlin: Malik, 1921.

Grosz, George. "Die Kunst ist in Gefahr." In Manifeste, Manifeste. Ed. D. Schmidt. Dresden: Verlag der Kunst, 1965.

Grunberger, Richard. The 12-Year Reich. A Social History of Nazi Germany 1933-1945. New York: Holt, Rinehart, and Winston, 1971.

Gunz, A. Die deklamatorische Rhetorik in der Germania des Tacitus. Lausanne: A. Bovard-Giddey, 1934.

Habermas, Jürgen. Erkenntnis und Interesse. Frankfurt am Main: Suhrkamp, 1973. Tr. Knowledge and Human Interests, Jeremy J. Shapiro. Boston: Beacon Press, 1971.

Habermas, Jürgen. Technik und Wissenschaft als "Ideologie." Frankfurt am Main: Suhrkamp, 1968.

Habermas, Jürgen. Zur Logik der Sozialwissenschaften. Materialien. Frankfurt am Main: Suhrkamp, 1970.

Hachmann, Rolf, Georg Kossack, and Hans Kuhn. Völker zwischen Germanen und Kelten. Schriftquellen, Bodenfunde und Namengut zur Geschichte des nördlichen Westdeutschlands um Christi Geburt. Neumünster: K. Wachholtz, 1962.

Hartman, Geoffrey. "Ghostlier Demarcations: The Sweet Science of Northrop Frye." In Beyond Formalism. New Haven: Yale University Press, 1970. Pp. 24-41.

Hartmann, Eduard von. Die moderne Psychologie. Eine kritische Geschichte der deutschen Psychologie in der zweiten Hälfte des neunzehnten Jahrhunderts. Leipzig: Haacke, 1901.

Hartmann, Eduard von. Philosophie des Unbewußten . Berlin: Altenburg, 1869. (English: Philosophy of the Unconscious. New York: Harcourt, Brace and Company, 1931.)

Hauff, Jürgen, Albrecht Heller, Bernd Hüppauf, Lothar Köhn, and Klaus-Peter Philipi. Methodendiskussion. Arbeitsbuch zur Literaturwissenschaft. 2 vols. Königstein: Athenäum, 1971.

Hecht, Werner, Hans-Joachim Bunge, and Käthe Rülicke-Weiler. Bertolt Brecht. Sein Leben und Werk. Berlin: Volk und Wissen, 1969.

Hellpach, Willy. Grundgedanken zur Wissenschaftslehre der Psychopathologie (Habilitationsschrift). Leipzig: Engelmann, 1906.

Hemingway, Ernest. A Farewell to Arms. New York: Scribner, 1929.

Hermand, Jost. Synthetisches Interpretieren: Zur Methodik der Literaturwissenschaft. Munich: Nymphenburger Verlagshandlung, 1968.

Herzog, Wilhelm. "Besinnt Euch!" Das Forum 3, No. 3 (1918), pp. 185-88.

Herzog, Wilhelm. "Der Geistige Typus des Revolutionärs." Das Forum 3, No. 3 (1918), pp. 181-85.

Herzog, Wilhelm. "Der Triumph des Krieges." Das Forum 1, No. 5/6 (1914), pp. 257-85.

Herzog, Wilhelm. "Der Unfug der Moral." Das Forum 1, No. 9 (1914), pp. 458-60.

Heubner, H. "Sprache, Stil und Sache bei Tacitus." Interpretationen. Beiheft 4 to Gymnasium. Heidelberg: 1964. Pp. 133-148.

Hexter, Jack H. Doing History. Bloomington: Indiana University Press, 1971.

Hilary of Poitiers, St. De Trinitate. Bk. V, No. 14. In Vol. II of Opera Omnia, ed. J.-P. Migne. Paris: Vrayet, 1844-45.

Hill, Thomas E. The Concept of Meaning. New York: Humanities Press, 1971.

Hiller, Kurt. "Antworten." Die Weltbühne 14, No. 50 (1918).

Hiller, Kurt. Leben gegen die Zeit. Hamburg: Rowohlt, 1969ff.

Hiller, Kurt, ed. Zieljahrbuch. Vol. I. Munich: G. Müller, 1916; Vol. II. Munich: G. Müller, 1918; Vol. III. Leipzig: K. Wolff, 1919; Vol. IV. Leipzig: K. Wolff, 1920.

Höhne, Heinz. Canaris: Patriot im Zwielicht. Munich: C. Bertelsmann, 1976.

Höhne, Heinz. The Order of the Death's Head: The Story of Hitler's SS. Tr. Richard Barry. New York: Coward, McCann, and Geoghegan, 1970. (Orig.: Der Orden unter dem Totenkopf; die Geschichte der SS. Gütersloh: S. Mohn, 1967.)

Hölzle, E. "Die amerikanische und die bolschewistische Weltrevolution." In Weltwende 1917. Monarchie, Weltrevolution, Demokratie. Ed. Hellmuth Rössler. Göttingen: Musterschmidt-Verlag, 1965.

Housman, Alfred E., ed. M. Manilii Astronomicon Liber Primus. 2nd ed. Cambridge: Cambridge University Press, 1937.

Howe, Richard Herbert. "Max Weber's Elective Affinities: Sociology within the Bounds of Pure Reason." American Journal of Sociology 84, No. 2 (1978), pp. 366-385.

Hüppauf, Bernd, ed. Literaturgeschichte zwischen Revolution and Reaktion. Aus den Anfängen der Germanistik, 1830-1870. Wiesbaden: Akademische Verlagsgesellschaft Athenaion, 1972.

Hughes, H. Stuart. History as Art and as Science. Chicago: University of Chicago Press, 1975.

Huizinga, Johan. Verzamelde Werken. 9 vols. Haarlem: H.D. Tjeenk Willink, 1948ff.

Hume, David. An Inquiry Concerning Human Understanding. Indianapolis: Bobbs-Merrill, 1955.

Hutton, Maurice, tr. Tacitus: Dialogus, Agricola, Germania. London: MacMillan, 1914.

Hyman, Stanley Edgar. The Tangled Bank. Darwin, Marx, Frazer and Freud as Imaginative Writers. New York: Atheneum, 1962.

Iggers, Georg G. The German Conception of History: The National Tradition of Historical Thought from Herder to the Present. Middletown, Conn.: Wesleyan University Press, 1968.

Iggers, Georg and Konrad von Moltke, ed. Theory and Practice of History. Tr. Wilma Iggers and Konrad von Moltke. Indianapolis: Bobbs-Merrill, 1973.

Jameson, Fredric. Fables of Aggression: Wyndham Lewis, the Modernist as Fascist. Berkeley: University of California Press, 1979.

Jameson, Fredric. "The Vanishing Mediator: Narrative Structures in Max Weber." New German Critique 1, No. 1 (1974), pp. 52-89.

Jauß, Hans Robert, "Geschichte der Kunst und Historie," in Geschichte: Ereignis und Erzählung. Ed. Reinhart Koselleck and Wolf-Dieter Stempel. Konstanz: Universitätsverlag, 1976. Pp. 174-211, 559-60.

Jay, Martin. The Dialectical Imagination. A History of the Frankfurt School and the Institute of Social Research 1923-1950. London: Heinemann, 1973.

Jones, Ernest. "Years of Maturity, 1901-1919." In The Life and Work of Sigmund Freud. Vol. 2. New York: Basic Books, 1955.

Kanzer, Mark. "Freud and His Literary Doubles." American Imago 33, No. 3 (1976), pp. 231-243.

Kern, Stephen. "Freud and the Birth of Child Psychiatry." Journal of the History of the Behavioral Sciences 9 (1973), pp. 360-368.

Kessel, Eberhard. "Rankes Idee der Universalhistorie." Historische Zeitschrift 178 (1954), pp. 269-308.

Kettner, G. "Die Composition des ethnographischen Teils der Germania des Tacitus." Zeitschrift für deutsche Philologie 19 (1887), pp. 257-274.

Kierkegaard, Søren. Concluding unscientific Postscript. Tr. David F. Swenson, ed. Walter Lowrie. Princeton: Princeton University Press, 1941.
Kierkegaard, Søren. Training in Christianity. Tr. Walter Lowrie. London: H. Milford and Oxford University Press, 1944.
Kluge, Ulrich. Soldatenräte und Revolution: Studien zur Militärpolitik in Deutschland 1918/19. Göttingen: Vandenhoeck and Ruprecht, 1975.
Kneissl, Peter. Die Siegestitulatur der römischen Kaiser. Göttingen: Vandenhoeck and Ruprecht, 1969.
Kocka, Jürgen. Klassengesellschaft im Krieg: deutsche Sozialgeschichte 1914-1918. Göttingen: Vandenhoeck and Ruprecht, 1973.
Koehl, R. "Feudal Aspects of National Socialism." American Political Science Review 54 (1960), pp. 921-933.
Kolb, Eberhard. Die Arbeiterräte in der deutschen Innenpolitik, 1918-1919. Düsseldorf: Droste, 1962.
Kolb, Eberhard, ed. Vom Kaiserreich zur Weimarer Republik. Cologne: Kiepenheuer and Witsch, 1972.
Kolinsky, Eva. Engagierter Expressionismus. Politik und Literatur zwischen Weltkrieg und Weimarer Republik. Eine Analyse expressionistischer Zeitschriften. Stuttgart: J.B. Metzler, 1970.
Kraggerud, E. "Verknüpfung in Tacitus' Germania." Symbolae Osloensis 47 (1972), pp. 7-35.
Krieger, Leonard. The Meaning of History. Chicago: University of Chicago Press, 1977.
Kroll, Wilhelm. Studien zum Verständnis der römischen Literatur. Stuttgart: J.B. Metzler, 1924.
Kuczynski, Jürgen and Wolfgang Heise. Bild und Begriff. Studien über die Beziehungen zwischen Kunst und Wissenschaft. Berlin (GDR)/Weimar: Aufbau Verlag, 1975.
Külpe, Oswald. Grundriß der Psychologie, auf experimenteller Grundlage dargestellt. Leipzig: W. Engelmann, 1893. (English: Outlines of Psychology: Based upon the Results of Experimental Investigation. New York: Macmillan, 1909.)
Kuhn, Thomas S. The Structure of Scientific Revolutions. Chicago: University of Chicago Press, 1962.
Kusminski, Adrian. "Defending Historical Realism." History and Theory: Studies in the Philosophy of History 18 (1979), pp. 316-349.
Kusminski, Adrian. "A New Science?" Rev. of Metahistory, by Hayden White. Comparative Studies in Society and History 18 (1976), pp. 129-43.

Lacan, Jacques. Ecrits. Paris: Editions du Seuil, 1966.
Lafargue, Paul. "Reminiscences of Marx." In Karl Marx, Selected Works in two volumes. Ed. V. Adoratsky. Vol. 1. New York: International Publishers, n.d. Pp. 81-101.
Lawler, James R., ed. Paul Valéry: An Anthology. Princeton: Princeton University Press, 1956.

Leeman, Anton D. Orationis Ratio. The Stylistic Theories and Practice of the Roman Orators, Historians and Philosophers. Amsterdam: A.M. Hakkert, 1963.

Lepenies, Wolf. "Anthropological Perspectives in the Sociology of Science." In Cognitive and Historical Sociology of Scientific Knowledge. Eds. Yehuda Elkana and Everett Mendelsohn. Dordrecht: Reidel, 1980.

Lepenies, Wolf. Das Ende der Naturgeschichte. Wandel kultureller Selbstverständlichkeiten in den Wissenschaften des 18. und 19. Jahrhunderts. Munich: Hanser, 1976.

Lepenies, Wolf. "Der Wissenschaftler als Autor. Über konservierende Funktionen der Literatur." Akzente 2 (1978), pp. 129-147.

Leroy, Maxime. Taine. Paris: Reider, 1933.

Levin, Norman Gordon. Woodrow Wilson and World Politics. America's Response to War and Revolution. New York: Oxford University Press, 1968.

Lewis, Bernard. History. Remembered, Recovered, Invented. Princeton: Princeton University Press, 1975.

Ley-Piscator, Maria. The Piscator Experiment: The Political Theater. New York: J.H. Heineman, 1967.

Loos, Adolf. Sämtliche Schriften. Vienna: Herold, 1962ff.

Losemann, Volker. Nationalsozialismus und Antike. Studien zur Entwicklung des Faches Alte Geschichte 1933-1945. Hamburg: Hoffmann and Campe, 1977.

Lucas, J. "La rélation de Cicéron à son public." In Ciceroniana. Hommages à Kazmierz Kumaniecki. Ed. Alain Michel and R. Verdière. Leiden: E.J. Brill, 1975. Pp. 150-159.

Lukács, Georg. "Georg Simmel." In Buch des Dankes an Georg Simmel. Briefe, Erinnerungen, Bibliographie. Zu seinem 100. Geburtstag am 1. März 1958 Ed. Kurt Gassen and Michael Landmann. Berlin: 1958. pp. 171-176.

Lukács, Georg. Werke. Neuwied am Rhein: Luchterhand, 1960ff.

Lutzhöft, Hans-Jürgen. Der nordische Gedanke in Deutschland 1920-1940. Stuttgart: E. Klett, 1971.

McCarry, Charles. The Secret Lovers. New York: E.P. Dutton, 1977.

Mack, Dietrich. Senatsreden und Volksreden bei Cicero. Würzburg: K. Triltsch, 1937.

Maier, Charles S. Recasting Bourgeois Europe. Stabilization in France, Germany, and Italy in the Decade after World War I. Englewood Cliffs, N.J.: Prentice-Hall, 1975.

Mann, Thomas. Gesammelte Werke. Frankfurt: S. Fischer, 1960.

Mann, Thomas. Tagebücher. 4 vols. Ed. Peter de Mendelssohn. Frankfurt: S. Fischer, 1980-82.

Marcuse, Herbert. Eros and Civilization. A Philosophical Inquiry into Freud. Boston: Beacon Press, 1956.

Marcuse, Herbert. "Industrialization and Capitalism in the Work of Max Weber." In Negations. Tr. Jeremy J. Shapiro. Boston: Beacon Press, 1968. Pp. 201-226.

Marx, Karl. The Eighteenth Brumaire of Louis Bonaparte. New York: International Publishers, 1972.

Marx, Karl and Frederick Engels. Selected Correspondence. London: Lawrence and Wishart, 1956.

Mayer, Arno J., ed. History, Choice and Commitment. Cambridge: Harvard University Press, 1977.

Mayer, Hans, ed. Deutsche Literaturkritik in 19. Jahrhundert. Frankfurt am Main: Suhrkamp, 1974.

Mehring, Walter. Berlin Dada. Eine Chronik mit Photos und Dokumenten. Zürich: Verlag der Arche, 1959.

Melin, B. "Zum Eingangskapitel der Germania." Eranos 58 (1960), pp. 112-131.

Mendel, Arthur P., ed. Essential Works of Marxism. New York: Bantam Books, 1961.

Mendell, Clarence W. Tacitus: the Man and his Work. New Haven: Yale University Press, 1957.

Mendelsohn, Erich. Rußland, Europa, Amerika. Ein architektonischer Querschnitt. Berlin: R. Mosse, 1929. Rpt. as Russia, Europe, America in Images: Reprint of Four Volumes of Architecture published in Germany in the Twenties. Ed. Charlotte and Timothy Benton. Great Britain: Open University Press, 1975.

Mennemeier, F.N. Modernes Deutsches Drama. Kritiken und Charakteristiken, Vol. II: 1933 bis zur Gegenwart. Munich: W. Fink, 1979.

Merton, Robert K. The Sociology of Science. An Episodic Memoir. Carbondale, Ill.: Southern Illinois University Press, 1979.

Michel, Alain and R. Verdière, eds. Ciceroniana. Hommages à Kazimierz Kumaniecki. Leiden: E.J. Brill, 1975.

Michel, Alain. Tacite et le destin de l'empire. Paris: Arthaud, 1966.

Mills, C. Wright. The Sociological Imagination. New York: Oxford University Press, 1959.

Misch, Clara. Der junge Dilthey. Ein Lebensbild in Briefen und Tagebüchern, 1852-1870. Stuttgart: B.G. Teubner, 1960.

Momigliano, Arnaldo. Studies in Historiography. London: Weidenfeld and Nicolson; New York: Harper and Row, 1966.

Mongardini, Carlo. Storia e sociologia nell'opera di H. Taine. Milan: Guiffré, 1965.

Morgan, David W. The Socialist Left and the German Revolution. A History of the German Independent Social Democratic Party, 1917-1922. Ithaca: Cornell University Press, 1975.

Mosse, George L. The Crisis of German Ideology: Intellectual Origins of the Third Reich. New York: Grosset and Dunlap, 1964.

Motherwell, R., ed. The Dada Painters and Poets: An Anthology. New York: Wittenborn, Schultz, 1951.

Much, Rudolf, ed. Die Germania des Tacitus. 3rd Ed. Heidelberg: C. Winter, 1967.

Müllenhoff, Karl V. Deutsche Altertumskunde. Berlin: Weidmann, 1887-1900. Vol IV.

Muschg, Walter. Psychoanalyse und Literaturwissenschaft. Antrittsvorlesung gehalten an der Universität Zürich. Berlin: Junker and Dünnhaupt, 1930.

Muthesius, Hermann. Kultur und Kunst. Gesammelte Aufsätze über künstlerische Fragen der Gegenwart. Jena: E. Diederich, 1904.

Neff, Emery. The Poetry of History. New York: Columbia University Press, 1947.

Nelson, John S. Rev. of Metahistory, by Hayden White. History and Theory: Studies in the Philosophy of History 14 (1975), p. 89.

Niederland, William G. "Freud's Literary Style: Some Observations." American Imago 28, No. 1 (1971), pp. 17-23.

Nierhaus, Rolf. Das swebische Gräberfeld von Diersheim. Berlin: Walter de Gruyter, 1966.

Nietzsche, Friedrich. Jenseits von Gut und Böse in Werke in Drei Bänden. Ed. Karl Schlechta. Munich: Hanser, 1960. II, 563-760. Tr. by Walter Kaufmann as Beyond Good and Evil. New York: Random House, 1966.

Nietzsche, Friedrich. Vom Nutzen und Nachteil der Historie für das Leben. In Werke in drei Bänden. Ed. Karl Schlechta. Munich: Hanser, 1960. I, 209-285. Tr. by Adrian Collins as The Use and Abuse of History (Indianapolis: Bobbs-Merrill, 1957).

Nisbet, Robert. Sociology as an Art Form. 2nd ed. London: Oxford University Press, 1976.

Norden, Eduard. Die antike Kunstprosa vom VI. Jahrhundert v. Chr. bis in die Zeit der Renaissance. Stuttgart: B.G. Teubner, 1958. (Orig. published Leipzig: Teubner, 1915.)

Norden, Eduard. Die germanische Urgeschichte in Tacitus Germania. Leipzig: B.G. Teubner, 1923.

Obermeit, Werner. Das unsichtbare Ding, das Seele heißt. Die Entdeckung der Psyche im bürgerlichen Zeitalter. Frankfurt: Syndikat, 1980.

Örtzen, Peter von. Betriebsräte in der Novemberrevolution. Düsseldorf: Droste, 1963.

Ogilvie, Robert M. and Ian Richmond, eds. Corneli Taciti de vita Agricolae. Oxford: Clarendon Press, 1967.

Pekkanan, T. "Tac. Germ. 2, 3 and the Name Germani." Arctos 7 (1972), pp. 107-138.

Perret, Jacques, ed. Tacite, La Germanie. Paris: Belles Lettres, 1962.

Peschel, K. "Die Sueben in Ethnographie und Archäologie." Klio 60 (1978), pp. 259-309.

Peschken, Bernd. Versuch einer germanistischen Ideologiekritik. Stuttgart: J.B. Metzler, 1972.

Peter, Lothar. Literarische Intelligenz und Klassenkampf: "Die Aktion" 1911-1932. Cologne: Pahl-Rugenstein, 1972.

Peters, R.S., ed. Brett's History of Psychology. London: Allen and Unwin, 1953.

Pfemfert, Franz. "Aufruf der Antinationalen Sozialistischen Partei Gruppe Deutschland." Die Aktion 8, No. 45/46 (1918), pp. 584-85.

Pfemfert, Franz. "Freunde, Kameraden der Aktion." Die Aktion 8, No. 41/42 (1918), pp. 523-27.

Pfemfert, Franz. "Nationalversammlung ist Konterrevolution!" Die Aktion 8, No. 47/48 (1918), pp. 613-20.

Pfemfert, Franz. "Soldaten! Kameraden der A.S.P.! Freunde der Aktion!" Die Aktion 8, Nr. 45/46 (1918), p. 588.

Pfister, F. "Tacitus und die Germanen." In Studien zu Tacitus Carl Hosius dargebracht. Ed. Hildebrecht Hommel, Karl Keyssner, Josef Martin, Friedrich Pfister, Joseph Vogt. Stuttgart: W. Kohlhammer, 1936. Pp. 53-93.

Pfister, Oskar Robert. The Psychoanalytic Method. Tr. Charles Rockwell Payne. New York: Moffat, Yard and Co., 1917.

Pinthus, Kurt, ed. Menschheitsdämmerung. Berlin: E. Rowohlt, 1920. Rpt. Hamburg: Rowohlt, 1960.

Platnauer, Maurice, ed. Fifty Years (and Twelve) of Classical Scholarship. New York: Barnes and Noble, 1968.

Pörtner, Paul, ed. Literaturrevolution 1910-1925. Dokumente, Manifeste, Programme. Darmstadt: Luchterhand, 1960.

Pöschl, V. "Zur Einbeziehung anwesender Personen und sichtbarer Objekte in Cieros Reden." In Ciceroniana: Hommages à Kazmierz Kumaniecki. Ed. Alain Michel and R. Verdière. Leiden: E.J. Brill, 1975. Pp. 206-226.

Polomé, Edgar. "A propos de la déese Nerthus." Latomus 13 (1954), pp. 167-200.

Popper, Karl R. The Logic of Scientific Discovery. Tr. by the author, Julius Freed, and Lan Freed. London: Hutchinson, 1959. (Orig.: Logik der Forschung. Vienna: 1935.)

Pound, Ezra. Selected Poems. Ed. T.S. Eliot. London: Faber and Gwyer, 1928.

Preyer, William. The Mind of the Child. Tr. H.W. Brown. New York: Arno, 1890.

Prutz, Robert E. Die deutsche Literatur der Gegenwart. 1848 bis 1858. 2nd Edition. Leipzig: Ernst Julius Günther, 1870.

Raabe, Paul, ed. The Era of Expressionism. Tr. J.M. Ritchie. London: Calder and Boyers, 1974.

Raabe, Paul, ed. Expressionismus: Der Kampf um eine literarische Bewegung. Munich: Deutscher Taschenbuch Verlag, 1965.

Raabe, Paul, ed. Ich schneide die Zeit aus: Expressionismus in Franz Pfemferts "Aktion." Munich: Deutscher Taschenbuch Verlag, 1964.

Rabinbach, Anson. "Ernst Bloch's Heritage of our Times and Fascism." New German Critique 11 (Spring, 1977), pp. 5-21.

Rademacher, Uwe. Die Bildkunst des Tacitus. Hildesheim, New York: G. Olms, 1975.

Ranke, Leopold von. Memoirs of the House of Brandenburg and History of Prussia during the Seventeenth and Eighteenth Centuries. 3 vols. Tr. A. and D. Gordon. New York: Greenwood Press, 1968.

Ranke, Leopold von. "Preface to The Histories of the Latin and Germanic Peoples." In The Varieties of History: From Voltaire to the Present. Ed. Fritz Stern. New York: Random House, 1973. Pp. 54-63.

Reeb, Wilhelm, ed. Tacitus Germania. Leipzig: B.G. Teubner, 1930.

Ribot, Théodule Armand. La Psychologie allemande contemporaine. Ecole expérimentale. Paris: F. Alcan, 1879. (English: German Psychology of Today: The Empirical School. 2nd Ed. New York: Scribner, 1885.)

Ritter, Heinrich. An Leopold von Ranke über deutsche Geschichtsschreibung. Ein offener Brief. Leipzig: Fues's Verlag, 1867.

Rolland, Romain. Demain: Pages et Documents, 11/12 (1916), in Arno J. Mayer, Political Origins of the New Diplomacy, 1917-1918. New York: H. Fertig, 1969.

Roscher, W.H. Ausführliches Lexicon der griechischen und römischen Mythologie. Leipzig: Teubner, 1884-1890.

Rose, Margaret. Parody/Meta-Fiction. London: Croom Helm, 1979.

Rose, Margaret. "Die strukturelle Einheit von Heines 'Rabbi von Bacherach'." In Heine Jahrbuch. Düsseldorf: Heine-Archiv, 1976. Pp. 38-51.

Rosenberg, Arthur. A History of the German Republic. Tr. Ian F.D. Morrow and L. Marie Sieveking. London: Methuen, 1936.

Rothe, Wolfgang, ed. Der Aktivismus 1915-1920. Munich: Deutscher Taschenbuch Verlag, 1969.

Royce, Josiah. The Philosophy of Loyalty. New York: MacMillan, 1924.

Rürup, Reinhard. "Problems of the German Revolution of 1918-1919." Journal of Contemporary History 3, No. 4 (1961), pp. 109-36.

Ryberg, Inez Scott. "Tacitus' Art of Innuendo." Transactions of the American Philological Association 73 (1942), pp. 383-404.

Salm, Peter. Three Modes of Criticism: The Literary Theories of Scherer, Walzel, and Staiger. Cleveland: Press of Case Western Reserve University, 1968.

Schellhase, Kenneth C. Tacitus in Renaissance Political Thought. Chicago: University of Chicago Press, 1975.

Schieder, Theodor, ed. Hundert Jahre Historische Zeitschrift 1859-1959. Beiträge zur Geschichte der Historiographie in den deutschsprachigen Ländern. Munich: Oldenbourg, 1959.

Schieder, Theodor. "Die Krise des bürgerlichen Liberalismus." In Liberalismus. Ed. Lothar Gall. Meisenheim: Anton Hain, 1979. Pp. 187-207.

Scheliha, Renata von. Die Wassergrenze im Altertum. Breslau: Markus, 1931.

Schickele, René. "Revolution, Bolschewismus und Ideal." Die Weißen Blätter 5, No. 6 (1918), pp. 97-130.

Schmidt, D., ed. Manifeste, Manifeste. Dresden: Verlag der Kunst, 1965.

Schönau, Walter. Sigmund Freuds Prosa: Literarische Elemente seines Stils. Stuttgart: Metzlersche Verlagsbuchhandlung, 1968.

Schrey, Gisela. Literaturästhetik der Psychoanalyse und ihre Rezeption in der deutschen Germanistik vor 1933. Frankfurt am Main: Athenaion, 1975.

Scobie, Alexander. Aspects of the Ancient Romance and its Heritage. Essays on Apuleius, Petronius, and the Greek Romances. Meisenheim a. Glan: Anton Hain, 1969.

Sherwin-White, Adrian N. Racial Prejudice in Imperial Rome. Cambridge: Cambridge University Press, 1967.

Simmel, Georg. Philosophie des Geldes (1900). 2nd ed. Leipzig: Duncker and Humblot, 1907. (English: The Philosophy of Money. London: Routledge and Kegan Paul, 1978.)

Simmel, Georg. Soziologie. Untersuchungen über die Formen der Vergesellschaftung. Leipzig: Duncker and Humblot, 1908.

Skinner, B.F. "Critique of Psychoanalytic Concepts and Theories." In The Foundations of Science and the Concepts of Psychology and Psychoanalysis. Eds. Herbert Feigl and Michael Scriven. Minneapolis: University of Minnesota Press, 1956. Pp. 77-87.

Sohn-Rethel, Alfred. Intellectual and Manual Labour. A Critique of Epistemology. London: Humanities Press, 1978.

Solzhenitsyn, Alexander. The Gulag Archipelago. New York: Harper-Row, 1974.

Stackelberg, Jürgen von. Tacitus in der Romania: Studien zur literarischen Rezeption des Tacitus in Italien und Frankreich. Tübingen: Max Niemeyer, 1960.

Staiger, Emil. Die Zeit als Einbildungskraft des Dichters: Untersuchen zu Gedichten von Brentano, Goethe und Keller. Zurich and Leipzig: Max Niehans Verlag, 1939.

Steidle, W. "Tacitusprobleme." Museum Helveticum 22 (1965), pp. 81-114.

Stern, Fritz. The Politics of Cultural Despair: A Study in the Rise of the German Ideology. Berkeley: University of California Press, 1961.

Stern, Fritz. Varieties of History: From Voltaire to the Present. New York: Random House, 1973.

Stern, William. No title. In A History of Psychology in Autobiography. Vol. I. Ed. Carl Murchison. Worcester, Mass.: Clark University Press, 1930. Pp. 335-388.

Stone, Lawrence. "The Revival of Narrative: Reflections on a New Old History." Past and Present 85 (1979), pp. 3-24.
Sullivan, John P., ed. Critical Essays on Roman Literature: Elegy and Lyric. Cambridge: Harvard University Press, 1962.
Sutherland, Carol H.V. The Emperor and the Coinage: Julio-Claudian Studies. London: Spink, 1976.
Sybel, Heinrich von. "Vorwort." Historische Zeitschrift, I (1859), pp. iii-v.
Syme, Ronald. Tacitus. Oxford: Clarendon Press, 1958.

Tackenberg, K. "Die Germania des Tacitus und das Fach der Vorgeschichte." In Festschrift Max Wegner. Ed. Dieter Ahrens. Münster: Aschendorff, 1962. Pp. 55-70.
Taine, Hippolyte. Balzac. A Critical Study (1906). Tr. Lorenzo O'Rourke. New York: Haskell House, 1973.
Thiel, Johannes H. Studies on the History of Roman Sea-Power in Republican Times. Amsterdam: North-Holland Publishing Company, 1946.
Timpe, Dieter. Arminius-Studien. Heidelberg: Carl Winter, 1970.
Trotzki, Leon. Literature and Revolution. Tr. Rose Strunsky. New York: Russell and Russell, 1957.
Trüdinger, Karl. Studien zur Geschichte der griechisch-römischen Ethnographie. Basel: Emil Birkhauser, 1918.
Tucholsky, Kurt. Gesammelte Werke. Ed. Mary Gerold-Tucholsky and Fritz J. Raddatz. Hamburg: Rowohlt, 1960ff.

Utitz, Emil. "Simmel und die Philosophie der Kunst." Zeitschrift für Aesthetik und allgemeine Kunstwissenschaft 14 (1920), pp. 1-41.

Veith, I. Hysteria: The History of a Disease. Chicago: The University of Chicago Press, 1965.
Vogt, Joseph. Orbis: ausgewählte Schriften zur Geschichte des Altertums. Ed. Fritz Taeger and Karl Christ. Freiburg: Herder, 1960.

Wagner-Liszt, Cosima. Die Tagebücher. 4 vols. Ed. Martin Gregor-Dellin and Dietrich Mack. Munich: Piper, 1982.
Wahl, Rainer. "Der preußische Verfassungskonflikt und das konstitutionelle System des Kaiserreichs." In Moderne Deutsche Verfassungsgeschichte (1815-1918). Ed. Ernst Wolf Böckenförde. Cologne: Kiepenhauser and Witsch, 1972. Pp. 171-194.
Waitz, Georg. "Falsche Richtungen. Schreiben an den Herausgeber." Historische Zeitschrift I (1859), pp. 17-28.
Walker, Bessie. The Annals of Tacitus: A Study in the Writing of History. Manchester: Manchester University Press, 1960.
Walser, Gerold. Caesar und die Germanen. Einzelschrift 1 to Historia. Wiesbaden: 1956.
Walser, Gerold. Rom, das Reich und die fremden Völker in der Geschichtsschreibung der frühen Kaiserzeit. Studien zur Glaub-

würdigkeit des Tacitus. Baden-Baden: Verlag für Kunst und Wissenschaft, 1951.

Weber, Max. Economy and Society. An Outline of Interpretive Sociology. Ed. Guenther Roth and Claus Wittich. New York: Bedminster Press, 1968.

Weber, Max. "Georg Simmel as Sociologist" (1908). Intro. by Donald N. Levine. Social Research 39 (1972), pp. 155-163.

Wederkop, Hermann von. "Querschnitt durch 1923." Der Querschnitt III, pp. viii-xvi. Rpt. Nendeln, Liechtenstein: Kraus, 1970.

Weimar, Klaus. "Zur Geschichte der Literaturwissenschaft. Forschungsbericht." DVLG 50 (1976), pp. 298-363.

Weisz, George. "Scientists and Sectarians: The Case of Psychoanalysis." Journal of the History of the Behavioral Sciences 11 (1975), pp. 350-364.

Wekwerth, Manfred. Notate. Über die Arbeit des Berliner Ensembles 1956 bis 1966. Frankfurt am Main: Suhrkamp, 1967.

Werfel, Franz. "Die christliche Sendung: Offener Brief an Kurt Hiller." In Tätiger Geist. Zieljahrbuch II. Ed. Kurt Hiller. Munich: G. Müller, 1918.

Weymar, Ernst. Das Selbstverständnis der Deutschen. Stuttgart: Klett, 1961.

White, Hayden V. "The Historical Text as Literary Artifact." In The Writing of History: Literary Form and Historical Understanding. Ed. Robert H. Canary and Henry Kozicki. Madison: University of Wisconsin Press, 1978.

White, Hayden V. Metahistory. The Historical Imagination in Nineteenth-Century Europe. Baltimore: The Johns Hopkins University Press, 1973.

White, Hayden V. Tropics of Discourse. Essays in Cultural Criticism. Baltimore: Johns Hopkins University Press, 1978.

Williams, Gordon W. Change and Decline: Roman Literature in the Early Empire. Berkeley: University of California Press, 1978.

Williams, Gordon W. Tradition and Originality in Roman Poetry. Oxford: Clarendon Press, 1968.

Winckler, Lutz, ed. Antifaschistische Literatur. Programme, Autoren, Werke. Vol. I: Konspekt I. Kronberg/Ts.: Scriptor-Verlag, 1977.

Wolfenstein, Alfred, ed. Die Erhebung. Jahrbuch für neue Dichtung und Wertung. Vol. I (1919) and Vol. II (1920). Rpt. Nendeln, Liechtenstein: Kraus, n.d.

Wolff, E. "Das geschichtliche Verstehen in Tacitus Germania." Hermes 69 (1934), pp. 121-166.

Wolff, Kurt H., ed. The Sociology of Georg Simmel. New York: The Free Press, 1950.

Wolfradt, Willy. "George Grosz," Jahrbuch der jungen Kunst. Leipzig: Klinkhardt and Biermann, 1921. Pp. 97-112.

Wundt, Wilhelm. Erlebtes und Erkanntes. 2nd Ed. Stuttgart: Alfred Kroener, 1921.

Wundt, Wilhelm. Grundzüge der physiologischen Psychologie. Leipzig: Engelmann, 1873. (English: Principles of Physiological Psychology. New York: Macmillan, 1904.)

Zilsel, Edgar. "The Sociological Roots of Science." American Journal of Sociology 47 (1942), pp. 245-279.

Zockler, Christopher. Dilthey und die Hermeneutik. Stuttgart: J.B. Metzler, 1975.

INDEX